Ciao Italia

My Lifelong Food Adventures in Italy

Other titles by Mary Ann Esposito

Ciao Italia Family Classics

Ciao Italia Five-Ingredient Favorites:
Quick and Delicious Recipes from an Italian Kitchen

Ciao Italia Slow and Easy:
Casseroles, Braises, Lasagne, and Stews from an Italian Kitchen

Ciao Italia Pronto!
30-Minute Recipes from an Italian Kitchen

Ciao Italia in Tuscany:
Traditional Recipes from One of Italy's Most Famous Regions

Ciao Italia

Celebrations, Italian Style:
Recipes and Menus for Special Occasions and Seasons of the Year

Nella Cucina:
More Italian Cooking from the Host of Ciao Italia

What You Knead

Mangia Pasta!
Easy-To-Make Recipes for Company and Every Day

Ciao Italia—Bringing Italy Home

Ciao Italia in Umbria:
Recipes and Reflections from the Heart of Italy

Ciao Italia

My Lifelong Food Adventures in Italy

Mary Ann Esposito

Host of PBS' *Ciao Italia*™

Food Photography by John W. Hession

Published by

Ciao Italia™

An imprint of

Peter E. Randall Publisher

Portsmouth, NH

2018

Esposito accepting the Premio Artusi award in Forlimpopoli, Italy, home to Italian writer Pellegrino Artusi for whom the award is named. Artusi wrote the definitive work, *The Art of Eating Well*, which became the benchmark cookbook for all Italians.

© 2018 Mary Ann Esposito

ISBN 13: 978-1-942155-17-1
Library of Congress No. 2018949379

Published by
Ciao Italia™
An imprint of
Peter E. Randall Publisher
5 Greenleaf Woods Drive, #102
Portsmouth, New Hampshire 03801
www.perpublisher.com

www.CiaoItalia.com
Facebook.com/MaryAnnEsposito
Twitter: @CiaoItaliaShow
Instagram @CiaoItaliaShow
Pinterest @CiaoItaliaShow

Cover photo and food photography by John W. Hession

For my family, don't forget

Contents

Assisi street scene

Foreword

I remember the first time I was a guest on Ciao Italia many moons ago. After a warm greeting from Mary Ann and Paul Lally (the director), I began prepping for my spot and immediately picked up on a "whistle while you work" vibe. The film crew and kitchen crew were busy but even during the chaos of getting everything just right at the last minute for the shoot, they appeared light hearted and happy. Mary Ann had infused this All-American crew with the spirit of Italy! A few minutes before we filmed, I went into makeup and was pleasantly surprised to see Phoebe Rambler, who I knew from working with Julia Child. As she did her best to make me presentable, she raved about working with Mary Ann and about the delicious food they all got to eat after the production was over. I don't remember the dish I cooked that day but I clearly remember that working with Mary Ann was stress-free. Like the other great pros I had worked with, she knew how to keep things moving along smoothly. When Paul declared it a "wrap", the entire crew, including Phoebe, descended on the food. It was a joyous moment. I appeared on Ciao Italia once every season after that and always looked forward to it.

Mary Ann's love for food and for people is one and the same. That is the moral my grandmother, Aida Podagrosi, who was born in Ferentino, an ancient castle town between Rome and Naples, taught me. I find their spirits to be kindred . . . one where cooking is an act of love and generosity, and where ingredients are subjected to great discernment and then prepared simply to maintain their integrity.

Saint Francis and the wolf

"Antipasto gets the conversation going" says Mary Ann. The magic isn't just in the cooking but happens at the table where talk, laughter, kindness and comradery combine with cuisine. In this wonderful book, Mary Ann ties people to the ingredients and recipes in a way that displays her beautiful Sicilian heart.

This impressive work isn't just another cookbook by a prolific and talented author and teacher; this is a very personal collection of recipes and stories that reflect a lifetime of travel and tasting the best that Italy has to offer. With a mix of esoteric and classic dishes culled from home cooks, farmers, winemakers, cheesemakers and even a couple professional chefs from every corner of Italy, Mary Ann has transcribed those flavors for the American home cook making each recipe approachable. I loved the interesting variety of dishes offered in the pages that follow—many that I have never heard of - like "Frascarelli" a type of pasta that is grated right into the boiling water then tossed with butter and sage leaves, or a salad made with Agretti, a type of green that I have never seen during my travels to Italy or elsewhere. There are many excellent recipes for soups, risottos, vegetables, seafood, meats, salads, breads, fruits and desserts—each one with a special connection to Mary Ann. And, of course, pasta is given extra attention, with very knowledgeable directions and advice. The headnotes preceding each recipe explain the origins and subtleties of each dish and will definitely inspire the home cook to venture into Mary Ann's Italy. I know I am anxious to.

Fabulous recipes aside, this book is worth possessing just for the in depth dissertations Mary Ann gives on so many ingredients like olive oil, cheese, rice, lentils, pasta, pasta sauces, tomatoes, bread, artichokes, radicchio, prosciutto, mortadella, balsamic vinegar and other stars of Italian cuisine. She teaches the importance of each and their connections to particular regions, cities and villages with a knowledge that can only come from firsthand experience. Mary Ann tells fun stories of Saints and extraordinary people and their connections to particular customs, history, holidays, farming and techniques of food preparation. These delightful tales, like the one of her grandmother preparing elaborate dishes honoring St. Joseph for granting her wish of saving her husband's life, give us a deeper understanding of how food is so much more than fuel for the body. It is a celebration of love and of life.

Mary Ann Esposito has spent her life cooking, traveling and teaching. The pages that follow are the culmination of her amazing career accomplishments, vast experience, intelligence, and most of all her connection to the food and the people she loves. Grazia, Mary Ann, for sharing your great adventure with us.

Jasper White,
chef, restauranteur and author

Introduction

In 1991, my first cookbook, *Ciao Italia*, was published as a companion to the PBS series of the same name. After nearly twenty-eight years of continuous national broadcast and travel throughout the magical boot, I've found that Italy has changed me in ways that I could not have imagined possible. When I page through my library of personal travel journals that I have written for each trip, they become for me a time machine, each page transporting me to a vividly remembered moment of people, places, and, of course, food.

I really started writing this book subconsciously when I was just a kid, exposed every day to the from-scratch southern Italian foods that have defined me. I think of this book as a capstone of the many opportunities that I have had to get to know what Italian food is really all about, and with this knowledge I find myself in a new place that is far different from my experiences in 1991. Since then, I have traveled to all the regions of Italy, meeting with farmers, cooking with chefs and home cooks, listening to their stories, studying their techniques, and delving into Italy's complex food history.

Each time I savor a piece of Parmigiano-Reggiano cheese, I recall how it is made, what the rules and nuances of this cheese are, and how it is used in cooking. And when the cheese makers made the sign of the cross over the newly formed curds as they were lifted from their whey, I was there to witness the pride in artisan workmanship.

How fortunate I have been to be able to stomp through a radicchio farm in the Veneto, surrounded by rows of royal magenta-colored plants with white veining or to have the experience of making emerald-green pesto on a farm in Liguria where miles of DOP basil plants perfume the air. How privileged I felt when I made bread dough in Sicily under the guidance of a master bread maker, kneading the golden yellow semolina flour in a wooden *madia* and baking it in an ancient outdoor stone oven fired with pruned olive branches.

My search for how regional foods are made led me to many places, such as Ristorante alla Borsa, in Valeggio Sul Mincio, where Nadia Pasquali and I made the most delicate see-through tortelli. On Capri, tasting the buffalo mozzarella was a visual and almost spiritual experience, as was finding the famous creamy vibrant green pistachio nuts, from Bronte, in a market in Palermo. With each experience, I came away with admiration for the reverence Italians have for their artisan-made foods and for the care and nurturing of the land. Travel and cooking in Italy have given me so much perspective and joy.

Italy is younger than the United States as a united country (1861), but its food history spans centuries. So many historical factors have influenced its food culture before unification that to suggest that it has a standard cuisine would be wrong. Yet people do, characterizing "Italian food" as pasta with red sauce. Years of travel have taught me that there is no such standard cuisine called "Italian food"; there is only regional food spread among twenty diverse areas, and that is what informs the recipes in this book. Along with the recipes are the stories and traditions that surround them and give them richness.

The world of food has changed dramatically, and Americans' relatively newfound interest in and awareness of where our foods come from and the purity of our ingredients is something that is just innate in Italy and has recently grown stronger here. Words like *sustainable*, *organic*, and *farm-to-table* are in our collective consciousness, and farmers' markets are more popular than ever. Italy has been at the forefront of this movement and awareness long before it was popular here, when Carlo Petrini founded the Slow

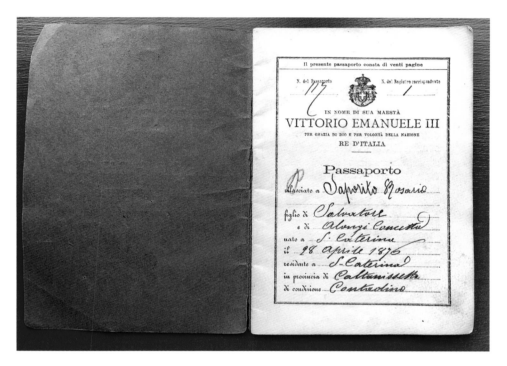

Food movement in 1986 in Bra, in the Piedmont region. Essentially this movement strives to preserve traditional, regional cuisine.

When I wrote my first book, the merits of using olive oil were just gaining national attention. The news buzz was that the Mediterranean diet was the one to emulate, with its emphasis on olive oil—a monounsaturated "good fat"—as well as a focus on eating less meat, more fish, and lots more vegetables, fruits, and whole grains.

Gathered here are recipes and food experiences from all over the boot, along with stories that bring them to life. I am grateful for the opportunity to catalogue them because in Italy, as in our own country, many traditional regional recipes are being lost to future generations who have neither the time nor interest in preserving them. It is my hope that this book will keep the soul of Italian regional cooking alive and that you will travel with me in these pages and come away with a new appreciation for the foods of Italy.

✦✦✦

A Few Words about Salt

There seems to be much confusion about which salt is best for specific cooking needs. First, let's be clear about what salt is: a mineral that contains compounds of chlorine and sodium. Salt comes from either the evaporation of briny seawater or from mining underground salt deposits formed eons ago.

Today we have so many choices of salts from regular table salt to flavored salts to pretzel salt and salt for margaritas. But we are told to limit our intake to a mere teaspoon a day. That would be hard to do for most people! Too much salt can have adverse affects on our health like high blood pressure.

There is no question that adding salt to a dish brightens its flavor, and how much salt to add is really a personal choice. If you feel a recipe is too skimpy on salt, you can always add more. My salt suggestions are only a guide. When you come right down to it, salt is salt, no matter what clever marketing messages Madison Avenue has thrown at us.

Iodized table salt comes from underground mines and contains anti-caking agents. It has a fine-grain texture and is combined with iodine, which is necessary for thyroid health. Use this salt in all recipes unless indicated otherwise.

Kosher salt is an additive-free coarse-grained salt that takes its name from the practice of salting kosher meats. It has a flaky texture, is less dense than table salt, and dissolves more quickly. If a recipe calls for table salt, use roughly double the amount of kosher salt because as the salt crystals increase in size, so does the amount of space between the grains. A tablespoon of fine sea salt will contain more salt by weight than a tablespoon of coarse salt because of the size difference of the grains.

Fine sea salt is derived from the natural evaporation of seawater. It is a finer, powdery grind of coarse salt. Both fine and coarse sea salts contain trace minerals including iron, calcium, and zinc.

Coarse sea salt is a larger crystallized version of fine sea salt. It is used to sprinkle over meats, fish, breads, and some baked goods to give them a polished gourmet look. A teaspoon of table salt equals about 1 ½ teaspoons of coarse salt.

Antipasto

"Eat and run" has never been part of the culinary language of Italy. In a country where the word *piano* (slow) is the password for eating well, the Italians could teach us how to eat mindfully for the full enjoyment of our food. We are told over and over again that the Mediterranean diet is the way to a healthy lifestyle, and there have been many scientific studies to support it.

For Italians, the table is set not just with plates and utensils but also with a proper beginning to the meal called *antipasto*, usually a parade of small plates offering local tastings of such things as pickled mushrooms and peppers, thin slices of grilled eggplant and zucchini, dried tomatoes in olive oil, and tiny cipolline onions. There would be tart olives and thin slices of *salumi* (local cured meats) like salame, prosciutto di Parma, and paper-thin slices of raw cured beef called carpaccio. There would also be marinated fish and shellfish such as anchovies, sardines, octopus, and cuttlefish.

Rustic breads would round out the setting, and all at the table would be welcomed first with a "cincin," clinking glasses of wine salute to longevity. No one would be in a hurry, checking a cell phone or tweeting. The focus would be on the food and the people enjoying it.

Antipasto is designed to get you in the right frame of mind for what foods will appear next at the table. There is perfect logic as to how Italians eat, in small courses, instead of a jam-packed plate of food with everything blending together.

After antipasto comes the *primo piatto* (first course), usually consisting of soup, risotto, or pasta. In the movie *Big Night*, two Italian brothers played by Stanley Tucci as Secondo and Tony Shalhoub as Primo, have opened a restaurant in New Jersey. In one unforgettable scene, a couple is ordering off the menu and the woman orders risotto *and* pasta. This does not sit well with chef

Primo, who tells his brother in no uncertain terms that she can have one or the other but not both! Two first courses? Unthinkable in Italy.

The *secondo piatto* (second course) follows with some type of fish, meat, or poultry that is grilled, pan-fried, or roasted. This may be accompanied by tiny potatoes and seasonal vegetables.

Insalata (salad) was traditionally served last, but these days it may be served before, with, or at the end of the meal. The reason for serving it last was the belief that it was looked upon as a *digestivo*, a way to settle down the meal just consumed.

A traditional Italian meal ends with fruit and nuts, not sweets. Those are reserved for special occasions like baptisms, engagements, and name days.

Naturally this way of eating takes time, the one thing that most of us do not have. Travelers are amazed that hours have passed and they are still at the table! For Italians, being at the table leads to conversation, relaxation, and mindfulness.

Antipasto can be light and simply prepared or hearty and elaborate. The important thing to keep in mind is to make sure that the type of antipasto offered fits the type of meal being served. A formal five-course dinner calls for something light to start, like the classic prosciutto di Parma, thin ribbon slices of raw cured ham matched with melon or figs. On the other hand, for a simple meal consisting of just one or two courses, more substantial antipasto could be offered, like fried polenta squares with a drizzle of extra-virgin olive oil or soft cheese over the top.

Antipasto gets the conversation going.

Sedano Ripieno di Tonno

Tuna-Stuffed Celery

2 (6-ounce) cans tuna fillets in olive oil

2 hard-boiled eggs, mashed

2 tablespoons minced red onion or shallot

2 tablespoons capers in vinegar, drained and minced

Salt and freshly ground black pepper to taste

4 crisp ribs celery, cut into 1-inch lengths

A good-quality canned tuna fillets in olive oil can work magic in minutes in the kitchen; team it with pasta and fresh lemon; stuff it into the cavities of juicy sweet bell peppers, or make this quick and healthy antipasto. **Serves 8 to 10**

Put the tuna and its oil in a bowl and flake with a fork; add the mashed eggs, onion, and capers and season with salt and pepper. Make a smooth mixture.

Fill the celery cavities with the tuna mixture. Arrange them on a dish and serve, or cover, and refrigerate. Bring to room temperature 1 hour before serving.

Bruschetta

Grilled Bread with Garlic and Olive Oil

Bruschetta—grilled bread rubbed with fresh garlic and served with a generous drizzle of extra-virgin olive oil over the top—is a popular antipasto throughout Italy. The secret to its success is to use a dense, crusty loaf with a tight crumb. Using a spongy store-bought bread is courting disaster because it will shred and is not dense enough to hold a good extra-virgin olive oil. Bruschetta varies from region to region, from the smooth liver pâté of Tuscany to the whipped cod of the Veneto to the chopped tomato and basil found in Campania.   **Serves 6**

6 (1-inch-thick) slices crusty country-style bread

2 to 3 cloves garlic, peeled and halved

Extra-virgin olive oil

Freshly ground black pepper (optional)

Grill the bread slices or toast them in the oven on a baking sheet until nicely browned on both sides, about 5 minutes.

Rub each slice on one side only with the cut side of a clove of garlic. As you do, tiny flecks of garlic will be caught in the crevices of the bread. Place each slice on an individual serving plate and drizzle the top with extra-virgin olive oil. Grind black pepper over the slices, if you wish, and serve.

Crostini di Spinaci e Gorgonzola

Spinach Toasts with Gorgonzola Cheese

Crostini are small baguette bread slices fried in olive oil or butter and topped with anything from black truffle paste to this simple yet elegant combination of spinach and melted Gorgonzola cheese.   **Serves 6**

Heat the olive oil in a large sauté pan over medium heat until it begins to shimmer. Add the bread slices, a few at a time, and fry them on both sides until golden brown. Drain the slices on absorbent paper.

In a small saucepan, melt the cheese over low heat, stirring constantly. Stir in the spinach. Mix well. Spread each bread slice with some of the mixture. Serve immediately.

1½ cups extra-virgin olive oil

12 (1-inch thick) slices baguette-style bread

1½ cups (about 2 ounces) crumbled Gorgonzola dolce cheese

1 cup cooked spinach, squeezed dry and finely chopped

Crostini di Fegatini

Little Toasts with Chicken Liver

1½ cups extra-virgin olive oil

12 (1-inch-thick) slices baguette-style bread

1 tablespoon unsalted butter

¼ cup finely minced red onion

2 thin slices prosciutto di Parma, finely minced

1½ pounds chicken livers, trimmed and chopped

14 fresh sage leaves, 2 minced and 12 left whole

Salt and freshly ground black pepper to taste

1 teaspoon unbleached all-purpose flour

¼ cup chicken broth, homemade (page 38) or store-bought

1 tablespoon capers in salt, well rinsed and drained

I enjoyed these delicious chicken liver crostini in Edgardo Sandoli's restaurant, La Cucina di Edgardo. They are a specialty of his home in Venice. **Serves 6**

Heat the oil in a large sauté pan over medium heat until it begins to shimmer. Add the bread slices, a few at a time, and fry them on both sides until golden brown. Drain the slices on absorbent paper.

Wipe out the frying pan with paper towels and melt the butter over medium heat. Add the onion and sauté until soft. Add the prosciutto, chicken livers, minced sage, and salt and pepper, increase the heat to medium-high, and cook until the livers are browned. Sprinkle the flour over the top and stir in the broth. Add the capers and cook until the mixture thickens slightly.

Transfer the mixture to a blender or processor and puree. Spread the mixture evenly over the bread slices and top each with a sage leaf. Serve immediately.

Crostini di Pomodori

Little Tomato Toasts

The secret to the success of these vibrant tomato-topped crostini is to use ripe plum tomatoes and fresh basil in season. Make these for a summer cookout and serve them while the rest of the meal is cooking on the grill.   **Serves 6**

Put the tomatoes in a strainer and set aside to drain. Grill or toast the bread slices. Rub each slice with a cut side of a clove of garlic and drizzle each with ½ teaspoon oil.

Transfer the tomatoes to a bowl and add the basil, oregano, salt, and pepper. Mix well. Divide the mixture and top the bread slices evenly. Serve immediately.

1½ cups seeded and chopped plum tomatoes (about 3)

12 (1-inch-thick) slices baguette-style bread

2 cloves garlic, peeled and halved

2 tablespoons extra-virgin olive oil

1 tablespoon minced fresh basil

1 tablespoon minced fresh oregano

Salt and freshly ground black pepper to taste

Ode to Olive Oil

"His Holiness would like the olive oil sent to the Vatican." So goes the traditional papal request for extra-virgin olive oil from Umbria. For centuries even popes have recognized and appreciated the superiority of the olive oil from trees in this region and paid farmers to plant them on the middle hills, and in the chalky soil of the Umbrian countryside. To this day, Umbrian olive oil still graces the table in the Vatican and is considered some of the best in Italy. But even before popes recognized its worth, it was held in high regard in biblical times, and its branches became a symbol of peace for the world. The ancient Etruscans, Greeks, and Romans understood olive oil's worthiness for culinary purposes. Pliny the Elder once wrote, "There is no plant which bears a fruit of as great importance as the olive." Its use also extended to oil for their lamps, for rubbing on the body, for sale as a profitable trading product, and for medicinal purposes. Roman soldiers even rubbed olive oil on their skin.

I especially love the stately, silver-leafed olive trees that dot the countryside of Tuscany and Umbria, their graceful beauty immortalized by great artists like Giotto and Perugino. There are hundreds of varieties of olive trees in Italy. The regions of Tuscany, Umbria, Sicily, Calabria, Liguria, Puglia, and Campania produce some of the best olive oils in the world, and each one has its own particular flavor, color, and density, depending on the type of olive and the type of soil. Lower acidity in the soil produces a better olive oil.

In the American kitchen, the role of olive oil is misunderstood, and there is often confusion as to which olive oil to use. Should one cook with extra-virgin olive oil or reserve it solely for dressing salads? Can it be used to deep-fry foods? Which is the best one to buy? Where should I store it? What is pomace?

Olives are harvested for oil production from mid-October to early November. Billowing nets are draped under the olive branches to protect the falling olives from bruising as they drop from the trees. Olives contain only 20 percent oil; the rest is 40 percent water and 40 percent pulp. Once the olives are picked, they are dumped into the top of a large crushing machine, where thousands of knifelike blades pierce the pulp and oil begins to drip into collection vats. The pulp is whirled at high speed with cold water to separate the oil from the pulp. This is where the term *cold-pressed* comes from.

By definition, and by Italian law, extra-virgin olive oil must not contain more that 1 percent acidity, the oil must come from the first pressing of the olives, and no mechanical heat can be used to extract the oil. Only then is an olive oil characterized as extra-virgin. Other grades have higher amounts of acidity and may come from multiple pressings. The color of olive oil can vary from golden yellow to yellow-green to dark green, depending on the type of olive and the method used to process it.

In the case of pomace, which is the pulp that remains after pressing the olives, any remaining oil is extracted with the use of solvents. This oil is refined and blended with a small percentage of virgin olive oil (higher acidity), and sold at much cheaper prices—but, in my opinion, you get what you pay for.

I have been cooking with low-acidity extra-virgin olive oil for years and I know what I like: fruity olive oil for salads and slightly peppery olive oil for light sautéing. Selecting olive oil is a lot like selecting a bottle of wine. It can be a daunting task, but if you know what you like, the job becomes easier. Just as there are hundreds of wines to choose from, so, too, the dilemma exists in the multiple choices for olive oil. Everything is dependent on your palate and whether or not you like fruity, dense, spicy, mild, or peppery as a flavor characteristic. The best way to determine this is to sample different types of olive oils from various regions of Italy.

To really taste-test olive oil correctly, take a sip and roll it around in your mouth, but do not swallow yet! Taste it at the tip of your tongue, the roof of your mouth, the center of the tongue, and the back of the tongue. Now swallow it for a throat "finish." The different areas of the mouth will produce a variety of tastes like nutty, peppery, heavy, intense, light, sweet, earthy, grassy, and buttery. If you follow this technique, you will come to appreciate the many properties of olive oil.

Last, a word about storing olive oil: It is best to keep it in a cool, dark place, not in the refrigerator where temperature extremes can affect its flavor. Olive oil is best used within a year of its purchase, otherwise it could become rancid, so only buy as much as you can use up in a short period of time. Following these guidelines will ensure that you will be using and enjoying olive oil according to Italian tradition.

Peperoni Sott'Olio e Aceto

Sweet Bell Peppers with Oil and Vinegar

The last time I visited Ristorante M.R. in Perugia, I ate nothing but antipasti. Mario Ragni, the "M.R." of the establishment's name, is a wonderful chef who combines fresh Italian ingredients in new ways. His antipasto bar is all one needs to feel really satisfied. The sweet peppers marinated in fruity olive oil and intense red wine vinegar were outstanding and reminded me of the pepper salad I make at home.   **Serves 8 to 10**

Preheat the broiler. Lightly grease a rimmed baking sheet.

Place the peppers on the baking sheet and broil, turning them occasionally, until they are blackened all over, about 15 minutes. Put the peppers in a paper bag, close it tightly, and let them cool for 20 minutes.

Meanwhile, in a large, shallow nonmetal dish, mix the olive oil, vinegar, garlic, salt, and pepper well. Set aside.

When cool, peel the peppers and remove the stems, cores, and seeds. Cut the peppers into thin strips. Add them to the dressing, mix well, cover, and allow them to marinate at room temperature for 1 hour before serving.

8 medium bell peppers (an assortment of yellow, red, and green)

½ to ⅔ cup extra-virgin olive oil, depending on size of peppers

2 tablespoons balsamic vinegar

3 tablespoons chopped garlic

Salt and freshly ground black pepper to taste

Salumi in Pasta Sfoglia

Puff Pastry with Italian Cured Meats

Here's a quick puff pastry pinwheel that can have a variety of fillings. **Makes about 4 dozen**

Preheat the oven to 425°F. Line two rimmed baking sheets with parchment paper.

Work with one sheet of puff pastry at a time, keeping the rest wrapped so that the pastry does not dry out.

Roll out each sheet on a lightly floured surface into a 14-inch square. Brush each sheet with 2 tablespoons of mustard. Layer the cured meats on the pastry, slightly overlapping, but leave a ½-inch border all around. Sprinkle the cheese over the top.

Tightly roll up each sheet like a jellyroll. Pinch the seam closed and tuck and seal the ends of the roll.

Cut each roll into 1-inch-thick rounds and lay them about 1 inch apart on the baking sheets. Bake the pinwheels until golden brown, about 12 minutes. Transfer them to a cooling rack to cool a bit. Serve warm.

2 (1-pound) packages frozen puff pastry (2 sheets each), thawed

8 tablespoons Dijon mustard

12 ounces assorted thinly sliced Italian cured meats

8 ounces (about 2 cups) shredded sharp Provolone cheese

Torta al Pesto

Pesto Tart

½ cup pine nuts

1 pound (4 sticks) unsalted butter, at room temperature

12 ounces cream cheese, at room temperature

4 ounces mascarpone cheese, home-made (page 329) or store-bought, at room temperature

A few fresh basil leaves

¾ cup Pesto (page 144)

1-1½ cups extra-virgin olive oil, plus more if needed

24 (1-inch-thick) slices baguette-style bread

Pesto is a classic sauce from Genoa made from peppery, spicy basil leaves. The Genovese use very small leaves to make pesto, removing the stems and center vein of each leaf first. A mortar and pestle is the traditional way to prepare pesto, but it can also be made in a food processor to save time. Try to use small basil leaves and tear them into pieces by hand first to minimize having to pulse them for too long. This will prevent the leaves from bruising and turning brown. This torta can be prepared up to 3 days ahead and is perfect crowd food.   **Serves 10 to 15**

Preheat the oven to 350° F.

Spread the pine nuts on a baking sheet and toast them until golden brown, about 5 minutes; be careful not to burn them. Let cool.

In a food processor or bowl, combine the butter, cream cheese, and mascarpone cheese. Process or beat with a wooden spoon until the mixture is very smooth. Set aside.

Line a 6-cup round mold or a 9 x 5-inch loaf pan with a double thickness of damp cheesecloth large enough to hang over the sides of the mold. Scatter some of the toasted pine nuts in the bottom of the mold and arrange the basil leaves in the base of the mold, shiny side down, to make an attractive design.

Spoon one-third of the cheese mixture into the mold and smooth it to make an even layer. Carefully spoon half of the pesto on top of the cheese layer and sprinkle with the remaining toasted pine nuts. Add another layer of the cheese mixture, spoon the remaining pesto over it, and top with the remainder of the cheese mixture. Bring the cheesecloth edges up over the top of the mold. Press lightly on the top of the mold to settle the ingredients. Cover the mold with foil and refrigerate it for several hours, or up to 3 days.

To serve, remove the foil and turn the mold upside down onto a serving dish. Remove the cheesecloth and let the torta come to room temperature.

In a large sauté pan, heat the olive oil over medium heat until it begins to shimmer. Add the bread slices, a few at a time, and fry them until golden brown on both sides. Serve the torta with the bread slices.

Basil Farm, Liguria

An Alphabet of Cheese

The uses of cheeses in Italian cooking have antique origins that have continued to today. Almost every region of Italy boasts locally made cheeses, and they number into the hundreds, which would make it a tremendous job to try to describe all of them. But mention should be made of the more familiar ones, their particular characteristics, and usage.

Many artisan cheeses carry a DOP designation. What exactly does this mean? DOP stands for Denominazione di Origine Protetta, or Protected Designation of Origin. This guarantees that the product is produced in a specified area with local ingredients and follows strict production guidelines. These marks also go for other artisan products like prosciutto di Parma, speck Alto Adige, San Marzano tomatoes, and many more.

For example, on the rind of Parmigiano-Reggiano cheese are embedded the DOP identifying letters. Consumers need to be savvy when buying it since there are many domestic "parmesan" cheeses bearing no resemblance to the real thing.

IGP stands for Indicazione Geografica Protetta, or Geographic Indication of Protection, and is another certification of a product's authenticity. In this case the rules are less rigid than for DOP. For a food product to receive this status, at least one of the ingredients must come from a specific region.

Asiago DOP: semi-hard cow's milk cheese made in the province of Vicenza, in the Veneto region. It has a pale yellow color and a pleasant nutty flavor that gets sharper as it ages. It is good for eating, grated over pasta, in frittatas, and in cream sauces.

Bel Paese: a semisoft cow's milk cheese with a mild taste. It pairs nicely with crusty bread and fresh pears.

Caciocavallo DOP: a stretched curd cow's milk cheese from Abruzzo, Calabria, Campania, and Sicily that is formed into a round or pear shape with a little knob on the top. It is a good table cheese with a hint of smokiness and is a good grating cheese once it ages.

Fior di Latte: a cow's milk cheese from southern Italy that is similar to fresh water buffalo mozzarella. Creamy white, it is best consumed the day it is made and is exceptional with ripe summer tomatoes and fresh basil.

Fontina DOP: a cow's milk cheese with a distinctive brown rind. It comes from a particular breed of cow in the Valle d'Aosta in northern Italy. It has a slightly nutty taste and a creamy texture. It is good as a table cheese and for cooking.

Gorgonzola DOP: a cow's milk cheese produced in Gorgonzola, Lombardy, in northern Italy, that has green mold running through it. It has a distinct flavor that becomes sharp as it ages. Gorgonzola dolce (sweet) is buttery and milder than Gorgonzola forte (sharp). Both are wonderful with crusty bread, and Gorgonzola dolce is delicious as a cream sauce for pasta dishes.

Grana Padano DOP: a grainy, cow's milk cheese produced in the Po River Valley Plain in northern Italy (excluding the provinces of Emilia, where Parmigiano-Reggiano is produced). It is a great table cheese as well as a grating cheese for many types of dishes.

Mascarpone: a very rich cow's milk cheese from Lombardy, with the texture of cream cheese. Used mainly in desserts like the classic tiramisù, it is very perishable. It pairs well with fresh figs or pears.

Mozzarella di Bufala Campana DOP: a soft delicate cheese made in the Campania region of southern Italy. It comes from the milk of the water buffalo and is both very perishable and expensive. Wonderful served with bread and a drizzle of olive oil, this cheese is at its peak on the day it is made. There is also a cow's milk version that is less rich tasting.

Parmigiano-Reggiano DOP: known as the king of Italian cheeses. Both the young and aged types are made from partially skimmed cow's milk. It is table ready at 12 months of aging and is pale yellow in color. As it ages, it becomes drier and granular in texture. Cheese, like bread, is one of man's most basic foods. The farmers of Italy have been making it for centuries, transforming the rich milk of cows, sheep, goats, and buffalo into distinctive cheese, both fresh and aged. Today, as in the past, making cheese is an artisan task adhering to time-honored methods of production. In all my years of travel from the top of the boot to the islands of Sicily and Sardinia, I have made it a point to visit as many local *caseifici* (cheese production houses) as possible. I remember my very first visit in the food-rich city of Reggio Emilia in the region of Emilia-Romagna, where the king of all Italian cheeses, Parmigiano-Reggiano, is made. There I received a personalized tour of a cheese factory from Sandro Iori, a man who knows a lot about Parmigiano-Reggiano's history and production. The making of this cheese is governed by law, and its name testifies to the fact that it must be produced in the Emilia-Romagna region, which includes the cities of Parma, Modena, Bologna, and Reggio Emilia. It may also be produced in Mantua in the region of Lombardia. The cheese must be made from cow's milk, from both a morning and evening milking, and it must be made between April and November of each year, when the best milk is obtainable.

Sandro is not a cheese maker but a high-ranking bank executive. He was born in Reggio Emilia and grew up near the pasturelands that feed the cows that yield the rich milk for this famous cheese. Parmigiano-Reggiano is so prized that the bank where he works owns huge warehouses full of aged golden wheels of the cheese, stacked floor to ceiling. He says this regarding the bank's view of this cheese: "Cheese is money."

Cheese is nothing more than the coagulated heated portion of milk, called curds. What causes the milk to coagulate is rennet, an enzyme produced from the stomach lining of sheep or from plants. The whey, the liquid left after the curds are removed, is used to make soft, fresh cheese called ricotta.

The principles of cheese making may be simple, but the quality of the final product is determined by a number of things: the type of milk used, its fat content, the temperature it is cooked at, the amount of aging time, the time of year the cheese is made, whether or not it has undergone a brine bath, and the ability of an experienced cheese maker to know when the cheese is ready for consumption.

Pecorino Romano DOP: A sheep's milk cheese made in the regions of Lazio, Tuscany, Sicily, and Sardinia. The best known is Pecorino Romano DOP, from the Lazio region. It has a salty taste and sharp flavor and is wonderful grated on tomato-based pasta dishes or as a table cheese.

Provolone ValPadana DOP: originally made from water buffalo milk, this cheese is now made from cow's milk. It develops a sharp flavor as it ages and can be used as a table cheese and in recipes with eggplant, pasta, and breads. In Sardinia, this cheese is grilled over hot stones.

Ricotta: means "recooked," and is technically not cheese but made from whey, the leftover liquid produced in the cheese-making process. It is cooked with rennet to produce a soft white cheese. Ricotta can be made from sheep or cow's milk whey, with sheep ricotta having a sharper taste. It is used in lasagne, as a sauce for pasta, or in desserts like cannoli. See page 332 for how to make it.

Scamorza: a southern Italian cheese made from cow's milk or a mixture of cow and sheep's milk. It is a molded, *pasta filata* (spun) cheese. It is good as a table cheese or grilled. There is also smoked scamorza DOP with a subtle smoky flavor and a brownish rind.

Taleggio DOP: a creamy cow's milk cheese from the Taleggio Valley in Bergamo, Lombardia. It is creamy, white, soft, and good with fresh fruit or crusty bread.

Salvia Fritta

Fried Sage Leaves

¼ cup cornstarch

⅓ cup unbleached all-purpose flour

½ cup unflavored sparkling water

16 fresh sage leaves, stemmed

Vegetable oil, for frying

Fine sea salt

Alla Borsa, one of my favorite restaurants, is in Valeggio Sul Mincio, near Verona. It serves a wonderful antipasto of fried sage leaves, a crispy and delightful surprise. Make the batter at least 2 hours ahead of time to allow it to thicken sufficiently, and use only fresh sage leaves. Serve them with chips of Parmigiano-Reggiano cheese and olives for a delicious and effortless antipasto.   **Serves 4**

In a small bowl, sift the cornstarch and flour together. Stir in the sparkling water. Cover the bowl and let it stand for 2 hours.

Add the sage leaves to the batter and use a spoon to coat each one well.

Heat 1 cup vegetable oil to 375°F in a deep-fryer or heavy-duty saucepan.

Drop the leaves a few at a time into the oil and fry until they are golden brown. With a slotted spoon, transfer the leaves to a dish lined with paper towels. Sprinkle with salt and serve hot.

Pizzette di Funghi

Little Mushroom Pizzas

Sometimes you have to think outside the box in the kitchen. That happened to me with three starting-to-shrivel portobello mushrooms that had been forgotten in the back of my refrigerator. What could be done with them? Make soup or a stir-fry? Instead I made these small pizzas (pizzette). **Serves 4**

Preheat the oven to 350°F. Brush a nonstick baking pan with olive oil.

Use a small spoon to scrape out the brown gills on the undersides of the mushroom caps, making sure not to puncture them. Brush the inside of the caps with olive oil and place them, cap side down, in a single layer on the baking sheet.

Scatter the cheese cubes evenly over each cap. Place 4 slices of tomato on each one. Drizzle extra-virgin olive oil over each cap and bake them for 25 to 30 minutes, or until the tomatoes look soft and the cheese has melted. Scatter the basil over the caps. Cut each cap into 4 wedges and serve.

3 large portobello mushrooms, stemmed

About 3 tablespoons extra-virgin olive oil

1½ cups cubed fresh mozzarella cheese

3 large cherry tomatoes, each cut into 4 round slices

½ cup shredded fresh basil leaves

Croccanti di Asparagi

Crunchy Asparagus Spears

Italians serve a variety of vegetables as antipasto. In this recipe for baked crunchy asparagus spears, the asparagus is coated in grated Parmigiano-Reggiano cheese and sesame seeds.   **Serves 4**

Preheat the oven to 350°F.

Pour the olive oil onto a nonstick rimmed baking sheet. Add the asparagus in a single layer and turn each spear several times to coat them in the oil.

Combine the cheese, salt and sesame seeds on a platter or on a sheet of wax paper. Roll each asparagus spear in the mixture to evenly coat them and place them on the baking sheet in a single layer.

Bake until the asparagus is easily pierced with a knife at its thickest part and they have started to brown. Transfer them to a serving dish and serve with lemon wedges.

2½ tablespoons extra-virgin olive oil

1 pound asparagus, trimmed

½ cup grated Parmigiano-Reggiano cheese

½ teaspoon salt

¼ cup sesame seeds

Lemon wedges, for serving

Carpaccio di Funghi
Mushroom Carpaccio

¼ cup plus 1 tablespoon extra-virgin olive oil

Juice of 2 lemons

1 clove garlic, finely minced

½ teaspoon salt, plus more to taste

¼ teaspoon red pepper flakes

Freshly ground black pepper to taste

8 ounces meaty mushrooms (porcini, king oyster, or button), stemmed and thinly sliced

2 tablespoons minced fresh flat-leaf parsley

1 cup arugula leaves

Shavings of Asiago cheese

Carpaccio usually refers to very thinly sliced raw meat or fish that is served with a drizzle of extra-virgin olive oil, but here it applies to thinly sliced raw mushrooms that are marinated and magically turned into an explosion of flavors for this earthy salad. To really get the most from mushrooms, do not store them in plastic bags that will trap moisture and make them slimy; mushrooms need to breathe, so store them in brown paper bags. **Serves 4**

In a bowl, whisk ¼ cup olive oil with the lemon juice, garlic, salt, red pepper flakes, and black pepper.

Put the mushroom slices in a baking dish and pour the dressing over them. Cover and allow them to marinate at room temperature for a couple of hours.

When ready to serve, transfer the mushrooms to a serving platter and sprinkle the parsley over them.

In a bowl, toss the arugula with the remaining 1 tablespoon olive oil and season with salt. Mound the arugula on top of the mushrooms in the center of the platter. Scatter the cheese shavings over the top and serve.

Crostini di Burrata e Balsamico

Little Toasts with Burrata and Balsamic Glaze

Burrata means "buttered" and is the new kid on the block when it comes to fresh Italian cheeses. I was first introduced to it years ago in Puglia, the gorgeous heel region of Italy. This rich, creamy-white, delicate cow's milk cheese is a softer version of mozzarella cheese that is shaped into a ball and filled with *stracciatella*, or stringy curds of mozzarella and a touch of cream. It is very perishable and in Italy is consumed *da giornata*, on the day it is made.   **Serves 4**

4 thick slices rustic bread, such as semolina bread

4 tablespoons extra-virgin olive oil

2 (4-ounce) balls burrata cheese

¼ cup balsamic glaze (page 30)

Heat the olive oil in a sauté pan over medium heat and brown the bread slices on both sides. Place a bread slice on each of four salad plates.

Cut the burrata balls in half with a serrated knife and place one half, cut side up, on top of each bread slice. Drizzle some of the balsamic glaze over each one and serve at room temperature.

Olive all'Ascolana

Stuffed Olives, Ascoli Piceno Style

You have to love them, because making these stuffed olives takes time. Olive all'Ascolana is one of the classic recipes of the Marche region; in 2005, the dish received IGP status from the European Commission. The large, fleshy, and aromatic olives called ascolane tenere contain between 16 and 18 percent oil and are preserved in salt brine with wild fennel seeds and local aromatic herbs. To stuff them requires removing the olive pit but keeping the olive whole so it can be filled with a tasty trio of minced cooked beef, pork, and chicken or turkey. Rolled in flour, tossed in beaten egg, and coated in breadcrumbs, they are fried in oil. They make the most delicious antipasto, and are often sold ready to eat in paper cones. This recipe makes a lot, but as they say in Ascoli Piceno, you need at least ten olives per person! They are that good. If you cannot find these olives in a specialty store or online, use large pitted Cerignola olives in brine. **Serves 8**

Heat 1 tablespoon olive oil in a 12-inch sauté pan over medium heat. Add the onion, celery, and carrot and cook until the mixture softens, about 5 minutes. Stir in the meats and cook for 10 minutes, stirring occasionally. Pour in the wine, allowing most of it to evaporate, then cook the meats on low heat for 15 minutes. No liquid should remain in the pan. Transfer the mixture to a food processor and finely chop the ingredients (or finely chop by hand). Transfer the mixture to a bowl and add the fresh breadcrumbs, 1 egg, cheese, nutmeg, lemon zest, cloves, and salt and pepper. Mix well and refrigerate while preparing the olives.

With a small knife, make a vertical slit in each olive, then cut around the pit as if you were removing the skin from an apple. The olive should remain intact. Stuff each olive with a marble-size amount of the meat filling.

Put the flour in a bowl. Beat the remaining 2 eggs in a third bowl. Put the 2 cups dry breadcrumbs in a second bowl. Coat each olive first in the flour, then in the egg, and lastly in the breadcrumbs. Place them on a rimmed baking sheet as you coat them.

Heat the olive oil to 375°F in a deep-fryer or deep, heavy-duty pot. Fry the olives until golden brown, about 5 minutes. Drain them on absorbent paper and serve hot.

1 tablespoon extra-virgin olive oil

1 small onion, minced

1 rib celery, minced

1 small carrot, minced

4 ounces chuck roast, cut into small pieces

4 ounces boneless pork, cut into small pieces

4 ounces boneless chicken or turkey breast, cut into small pieces

½ cup dry white wine

1 cup fresh breadcrumbs

3 large eggs

¼ teaspoon grated nutmeg

¼ cup grated Parmigiano-Reggiano cheese

Grated zest of 1 lemon

Pinch ground cloves

Salt and freshly ground black pepper to taste

2 pounds whole olives in brine, drained

2 cups unbleached all-purpose flour, for dredging

2 cups dry breadcrumbs

3 cups olive oil, for frying

Smalto Balsamico

Balsamic Glaze

3 cups balsamic
    vinegar
2 tablespoons honey
¼ teaspoon salt

Makes about 2 cups

Pour the balsamic vinegar into a small saucepan and bring to a boil over medium-high heat. Lower the heat to medium, stir in the honey and salt, and cook, stirring often, until the mixture reduces by half, looks thick and syrupy, and has the consistency of honey. When cool, transfer to an airtight jar. Keep in a cool place, but do not refrigerate.

Tools of the Trade

Every cook has different ways of making life in the kitchen manageable and efficient. Most Italian cooking does not require a lot of fancy cookware or gadgets, and I am a big fan of doing things *a mano* (by hand). There are some tools, however, that are indispensable to every cook. The list that follows includes those that I use most frequently. You can find these tools online or in kitchenware stores.

Baker's peel: This long-handled wooden paddle is handy for transferring pizza and bread to a hot baking stone in the oven.

Baking sheets: Rimmed and non-rimmed sheets, as well as nonstick baking sheets, should be of the best material, preferably stainless steel.

Baking stone: An unglazed stone placed in the bottom of the oven is essential for baking breads and pizza. A baking stone helps the bread rise while baking and gives it uniform color and texture and a crispy crust.

Bowls: Keep an assortment of sizes—you'll want several deep ones for making bread dough and oven-safe high-sided bowls for baking fruits and making molded vegetable and pasta dishes.

Cannoli forms: These stainless steel tubes are used to shape cannoli.

Cheese grater: The old-fashioned four- or six-sided stand-up box model is the best. A rotary grater is fine, too, but I like the control and texture that a hand grater allows me.

Colanders: Have several sizes for straining sauces and draining vegetables and pasta.

Cooling racks: These should be large, heavy duty and stackable.

Deep-fryer: This isn't essential, but it is handy for frying cenci, struffoli, pizza fritta, vegetables, and seafood.

Dehydrator: This appliance is indispensable for making dried tomatoes, eggplant, and zucchini preserved in olive oil. It is also great for drying stone fruit such as peaches and apricots.

Dowel rods: ¼-inch-thick wooden rods are used for drying homemade pasta such as fettuccine, spaghetti, and vermicelli.

Food processor: This is useful for many tasks, including making dough, mixing sauces, and pureeing soups.

Funnels: A variety of sizes will come in handy for decanting liquids into containers.

Garlic press: This is handy for recipes that call for garlic juice or mashed garlic.

Immersion blender: I use this when I don't need to use the countertop blender, for general pureeing, whipping cream, and making smoothies.

Kitchen shears: Use these for cutting everything from poultry to pizza.

Knife sharpener: Use either a whetstone or a sharpening steel, because a dull knife is an accident waiting to happen. Don't let it happen to you.

Knives: One of the most essential tools are knives; they should be of the highest quality and include an 8-inch chef's knife as well as carving, deboning, serrated, slicing, and paring knife.

Lemon reamer: This little gadget makes quick work of squeezing lemons, oranges, limes, and grapefruit.

Marble pastry slab: The cool surface is perfect for rolling out pastry dough.

Meat hammer or pounder: Weighted models with a smooth surface (no teeth) are best because they don't tear the meat.

Mezzaluna: This single-blade half-moon knife has two wooden handles; it is rocked back and forth when chopping vegetables and herbs.

Oil cans: Decanting olive oil into a spouted stainless steel oil can keeps counters and stovetops neat.

Pasta fork: This utensil is essential for lifting pasta directly from the pasta pot and into the sauce.

Pasta pots: Ideally you will want a 7- to 8-quart stainless steel three-piece set that includes one small and one large colander insert for draining pasta.

Pasta machine: There are many hand-crank brands on the market; Atlas, Cross, and Marcato are all good.

Pasta platters: Sauced pasta dishes are best served in shallow platters rather than bowls to prevent the sauce from settling at the bottom.

Pastry brushes: Assorted natural-bristle brushes can be used for glazing breads and fruit tarts and for greasing bowls and molds.

Pastry bags: A variety of cloth or disposable bags of various sizes can be used for decorating desserts and for filling pastries and stuffed pastas.

Pastry blender: Wooden-handled types are best for blending butter and flour for pastry dough and for mashing potatoes for gnocchi.

Peppermill: This can be used for grinding peppercorns and other spices.

Pizza pans: Round, perforated aluminum pans help create a nicely browned bottom crust.

Ravioli forms: The two-piece forms are inexpensive and can turn out dozens of ravioli at a time. The ravioli attachment for a hand-crank pasta machine is more expensive but also gets the job done quickly.

Rolling pins: Use a thin 27-inch-long wooden pin for pasta and a 16- to 18-inch pin for pastry.

Sausage funnels: Long- or short-necked funnels for making sausages in casings are available online and in kitchen stores.

Strainers: Long-handled strainers are ideal for scooping delicate filled pasta such as ravioli and gnocchi from the cooking water.

Tart pans: Removable-bottomed pans are available in various sizes from 9 to 12 inches.

Wooden board: Use this for rolling out pasta and kneading bread.

Wooden spoons: Have an assortment of sizes for a multitude of kitchen tasks.

Soup

Genoa Duomo

Italian soups can be meals in themselves. What makes them taste so good? A rich full-bodied broth as the base and fresh vegetables are key, along with additions such as dried beans, bread, pasta, rice, Parmigiano-Reggiano cheese rinds, or even eggs that can turn soup into a culinary wonder.

In my grandmother's day, making soup was an all-day affair. First came the trip to see the "chicken man" to buy just the right plump bird. Once that was done, it met its demise at the deft hands of my grandmother and mother, who then laboriously singed and plucked the feathers and cleaned the bird. They would often prepare several at a time. The chickens were put into huge pots, feet and all, and simmered with chunks of fresh vegetables, herbs, and spices. The kitchen smelled wonderful, and one of the lessons that I learned from them is that for any soup, the ingredients should simmer, not boil, because boiling evaporates the flavor, while simmering keeps all that flavor in the pot. These were smart women. While the soup simmered, pasta dough was made to be added later. My job was cutting pasta strips into tiny squares called quadrucci.

But that was then, and this is now. When I want to make a great-tasting broth, I buy cut-up chicken all ready for the pot.

There are some classic soups besides chicken, such as minestrone (big soup), so called because of the variety of vegetables that go into it. This was the original "kitchen sink" soup. In the southern region of Campania, minestrone is eaten at room temperature during the hot summer months. In the Veneto in the north, rice is a familiar staple in soup. Tuscans like their soup thick, with beans and stale bread, as in the classic *ribollita*, which means "reboiled" because the soup tastes even better when it is reheated the day after it is made. In Rome, *stracciatella*, a mixture of eggs and grated Parmigiano-Reggiano cheese, works magic when briskly whisked into boiling broth. Southern Italians love stylishly shaped macaroni, like little hollow ditalini, in their soup.

The base for soup can be meat, poultry, fish, or just vegetables. Meat broth is the most common in Italy. As with chicken broth, when meat broth was made at home, it began with a less tender cut of meat, usually a brisket, or beef shin and neck bones, and it was the cook's fancy as to what else went into it.

Today, people seem to have lost the art of making good soup, which is a pity because the ingredients to create them, like onions, carrots, celery, and parsley are probably in your refrigerator right now. Soups are some of the quickest and easiest dishes to prepare, and no canned, heavily salted variety can ever compare. Although good-quality canned chicken or beef broth may be used in these recipes, it is easy to make these broths ahead of time and freeze it for future use. Delicious, authentic soups can be made even easier using kitchen tools like food processors, mincers, immersion blenders, and slow cookers.

Brodo di Pollo

Chicken Broth

- 2 sprigs fresh flat-leaf parsley
- 2 sprigs fresh basil
- 5 whole black peppercorns
- 1 tablespoon whole cloves
- 4 pounds chicken necks, wings, and/or thighs
- 2 teaspoons coarse salt
- 1 clove garlic, peeled
- 1 large yellow onion, unpeeled and quartered
- 2 ribs celery with leaves, cut in 4 pieces
- 2 carrots, peeled and cut in half
- 2 plum tomatoes, fresh or canned, quartered
- 1 bay leaf
- Juice of 1 lemon

Making chicken broth was a sacred ritual at home. The bird would slowly simmer with cut-up vegetables, herbs, and spices. When it was done, the vegetables and chicken were cut into small pieces and served in some of the broth for one meal. The rest of the broth was strained and used later in the week as a base for other soups made with pasta, bread, or vegetables. Leave the onions unpeeled for a rich-looking color to this soup. **Makes 3½ to 4 quarts**

Tie the parsley and basil sprigs together with kitchen string. Wrap the peppercorns and whole cloves in a small piece of cheesecloth and tie it up with string.

Put the chicken pieces and salt in a large stockpot and add enough cold water to cover. Cover the pot and bring to a boil over medium-high heat. Skim off the foam that collects with a slotted spoon. Lower the heat to a simmer. Add all the remaining ingredients, including the herb bundle and cheesecloth bag. Cover the pot and cook for 45 minutes to 1 hour. Periodically skim off any additional foam that collects as the soup cooks.

Remove the chicken pieces with a slotted spoon and reserve the meat for another use or shred it and add it to the soup. Discard the onion, cheesecloth bag, and bay leaf. Pour the broth and remaining vegetables through a large strainer lined with cheesecloth into another pot or a large bowl. Transfer the vegetables to a cutting board. Cut them into bite-size pieces to add to the soup or serve them separately if you want a clear broth.

Cover the soup and refrigerate overnight. Skim off any fat that has collected and discard. The broth is ready to use or can be frozen for up to 3 months.

Cappelletti in Brodo

Little Hats Swimming in Broth

I have many wonderful memories of making *cappelletti* (little hats) stuffed with finely ground chicken, though on occasion they were stuffed with beef, pork, or veal. Thin slices of lemon and fresh spinach add extra flavor to the broth.　**Serves 8 to 10**

In a large pot, bring the chicken broth to a boil over medium heat. Add the cappelletti and cook them until they bob to the surface. If desired, add the spinach to the boiling broth just before the cappelletti bob to the surface. Ladle the soup into individual serving dishes and sprinkle with grated Parmigiano-Reggiano cheese. Add the lemon slices (if using) to each bowl just before serving.

4 quarts chicken broth, homemade (page 38) or store-bought

3 to 4 dozen Cappelletti (page 94)

2 cups shredded spinach leaves (optional)

Grated Parmigiano-Reggiano cheese

1 lemon, cut into thin slices (optional)

Brodo di Manzo

Beef Broth

5 whole black
  peppercorns

1 pound beef shin

1 pound beef brisket

2 or 3 beef neck
  bones

1 tablespoon sea salt

1 large yellow onion,
  unpeeled and
  quartered

2 carrots, peeled and
  cut in half

1 rib celery with
  leaves, cut in half

2 fresh or canned
  plum tomatoes,
  coarsely chopped

4 or 5 sprigs fresh
  flat-leaf parsley,
  tied together with
  kitchen string

A really rich-tasting beef broth begins with choosing hearty cuts of meat like beef shin or brisket; some cooks add beef shoulder and neck bones. This broth combines well with pasta or rice or can be used to create a sauce for roasted meats. The meats cooked in the broth are often shredded into small pieces and combined with the broth for a hearty soup or used in a second course.   **Makes 3½ to 4 quarts**

Wrap the peppercorns in a small piece of cheesecloth and tie it up with kitchen string.

Put the meat and salt in a large stockpot and add enough cold water to cover. Bring to a boil over medium-high heat and boil for 5 minutes. Skim off the foam that accumulates with a slotted spoon. Add all the remaining ingredients, including the cheesecloth bag. Stir well with a wooden spoon. Lower the heat to simmer and cook for 2½ to 3 hours. As the soup cooks, periodically skim off the foam that collects on the top with a slotted spoon.

When the meats are tender, remove them, along with the bones, and reserve the meat for another use or shred it and add it to the soup. Discard the onion and cheesecloth bag. Pour the broth and remaining vegetables through a large colander lined with cheesecloth into another pot or a large bowl. Press on the solids with the back of a wooden spoon to release the juices; discard the solids in the colander. The broth is ready for use or can be frozen for up to 3 months.

Zuppa di Pasta Grattata

Grated Pasta Soup

Adding coarsely grated pasta to boiling soup is a method all but forgotten by modern Italian cooks. This unusual pasta is flavored with lemon zest. **Serves 8 to 10**

In a bowl, mix the flour, breadcrumbs, and cheese. In another bowl, beat the eggs with the lemon zest and juice, 1 teaspoon of salt, and a grinding of pepper. Add the egg mixture to the flour mixture and combine into a rough ball of dough. The dough should hold together when a small amount is pinched between your fingers; if it seems dry, add a few teaspoons of water. Wrap the dough ball in plastic and refrigerate it for at least 6 hours, or until firm enough to grate.

Using the large holes of a box cheese grater, grate the dough over a clean towel. In a large stockpot, bring the broth to a boil over medium heat. Add the pasta and boil for about 4 minutes, or until it floats to the surface. Ladle the soup into bowls ands serve hot.

Note: Double the pasta recipe and freeze half to have on hand for a quick soup. Spread out the uncooked grated pasta on a floured baking sheet and freeze until hard. Transfer to plastic bags and store in the freezer. Do not defrost before cooking.

1½ cups plus 2 tablespoons unbleached all-purpose flour

1 cup fresh bread-crumbs, toasted

¾ cup grated Parmigiano-Reggiano cheese

2 large eggs

Grated zest and juice of 1 large lemon

Salt and freshly ground black pepper to taste

4 quarts chicken broth, store-bought or home-made (page 38), or beef broth (page 40)

Zuppa di Pane alla Nonna

Grandma's Bread Soup

This soup with tiny mosaic-size bread floating on top was a childhood favorite. It utilizes stale bread, giving it new life.   **Serves 8 to 10**

In a large stockpot, bring the broth to a boil over medium heat.

Meanwhile, in a large bowl, beat the eggs with the milk. In a large sauté pan, warm the olive oil over medium heat. Toss the bread cubes in the egg-milk mixture, coating them well. Remove the bread cubes with a slotted spoon and fry them, in batches, until browned on all sides. Transfer the bread to a plate and set aside.

When the broth comes to a boil, ladle it into soup bowls. Add some of the bread cubes to each bowl, sprinkle with grated Pecorino Romano cheese, and serve hot.

4 quarts chicken broth, homemade (page 38) or store-bought

2 large eggs

1½ cups milk

¼ cup extra-virgin olive oil

6 slices stale country bread, cut into ¼-inch cubes

Grated Pecorino Romano cheese, for sprinkling

Zuppa di Ceci
Chickpea Soup

1 cup dried chickpeas, covered with cold water and soaked overnight

1½ cups extra-virgin olive oil, plus more for drizzling

2 sprigs fresh rosemary *or* 1 teaspoon dried rosemary

2 cloves garlic, finely minced

1 tablespoon anchovy paste

1 tablespoon tomato paste

¼ cup water

2 cups chicken broth, homemade (page 38) or store-bought

3 cups crushed fresh or canned plum tomatoes (6 or 7 medium tomatoes)

1 cup cooked soup pasta, such as ditalini or elbow macaroni

Salt and freshly ground black pepper to taste

Soup made with *ceci* (chickpeas) is standard all over Italy. Bags of dried chickpeas were always in my grandmothers' cupboards. The beans need to be soaked in water overnight so that they will cook more quickly. To me it was magical, watching how they doubled in size after they had been soaked. Canned chickpeas can be used in this recipe; just be sure to rinse them well as they contain a lot of starchy liquid.   **Serves 6 to 8**

Drain the chickpeas, put them in a large saucepan, and add fresh cold water to cover. Bring to a boil over medium heat, lower the heat so that the beans are boiling gently, and cook them until tender, about 35 minutes. They should retain their shape and not be mushy. Drain and set aside.

In a large pot, heat the olive oil over medium heat. Add the rosemary and garlic and sauté over medium heat until the garlic is soft and the rosemary is limp. Discard the rosemary sprigs. Lower the heat slightly and stir in the anchovy paste. In a small cup, whisk the tomato paste into the ¼ cup water and add the mixture to the pot, along with the chicken broth, tomatoes, and half the cooked chickpeas. Stir, bring to a boil, and let simmer for about 15 minutes.

Meanwhile, in a food processor, puree the remaining chickpeas until smooth. Stir the chickpea puree into the soup and simmer for about 5 minutes. Add the pasta and simmer for 5 minutes more. Season with salt and pepper. Ladle into soup bowls, drizzle with olive oil, and serve hot.

Note: This soup tastes even better the day after it is made. If it seems too thick, thin it with a little chicken broth or water.

Zuppa della Regina

Queen's Soup

This is the perfect soup when you are under the weather; if no home-made broth is on hand, use a good canned one.   **Serves 6 to 8**

In a bowl, beat the egg yolks with a whisk or fork until light colored. Add 6 table-spoons flour and the cheese and beat until the batter is smooth and thin but not too runny; the consistency should be like that of thick pancake batter. If the batter seems too thin, add the remaining 1 tablespoon flour; if it's too thick, add a little broth.

In a large stockpot, bring the broth to a boil over medium heat. Hold a colander with holes about ⅛ inch in diameter over the top of the pot and pour the batter into the colander—it will stream out into the broth like strands of spaghetti. Boil for 3 minutes, or until the strands are set and not loose or runny. Season with salt and pepper and serve hot.

4 large egg yolks

6 to 7 tablespoons unbleached all-purpose flour

¼ cup grated Parmigiano-Reggiano cheese

6 cups chicken broth, homemade (page 38) or store-bought, or beef broth (page 40)

Salt and freshly ground black pepper to taste

Stufato di Pesce alla Sardo

Sardinian-Style Fish Stew

1 teaspoon saffron
   threads

½ cup hot chicken
   broth, homemade
   (page 38) or
   store-bought

5 tablespoons
   extra-virgin olive
   oil

½ cup thinly sliced
   onion

½ cup chopped
   fennel bulb plus
   1 tablespoon finely
   chopped leaves

2 cloves garlic,
   chopped

½ teaspoon red
   pepper flakes

1 tablespoon minced
   fresh flat-leaf
   parsley

1½ cups peeled and
   coarsely chopped
   fresh plum
   tomatoes

½ cup dry white wine

2½ pounds mixed
   fish and shellfish,
   such as a com-
   bination of tuna,
   swordfish, lobster,
   medium shrimp
   (26–30 count), and
   squid

Salt and freshly
   ground black
   pepper to taste

Some people aren't aware that the island of Sardinia is part of Italy. Its cooking is rooted deep in history; the best way to describe Sardinian cuisine is just to call it simple, taking the offerings from the land and sea and using them in unadulterated ways. You would think that fish would be the dominant part of the diet, but Sardinians actually prefer meat such as lamb and pork over fish. This has to do with their history and the many foreign invasions that took place there, which made the Sardinians fearful of the coast and drove them inland. That said, Sardinian waters offer a great variety of fish and shellfish, including bass, mullet, eel, tuna, spiny lobster, laguna fish, trout, and cuttlefish. While it is likely impossible to duplicate a Sardinian fish stew at home, a fresh assortment of at least four kinds of fish is a good rule to follow when making this dish. A signature ingredient in many Sardinian dishes is saffron. Yes, it is expensive; if that is a concern, you can certainly omit it.   **Serves 6**

Soak the saffron threads in the hot chicken broth; set aside.

In a large Dutch oven or similar heavy pot, heat the oil over medium heat. Add the onion and sauté for 2 minutes. Add the chopped fennel and sauté for 3 minutes. Add the garlic and red pepper flakes and sauté for 1 minute. Add the fennel leaves, parsley, tomatoes, and wine and stir well.

Pour the chicken broth through a fine-mesh strainer and into the pot, pressing on the saffron threads to extract all the liquid; discard the saffron. Stir well and simmer for 5 minutes.

Meanwhile, cut the tuna, swordfish, and lobster into bite-size pieces. Peel and devein the shrimp. Cut the squid into ¼-inch-thick rings. Add the squid to the pot and season with salt and pepper. Cook over medium heat for 8 to 10 minutes, or until the squid is barely al dente, still firm but not rubbery. Add the remaining fish and shellfish and cook for 10 minutes longer.

Place a bread slice in each of 6 soup bowls and carefully ladle the soup over the bread. Serve hot, passing grated Pecorino Romano cheese at the table for sprinkling, if desired.

Note: It is not customary in Italy to add grated cheese to fish dishes, but here the salty taste nicely complements the flavors of the seafood.

6 slices country style bread, toasted

Grated Pecorino Romano cheese, for sprinkling (optional)

Zuppa di Riso e Asparagi

Rice and Asparagus Soup

When making this delicious soup from Reggio Emilia, be sure to use very tender, thin asparagus. The best asparagus grows wild in Italy, but it has a short spring growing season. **Serves 4**

In a large sauté pan, melt the butter over medium heat. Add the onion and sauté until soft. In a small cup, whisk the tomato paste into the water and add the mixture to the pan, along with the salt and pepper. Add the asparagus, cover, and simmer until crisp-tender, about 3 to 4 minutes. Set aside.

In a large stockpot, bring the broth to a boil over medium heat. Add the rice, reduce the heat to low, and cook until the rice is al dente, about 15 minutes. Add the asparagus mixture to the rice and simmer for 2 to 3 minutes longer. Serve immediately, sprinkled with cheese.

2 tablespoons unsalted butter

1 small white onion, finely chopped

1 tablespoon tomato paste

1 cup water

1 teaspoon salt

½ teaspoon freshly ground black pepper

1 pound asparagus, trimmed and cut on the diagonal into 1-inch pieces

4 cups chicken broth, homemade (page 38) or store-bought, or beef broth (page 40)

¾ cup Arborio rice

Grated Parmigiano-Reggiano cheese

Zuppa di Scarola e Polpette

Escarole and Meatball Soup

8 ounces ground chicken

8 ounces ground pork

1 large egg, lightly beaten with a fork

¼ cup fresh breadcrumbs

1 tablespoon chopped fresh flat-leaf parsley

1 tablespoon minced fresh mint

Grated zest of 1 lemon

Salt and freshly ground black pepper to taste

4 cups chicken broth, homemade (page 38) or store-bought, or beef broth (page 40)

2 cups torn escarole (bite-size pieces)

¼ cup grated Pecorino Romano cheese

This soup with tiny meatballs and escarole has many cousins; sometimes it is called *minestra di maritata* (wedding soup), because the flavors are said to combine well together. In this version, chicken and pork provide exceptional flavor, though variations might include veal and often substitute spinach for the escarole.   **Serves 6 to 8**

Preheat the oven to 350°F. Lightly oil a rimmed baking sheet or shallow baking pan.

In a bowl, combine the ground meats, egg, breadcrumbs, parsley, mint, lemon zest, and salt and pepper. Mix well but do not overwork the mixture. Using your hands, form marble-size balls. Place them on the baking sheet and bake for 30 minutes. Drain off any fat with a spoon.

In a large pot, bring the broth to a boil over medium heat. Add the meatballs and reduce the heat to simmer. Add the escarole, cover, and simmer just until the escarole wilts. Stir in the cheese and serve immediately.

Minestra con Pane Sotto

Soup with Bread Under It

Years ago Aunt Santina gave me the recipe for this unusual soup that her mother, Mrs. B., used to carry to the workers in the fields near Veroli, in the region of Lazio. It is almost thick enough to eat with a fork. The story goes that Mrs. B. would twist a large kitchen towel around her head and tie it securely. A large bowl of this soup would be propped atop her head, and off she went to the fields, arriving just before the church bells tolled at noon. When she arrived, the workers knelt and prayed and then ate this soup. **Serves 8 to 10**

In a large pot, heat the olive oil over medium heat. Add the onion and cook until soft. Add the garlic and continue cooking until it softens. Add the tomatoes, basil, and salt and pepper. Stir well, cover, and let simmer for 20 minutes.

Meanwhile, bring a large saucepan of water to a boil over medium-high heat. Add the Swiss chard and cook until the leaves wilt. Scoop out the Swiss chard with a slotted spoon and add it to the tomato soup. Stir well and simmer for 5 minutes.

Place 4 bread slices in a single layer in the bottom of a deep casserole dish. Spread just enough of the soup over the bread to cover it. Sprinkle with ¼ cup of the Pecorino Romano cheese. Make a second layer of bread, tomato soup, and cheese. Continue to make two more layers to use all the bread, soup, and cheese. Let the soup stand for a few minutes in order for the bread to soak up some of the liquid, then scoop from the casserole dish to serve.

¼ cup extra-virgin olive oil

1 medium onion, chopped

2 cloves garlic, chopped

8 cups chopped fresh plum tomatoes (about 5 pounds) or canned tomatoes

2 or 3 sprigs fresh basil

Salt and freshly ground black pepper to taste

1 pound Swiss chard, stems removed and leaves torn into small pieces

16 (1-inch-thick) slices dense country-style bread

1 cup grated Pecorino Romano cheese

Zuppa di Zucca

Squash Soup

1½ pounds zucca gialla or butternut squash

2⅓ cups water

2 tablespoons unsalted butter

1 medium onion, finely chopped

2 to 2¼ cups chicken broth, homemade (page 38) or store-bought

1 cup half-and-half

1 tablespoon grated nutmeg

Salt and freshly ground black pepper to taste

¼ cup toasted pine nuts

1 tablespoon minced fresh thyme *or* 1 teaspoon dried thyme

The first time I saw stylish-looking zucca gialla (yellow squash) in Italian markets, with its knobby, ribbed forest-green skin and wood-like stems, I knew I had to grow it in my home garden. These squash have deep orange flesh and a sweeter taste than our own butternut type squash and are used mostly for making soup and stuffing pasta. Seeds for growing zucca gialla are available from GrowItalian.com.   **Serves 4 to 6**

Preheat the oven to 350° F.

Cut the squash in half and scrape out the seeds and stringy pulp. Place the halves, cut-side down, in a baking pan.

Add the water to the pan. Cover with foil and bake for 45 to 50 minutes, or until the squash is soft. Let cool, then scoop out the flesh. Puree the flesh in a food processor or blender until smooth.

In a large saucepan, heat the butter over medium heat. Cook the onion until very soft. Add the squash puree, 2 cups broth, the half-and-half, nutmeg, and salt and pepper and stir well. Bring to a boil, reduce the heat to medium-low, and simmer for 15 minutes. The soup should have the consistency of heavy cream; if it seems too thick, add up to ¼ cup more broth.

Scatter the pine nuts over the soup, sprinkle with the thyme, and serve.

Zuppa di Pomodoro, Porro e Riso

Tomato, Leek, and Rice Soup

This is one of my all-time favorite soups. Even though only a few ingredients go into this soup, it is very important that the tomatoes be in season for the best flavor. Cherry tomatoes have few seeds and are full of natural sweetness. In the summertime, I freeze them whole for winter use, when this soup is a staple dish. An added bonus is that this is fat-free, low-sodium soup. **Makes 1¼ quarts**

Put the leeks and tomatoes in a soup pot . Cover the pot and cook over very low heat, stirring occasionally, until the tomatoes are very soft, about 5 minutes. Add the basil leaves.

Use an immersion blender to puree the soup or transfer the mixture in batches to a food processor or blender and process until very smooth. Pour the soup in batches into a fine-mesh strainer set over a bowl. With a wooden spoon, press on the solids to extract the juices. Discard the seeds.

Return the soup to the soup pot. Stir in the sugar and salt and set aside.

Meanwhile, in a small saucepan, combine the rice and water and bring to a boil over medium heat. Lower the heat to simmer, cover the pot, and cook the rice until it has absorbed all the water, about 10 minutes. Stir the rice into the soup. Reheat the soup and serve hot.

Note: For variety, you can add fresh minced herbs such as parsley, mint, or dill, or add diced fresh mozzarella cheese just before serving.

2 medium leeks, dark green tops removed and discarded, leeks halved lengthwise, rinsed well and thinly sliced crosswise

2 pounds whole cherry tomatoes, stemmed

8 to 10 fresh basil leaves

1 teaspoon sugar

Salt to taste

½ cup long-grain rice

1 cup water

Jota Triestina

Bean Soup, Trieste Style

Jota (or yota) is a bean soup dish from Trieste, in northeast Italy, that over the centuries has undergone very few changes; the most significant dates back some four centuries ago when potatoes were introduced. It was considered a peasant dish, made with leftovers and two common ingredients, cranberry beans (also known as borlotti or shell beans) and sauerkraut. **Serves 6 to 8**

Drain the beans and put them in a large saucepan; cover with the vegetable broth and add the herbs. Bring to a boil over medium-high heat, then reduce the heat and cook at a medium boil until the beans are almost tender, about 30 minutes. Add the potatoes and continue cooking for about 20 minutes more.

Meanwhile, heat the olive oil in a medium skillet over medium heat. Add the onion and ham and cook until the onion is soft. Stir in the sauerkraut and cook for about 5 minutes more.

Melt the butter in a small skillet over medium heat, then add the flour and whisk the mixture to form a brown paste.

Add the onion mixture to the beans and stir to combine well. Reduce the heat to low and whisk in the brown paste until incorporated and hot. Taste and season with salt and pepper, then serve hot.

2 cups dried cranberry beans, covered with cold water and soaked overnight

Small bouquet fresh herbs, such as thyme, rosemary, and/or sage sprigs and bay leaves, tied with kitchen string

8 cups vegetable broth

2 all-purpose potatoes, peeled and cut into 1-inch dice

2 tablespoons extra-virgin olive oil

1 small onion, peeled and diced

1 cup diced cooked ham

1 (14-ounce) can sauerkraut, drained and rinsed

2 tablespoons unsalted butter

¼ cup unbleached all-purpose flour

Salt and freshly ground black pepper to taste

Zuppa di Pesce alla Napoletana

Neapolitan Fish Soup

4 pounds littleneck clams

1 cup dry white wine

¼ cup minced fresh flat-leaf parsley

4 cloves garlic, peeled and halved

¼ cup extra-virgin olive oil

1 large onion, chopped

1 cup chopped fennel

1 teaspoon red pepper flakes *or* ½ teaspoon red pepper paste

3 cups pureed plum tomatoes or passata (page 215)

1 pound squid rings

1 pound sea scallops, cut in half

1 pound medium shrimp (26–30 count), peeled and deveined

Salt and freshly ground black pepper to taste

Juice of 1 large lemon

8 country-style bread slices, toasted

It was Italian fishermen who invented fish soups and stews, using the trimmings of the daily catch. Thrown into a pot with some herbs, water, and maybe wine, these bits and pieces became a hearty fish soup. Over time the soup was refined with other ingredients like tomatoes and hot pepper.   **Serves 8**

Scrub the clams in cold water; discard any with cracked shells or those that do not close when tapped. Place them in a large sauté pan with the wine, parsley, and 4 garlic halves. Cover the pan and cook the clams over medium heat until they open; discard any clams that do not open.

Use a slotted spoon to transfer the clams to a bowl. Strain the liquid in the pan through a strainer lined with cheesecloth into a large glass measuring cup; you should have about 1 cup. Set the liquid aside. Remove the clam meat from the shells and set aside.

Heat the olive oil in a large soup pot over medium heat. Add the onion and fennel and cook until they begin to soften, about 4 minutes. Add the remaining 4 garlic halves and cook until they soften; stir in the pepper flakes and cook for a minute or two. Add the reserved clam cooking liquid and the pureed tomatoes; stir well and bring to a boil over medium-high heat. Boil for 2 minutes, then lower the heat to medium. Add the squid rings and cook for 5 minutes; add the scallops and continue cooking for 3 minutes; add the shrimp and cook for an additional 3 minutes. Season with salt and pepper. Add the clams and heat slowly over low heat until hot; stir in the lemon juice. Serve in large bowls ladled over slices of toasted bread.

Brodetto al Porto Recanati

Fish Chowder in the Style of Porto Recanati

½ cup extra virgin olive oil

1 large onion chopped

1 pound squid cut into ½ inch thick rings

1 teaspoon saffron dissolved in ½ cup warm water

2 cups fish stock or water

Flour

1 pound monkfish, cut into 1-inch pieces

1 pound cod, cut into 1-inch pieces

1 cup white wine

Salt and pepper to taste

Thick slices of toasted bread

Brodetto means broth and in the Marche, this name refers to fish chowder chocked full of at least nine and up to thirteen different kinds of fish typically found in Adriatic waters. The dish is said to have originated in Greece but six cities in the Marche also claim ownership, each one making the savory broth a little differently. The general consensus among brodetto afficianadoes is that the seaside town of Porto Recanati in the province of Macerata, on the eastern coast of the Adriatic, makes the best but that is not to say that Ancona, San Benedetto, Porto San Grigorio, Numana, Falconara and Senigalllia produces anything less worthy. It is just that they add different ingredients. What these cities all agree on is that a fresh catch of fish from the Adriatic must be used along with quality extra virgin olive oil.

I like to think that this fish chowder is a cousin to the cioppino of California, and was born out of fish market castoffs, where the unsellable pieces of fish were thrown into a pot with some seasonings, an onion or two, covered with water and slowly simmered. Or perhaps early sailors developed the dish with the catch of the day on their long voyages and ladled it over the hard tack biscuits that sustained them through much of their seafaring lives. It is easy to see that over time, brodetto has undergone many taste changes.

One thing is certain when making the brodetto di Porto Recanati, there must be scorfano (scorpion fish). As to the other types of fish, it is never the same, so whatever is available in the fish market will do like merluzzo, squid, shrimp, John Dory, rock fish and red mullet (triglia). Some cooks add the fish gutted and whole, while others cut the fish into chunks but add the heads for added flavor.

The brodetto of Porto di Recanati is so thick that you can hardly find the broth and the key ingredient are many kinds of fish including cuttlefish, a cousin of squid but hard to find. Saffron is also a key

continued on page 60

continued from page 58

ingredient. It would be ideal to taste this dish in its proper locale along the Adriatic but still a comparable brodetto can be made in your own kitchen by adhering to the same choosiness of buying local, fresh fish and employing the cooking techniques of the Marchigiani.   **Serves 4**

Heat the olive oil in a soup pot and add the onion; cook until it wilts and begins to brown. Add the squid (or cuttlefish) and cook a few minutes. Stir in the saffron and season with salt and pepper and add enough fish broth or water to cover the squid. Lower heat to simmer and cook until the squid or cuttlefish is tender. Flour the monkfish and cod and place layered on top of one another in a separate pot. Add the fish stock or water and wine, cover and cook on low heat for about 8 minutes or until the fish easily flakes when poked with a fork. Add the squid and liquid to the fish pouring it on top. Season the soup with salt and pepper, cover and heat for 5 minutes, Serve over slices of toasted bread.

Rice

Rice is a primary food source for over half the world's population, and one of the oldest. Stone Age paddy fields tended by the world's earliest known rice farmers have been uncovered in a swamp in China, showing that rice growing began in the wetlands of eastern China over 7,000 years ago. Once cultivation began, the hearty grain is thought to have spread quickly westward and had made its way to southern Europe by medieval times.

In ancient Rome, rice, introduced by way of India, was used to thicken food as well as a medicinal remedy for an upset stomach. It was an expensive imported commodity and not consumed as much as other cereal grains such as barley.

In the late fifteenth century, farmers in the Po River valley decided to plant some seeds, and that was the beginning of Italy becoming the largest rice producer in Europe. The regions of the Piedmont, Lombardy, and the Veneto in northern Italy are the prime rice-growing regions because they have the right climate and an abundance of water needed for the plants to grow.

Italy grows short-, medium-, and long-grain starchy rice that is perfect for making classic risotto, which requires a rice that can absorb a lot of liquid and produce a creamy consistency that the Venetians refer to as *all'onda* (on the wave). In other words, the rice must flow off the spoon in waves and not be lumpy and static.

There are several types of Italian rice: *comune* (common), *semifino*, (semifine), *fino* (fine), and *superfino* (superfine). Arborio rice is the best known of the superfino types and the most common type of medium-grain rice used for making risotto. The rice releases starches called amylose and amylopectin; both are necessary to create a creamy, not dry texture. Arborio is readily available in grocery stores or online. Another type of rice that is also good for risotto is Carnaroli, a medium-grain rice that grows in the Pavia,

Novara, and Vercelli areas of northern Italy. It has a longer grain than Arborio and a higher starch content. Vialone Nano, grown in Verona, is preferred by Venetians for making risotto; the shorter, rounder grain can absorb twice the amount of liquid to produce a very creamy texture.

To make risotto, start with a heavy-duty pot, which will deliver maximum heat during cooking. Second, make sure that the rice is well coated in the oil or butter before adding the liquid; this will help keep the grains separate, allowing for its finished state to flow freely off the spoon. Third, be sure that the liquid is hot when adding it to the rice; this will prevent the loss of cooking temperature. Fourth, don't be in a hurry when stirring in the liquid; each addition should be fully absorbed by the rice before adding more. Finally, know when to stop stirring. Stop when the rice is still firm but cooked through. Taste it; it should not be hard or mushy, just creamy.

Risotto is an ever-changing dish with an endless variety of ingredients that can be added to it. In Milan, saffron and Parmigiano-Reggiano cheese define the dish, whereas in Venice it's seafood, or peas for the classic *risi e bisi* (rice and peas). But that is just the beginning of what you can do to flavor it. Besides being a savory dish, rice finds its way into street food such as the famous arancine, Sicilian rice balls stuffed with meat or the Neapolitan sweet Easter pie known as pastiera.

Arancine Siciliane

Sicilian Rice Balls

3 tablespoons extra-virgin olive oil

¼ cup minced celery

¼ cup minced carrot

¼ cup minced onion

1 teaspoon red pepper flakes

1 pound ground beef or pork

2 cups crushed plum tomatoes

¼ cup dry red wine

½ cup fresh or frozen peas

Salt and freshly ground black pepper to taste

1 cup Arborio rice

2½ cups chicken broth, homemade (page 38) or store-bought

1 teaspoon saffron threads dissolved in ¼ cup warm water

½ cup grated Pecorino Romano cheese

4 large eggs

2 cups unbleached all-purpose flour

2 cups fine dry breadcrumbs

4 cups sunflower oil, for frying

Tomato sauce, for serving (optional)

Sitting on a bus on the clogged streets of Palermo, I listened to the bus driver having a heated argument with a woman passenger about fried rice balls. The bus driver was from Calabria and insisted that "arancino" (plural "arancini") was the correct pronunciation, while the determined woman waved her index finger back and forth to signal no, in Palermo it was pronounced "arancina" (plural "arancine"). The word translates to "little oranges," and arancine/i is an iconic Sicilian street food found in the vibrant outdoor markets like the Ballarò. They are shaped like small oranges enclosing a meaty ragù filling. The rice gets its bright orange color from saffron, which also accounts for the name. No matter what it is called, there is no disagreement when it comes to pronouncing the taste as *delizioso!* **Makes about 12**

Heat the olive oil in a small saucepan over medium heat. Cook the celery, carrot, and onion until the mixture softens, about 4 minutes. Stir in the pepper flakes. Add the meat and brown it well. Combine the tomatoes with the wine and add to the meat; stir the ingredients well. Reduce the heat to medium-low and cook for 45 minutes. The mixture should be thick, not watery. Stir in the peas. Season with salt and pepper. (The ragù can be made up to 3 days ahead of time; store in the refrigerator.)

Combine the rice and chicken broth in a small saucepan. Stir well and bring to a boil over medium heat. Lower the heat and allow the rice to cook, partially covered, until all the liquid has evaporated, about 20 minutes.

Strain the saffron threads and add the saffron water to the rice. Stir well. Off the heat, stir in the cheese and 2 of the eggs. Let cool. Add salt to taste.

To assemble the rice balls, scoop about ½ cup of the rice into the palm of your hand. Form a ball, then make an indentation in the center with your finger. Fill the indentation with a generous tablespoon of the ragù. Close the rice around the filling. Repeat until all the rice and ragù are used.

Put the flour in a shallow bowl. Beat the remaining 2 eggs with a fork in another shallow bowl. Put the breadcrumbs in a third shallow bowl. First dredge the rice balls in the flour, then dip them in the egg mixture. Finally, coat the balls in the breadcrumbs to cover them completely. Place on a rimmed baking sheet and refrigerate, uncovered, for several hours or overnight.

Heat the sunflower oil to 375°F in a deep-fryer or heavy-duty pot. Fry the arancine in the oil until nicely browned. Drain them on absorbent paper. Serve hot, with or without tomato sauce on the side.

Risotto di Lorenza

Lorenza's Risotto

Reggio Emilia is home to dear friend Lorenza Iori, who cooks risotto in a flavorful combination of a meat ragù and the soaking liquid from the porcini mushrooms used in the dish, instead of the traditional broth and wine. The only addition I have made to Lorenza's recipe is the grated Parmigiano-Reggiano cheese.   **Serves 8**

Put the porcini in a large bowl and add 4 cups of the hot water. Set aside to soak until they soften, about 30 minutes.

Meanwhile, in a large sauté pan, heat the olive oil over medium heat. Add the onion and cook until golden brown and almost caramelized, about 10 minutes. Add the sausage, breaking up the meat with a spoon, and brown it. Stir in the tomatoes, the remaining ½ cup water, and salt and mix well. Simmer the ingredients until thickened, about 15 minutes. Transfer to a food processor and blend until smooth. Transfer the ragù to a bowl and set aside.

Drain the porcini mushrooms in a strainer set over a bowl. Dice the porcini and set aside. Strain the porcini liquid through a fine-mesh sieve or a strainer lined with cheesecloth to remove any sediment. Pour the liquid into a saucepan and bring it to just under a boil, then lower the heat and keep warm.

In a large heavy-duty saucepan, melt the butter over medium heat. Add the rice and cook for 1 to 2 minutes, stirring to coat it well in the butter. When the rice begins to make a crackling sound, lower the heat to medium-low and add ¼ cup of the reserved porcini soaking liquid. Cook, stirring, until all the liquid is absorbed. Add ¼ cup of the ragù and cook, stirring, until the rice has absorbed the liquid. Slowly add the remaining porcini liquid and sauce to the rice in alternating additions, ¼ cup at a time, allowing the rice to absorb all the liquid each time before adding more. Add the diced porcini. You may not need to add all the porcini liquid; the rice should be al dente, not mushy. Stir in the heavy cream. Remove the rice from the heat and stir in the cheese. Serve immediately.

1 cup dried porcini mushrooms (about 1 ounce)

4½ cups hot water

¼ cup extra-virgin olive oil

1 white onion, thinly sliced

8 ounces sweet Italian sausage, casings removed

2 cups chopped fresh or canned plum tomatoes (about 4 medium tomatoes)

Salt to taste

6 tablespoons unsalted butter

2 cups Arborio rice

2 tablespoons heavy cream

½ cup grated Parmigiano-Reggiano cheese

Risotto alla Milanese

Risotto, Milan Style

1 teaspoon saffron
   threads

2 tablespoons warm
   water

4½ to 5 cups chicken
   broth, homemade
   (page 38) or
   store-bought

6 tablespoons
   unsalted butter

½ cup finely minced
   white onion

2 cups Arborio rice

1 cup dry white wine

¾ cup grated
   Parmigiano-
   Reggiano cheese

One cannot eat in Milan without trying risotto alla milanese, one of the city's defining classical and signature dishes.   **Serves 6**

Put the saffron threads in a small bowl and add the warm water. Set aside to soak for 20 minutes.

In a saucepan, bring the chicken broth to a simmer and keep warm.

In a large heavy-duty saucepan, melt the butter over medium heat. Add the onion and cook until very soft; do not allow it to brown. It should remain colorless and almost seem to dissolve in the butter. Add the rice, stirring to coat each grain with the butter and onion mixture. When the rice begins to make a crackling sound, reduce the heat to medium-low and add ½ cup of the white wine. Cook, stirring constantly, until all the wine is absorbed. Add ½ cup hot chicken broth and continue to stir until the rice has absorbed the liquid. Add the remaining ½ cup wine. Add 4 more cups of broth, ½ cup at a time and continue to stir, allowing the rice to absorb each addition of liquid. Test the rice for doneness: It should be al dente, not mushy and hold its shape. If necessary, add up to ½ cup more broth and cook, stirring, until the liquid is absorbed and the rice is al dente. Add the saffron threads with the water and mix well.

Remove the rice from the heat, stir in the Parmigiano-Reggiano cheese, and serve.

Risi e Bisi con Prosciutto

Rice and Peas with Ham

Risi e bisi is a Venetian specialty best made with spring peas. They are very delicate and sweet and are a succulent addition to the rice. Prosciutto adds additional flavor but can be omitted.   **Serves 6**

If the peas are large, cook them in boiling water until tender, about 2 minutes. Drain and set them aside. Small tender peas do not need cooking.

In a heavy-duty saucepan, melt the butter over medium heat. Add the onion and prosciutto and cook until the prosciutto begins to brown, about 3 to 4 minutes. Add the rice and stir to coat well with the butter and onion mixture. Add the wine and 4½ cups chicken broth, ½ cup at a time, stirring after each addition and allowing the rice to absorb all the liquid before adding more. Add the peas to the rice about 5 minutes before the rice is cooked. The rice should be creamy and al dente. If necessary, add up to ½ cup more broth and cook, stirring, until the liquid is absorbed and the rice is al dente.

Remove the rice from the heat, stir in the Parmigiano-Reggiano cheese and white pepper, and serve.

2 cups shelled fresh peas

4½ to 5 cups warm chicken broth, homemade (page 38) or store-bought

6 tablespoons unsalted butter

½ cup finely minced white onion

½ cup diced prosciutto (about 2 ounces)

1 cup dry white wine

2 cups Vialone Nano or Arborio rice

¾ cup grated Parmigiano-Reggiano cheese

1 teaspoon ground white pepper

Risotto con Mirtilli

Risotto with Blueberries

No one was more surprised than I when I was served a blueberry risotto for the first time in the Alto Adige region of Italy, close to the Swiss border. Not only was it attractive to look at, but its flavor was a fine example of Italian *alta cucina*, or innovative high-style cuisine.   **Serves 6**

In a saucepan, bring the broth to a simmer and keep warm.

In a large heavy-duty saucepan, melt the butter over medium heat. Add the onion and cook until very soft, about 5 minutes. Do not allow the onion to brown; it should remain colorless and almost seem to dissolve. Add the rice, stirring to coat each grain with the butter-onion mixture. Lower the heat to medium-low and add ½ cup of the white wine. Cook, stirring constantly, until all the wine is absorbed. Add ½ cup of the chicken broth and cook, continuing to stir, until the rice has absorbed the liquid. Add the remaining ½ cup wine. Add 4 more cups of the broth, ½ cup at a time, while continuing to stir and allowing the rice to absorb each addition of liquid. The rice should be al dente, not mushy. If necessary, add up to ½ cup more broth. Reduce the heat to low and add the blueberries. Cook, stirring, to mash the berries slightly, until they have softened. Serve at once.

4½ to 5 cups chicken broth, homemade (page 38) or store-bought

6 tablespoons unsalted butter

½ cup finely minced white onion

2 cups Arborio rice

1 cup dry white wine

1 cup fresh blueberries

Timballo di Riso

Rice Tart

Elegant is the only way to describe this rice tart boasting the rich taste combination of Parmigiano-Reggiano cheese, creamy mozzarella, and delicate mortadella, a cooked salumi product from Bologna (page 280), studded with small cubes of fat. **Serves 6 to 8**

Preheat the oven to 375°F.

Grease a 9-inch springform pan with some of the melted butter. Coat the bottom and sides of the pan with the breadcrumbs and set aside.

Heat the olive oil in a 3-quart saucepan and add the leek. Cook until soft, then add the rice all at once and stir to combine with the leek. Add the broth and stir the mixture well. Bring to a boil. Turn off the heat, cover the pan, and allow rice to stand for 20 minutes, or until all the liquid is absorbed.

Transfer the rice to a bowl and cool slightly. In a separate bowl, whisk the eggs and Parmigiano-Reggiano cheese together. Pour over the rice mixture and stir well.

Spread half the cheese over the breadcrumbs in the springform pan and pat evenly with a spoon. Overlap the mortadella slices over the rice and then layer the mozzarella cheese over the mortadella. Spread the remaining rice over the cheese to cover completely.

Cover the pan with aluminum foil and bake the rice cake for 45 to 50 minutes, or until the rice starts to look golden and is a bit crusty at the edges. Let cool for about 10 minutes, then unlatch the sides of the pan and place the tart on a serving dish. Cut into wedges, drizzle with melted butter, and serve warm.

2 tablespoons unsalted butter, melted

¼ cup breadcrumbs

3 tablespoons extra-virgin olive oil

2 medium leeks, finely diced, *or* 1 medium onion, diced

2 cups Arborio rice

3 cups hot chicken broth, homemade (page 38) or store-bought

2 large eggs

½ cup grated Parmigiano-Reggiano cheese

Salt and freshly ground black pepper to taste

12 ounces thinly sliced mortadella or ham

8 ounces fresh mozzarella cheese, sliced

Risotto ai Frutti di Mare
Risotto with Seafood

- 30 littleneck clams in the shell
- ¼ cup water
- 3 sprigs fresh flat-leaf parsley, plus ¼ cup coarsely chopped fresh flat-leaf parsley leaves
- 2 sprigs fresh thyme
- 1 clove garlic, peeled
- 4 cups fish stock, reduced-sodium fish broth, or clam juice
- ¼ cup extra-virgin olive oil, plus more for drizzling
- 1 medium yellow onion, finely chopped
- 1 cup Arborio or Carnaroli rice
- ½ cup dry white wine
- 8 ounces dry sea scallops
- Kosher salt and freshly ground black pepper to taste
- 8 ounces medium shrimp (26–30 count), peeled and deveined
- 8 ounces cleaned squid, cut into ½-inch thick rings
- Finely grated zest and juice of 1 medium lemon, plus lemon wedges for garnish

This impressive and rich seafood risotto can be served as a main course. Do not overcook the seafood. **Serves 4**

Scrub the clams with a brush and place them in a large sauté pan. Add the water, parsley sprigs, thyme sprigs, and garlic clove. Cover the pan and bring to a boil over medium-high heat. As soon as the clams open, drain them, saving the liquid. Shell the clams and set them aside. Discard any clams that do not open.

Combine the fish stock and reserved clam cooking liquid in a medium saucepan and bring to a simmer over medium heat. In a heavy-duty 2-quart pot, heat the oil over medium heat until it is shimmering. Add the onion and cook just until it begins to wilt. Add the rice and cook, stirring, until the kernels start to crackle, about 1 to 2 minutes. Do not let the mixture brown. Stir in the wine and let simmer, stirring often, until all the liquid has been absorbed, 2 to 4 minutes. Pour a ladleful of the hot broth over the rice. Let the rice simmer, stirring often, until it absorbs the liquid. Continue adding the broth, while stirring, and let it absorb enough liquid until the rice is al dente, 20 to 30 minutes (you may not need all the broth). The rice should be cooked through but firm and have a bit of a bite.

Meanwhile, pat the scallops dry with paper towels. Cut the scallops into ½-inch-thick round slices and season them with salt and pepper. Pat the shrimp and squid dry with paper towels and season them with salt and pepper. Keep each seafood separate because they will cook at different rates. Add enough oil to a large sauté pan to just film the bottom and heat the oil until it begins to shimmer. Add the scallops and sear them on one side without moving them until they are nearly opaque, about 2 minutes. Transfer the scallops to a rimmed baking sheet and spread them into a single layer. Add the shrimp to the sauté pan and cook, stirring occasionally, until just cooked through, about 3 minutes. Transfer to the baking sheet. Add the squid rings to the sauté pan and cook, stirring occasionally, until just cooked through, about 1 minute. Transfer to the baking sheet. Season all the shellfish with salt and pepper and set aside.

When the rice is done, remove it from the heat and gently fold in the seafood mixture, along with the reserved clams, chopped parsley, lemon zest, and lemon juice. Taste and season with more salt, pepper, and lemon juice. Serve with a drizzle of extra-virgin olive oil and serve with lemon wedges.

Risotto al Vino Rosso

Red Wine Risotto

4 ounces pancetta, minced

3 tablespoons extra-virgin olive oil

1 medium onion, minced

1½ cups Arborio, Carnaroli, or Vialone Nano rice

1½ cups dry red wine

5 cups hot fresh or bottled tomato juice

½ cup grated Asiago cheese

¼ cup minced fresh basil

This bold-tasting risotto preparation is a clear departure from the more classic northern Italian version that calls for chicken broth and white wine. Instead, a combination of red wine and tomato juice gives the rice a wonderful depth of flavor and a gorgeous color. Pancetta, unsmoked bacon, provides additional flavor in this dynamic dish.
Serves 4 to 6

In a heavy 2-quart saucepan, brown the pancetta over medium heat until crisp; transfer it to a small bowl and set aside.

Add the oil to the saucepan; when it is hot, stir in the onion. Cook it until it softens, but do not let it brown. Stir in the rice and cook, coating all the grains with the oil. Add the wine slowly and stir until it is almost absorbed by the rice.

Adjust the heat to medium-low and begin adding the tomato juice, a ladleful at a time, and stir until the rice absorbs each addition of the juice. Continue stirring until the rice looks creamy but still has a little bite to it. Stir the cheese, basil, and pancetta into the rice. Serve immediately.

Rice Worth the Price

"The greatest service which can be rendered any country is to add a useful plant to its culture: especially a bread grain; next in value is oil." These words expressed by Thomas Jefferson shed new light on the man who penned the Declaration of Independence. Jefferson was without a doubt a Renaissance man, not just concerned with man's inalienable rights but also with an insatiable curiosity for everything from astronomy and architecture to vegetable gardening. In fact, Jefferson recorded in his garden diaries that he planted over 300 varieties of 99 species of vegetables and herbs!

To say that Jefferson was also an Italophile would not be an exaggeration. From the name of his Virginia home, Monticello (meaning "little mountain"), to his liking for macaroni (and serving it to his guests at a state dinner in 1802), Jefferson certainly had a soft spot for Italy.

According to sources at Monticello, Jefferson paid a visit to Turin in the Piedmont region of Italy in 1787. He spent a few days in the city, admiring its art and architecture, but it was his journey to the rice-growing areas of Piedmont that really drew his curiosity. He had heard that Italian rice was far superior to South Carolina rice for its durability and whiteness, and the fact that it did not break easily in processing, and he was eager to talk to rice growers and workers about not only the cultivation of rice but also about the husking machinery used.

The cultivation of rice was something that Jefferson observed very closely. In one of his handwritten garden books, he notes, "The consumption of rice in [Italy] was very great. I thought it my duty to inform myself from what markets Italy draws supplies and in what proportions from ours." The man was obviously thinking of viable trading opportunities in the rice industry. He reasoned that Carolina rice could be sent to Europe for use in dishes prepared with milk and sugar (like rice pudding), because the rice held up much better than Italian rice. Likewise, Italian rice would be imported to the States for use in dishes prepared with fatty meats or fowl for which Italian rice was much better suited.

He was so impressed by his visit that he committed to memory a sketch of the mechanism used for husking the rice. He also broke the law: He had sacks of unhusked rice taken out of the Piedmont and sent by mule over the Apennine Mountains to Genoa, where it was loaded onto a ship bound for Monticello. Jefferson knew full well that the laws of Italy forbade the exportation of rice and that anyone caught doing so would be committing a crime that was punishable by death!

Not trusting that his shipment would arrive, Jefferson boldly and daringly stuffed his pockets with as much rice as they could hold, determined to plant it in Georgia and South Carolina. There it took root. But not everyone shared in Jefferson's enthusiasm for Italian rice. When he sent some to the South Carolina Agricultural Society, the members deemed it inferior to the Carolina variety and told Jefferson to send no more. That was a wise decision, because ultimately Jefferson's rice crop failed, as did his beloved olive trees and grape stock from Italy and France. Not to be deterred in his agricultural pursuits, Jefferson regarded these failures as a learning experience that for him was worth the price of a president smuggling rice under threat of death.

Pasta

Who invented pasta? Food historians have long debated this question, but most give the Chinese credit. However, if you study cooking manuscripts from different regions of the world, you will be amazed at how much similarity exists among various cuisines. In the case of stuffed pasta, for example, the Chinese have the wonton, a small piece of dough stuffed with a meat filling and served in soups, or fried. The Poles have pirogues. The Italians have ravioli, tortelli, cannelloni, cappelletti, and many other types that are added to soups or sauces.

But of course, no cuisine is pure Chinese, Italian, or Polish. People have been trading food ideas and food crops through invasions and migrations for centuries, and the ideas from one culture have been adopted and adapted by many others.

What is important to remember about Italy is what the Italians have done with pasta to make it their national dish. They layer it for lasagne, stuff it for tortellini, make narrow ribbons out of it for fettuccine, flavor the dough with vegetables, and form it into endless shapes.

Pasta is an old food for sure. In Rome, near the Quirinal Hill, is the National Pasta Museum, which traces the history of pasta. As their empire grew, the ancient Romans' need for more farmland became acute, and Sicily became the fertile breadbasket that Rome exploited for its grain to provide food for their military legions. Hard wheat, semolina, was one of those grains, mixed with water to become a sort of paste. The word *pasta* is derived from the word *paste*.

Naples perfected the art of making dried pasta, and it became the pasta epicenter for the rest of the world. Over time, hundreds of dried pasta forms—some with whimsical names like *gemelli* (twins), *fusilli* (twists), and *farfalle* (butterflies)—took shape in complex machines that extruded the dough through bronze dies.

In northern Italy, notably in the areas around Bologna, fresh pasta is made with eggs added to all-purpose flour known as *farina tipo 00* to produce richer and lighter pasta like tortellini, lasagna, and fettuccine. Many regions use a different ratio of flour to eggs for making the dough; some add more yolks than whole eggs, some add only egg whites, some add olive oil, and some flavor the pasta with spinach, carrot, beet, and herbs.

However pasta is made, it is loved the world over because of its versatility and ability to combine with just about any other food. It is filling, healthful and easy on the budget.

Of course, *pasta casarecce* (pasta made at home), is the best, but this is not to say that you can't buy good fresh or even dried pasta. There are many very good brands of dried imported pasta on the market. That being said, I will always prefer freshly made to dry. It is lighter, cooks faster, and has flavor and texture nuances that manufactured boxed pasta could never have. If you want to make your own pasta, follow these simple rules:

1. Do not make pasta at home using only coarse-ground semolina flour; it does not absorb liquid well, and the dough will be too hard to roll out. Semolina flour–based pasta is best made in large commercial machines. At home, use a ratio of 3 cups unbleached all-purpose flour with a high protein content (11 to 13 percent) mixed with 1 cup coarse-ground semolina. Do not confuse coarse-ground semolina flour with durum semolina, a finer grind of the same flour.

2. Use large eggs. Egg size determines how much flour will be needed to make the dough. There is no exact proportion for

this; you will know when you have added enough flour by the feel of the dough. It should be neither too wet nor too sticky; a sticky dough needs more flour while a dry dough needs more water. Making dough means striving for balance through trial and error.

3. Always let the dough rest to relax the gluten in the flour after you have kneaded it. This step will make it easier to roll out. If the dough is not relaxed, it will resist and snap back.

4. Work on a floured surface when rolling out and cutting the dough. A wood surface is ideal because there is more control over the dough; on a stainless steel surface, the dough is too slippery.

5. Invest in a hand-crank pasta machine and some wooden dowel rods over which to hang the pasta to dry. Use a long, thin rolling pin for rolling and thinning the dough.

6. Allow the pasta to dry completely before storing it or it will get moldy. On humid days, drying will take longer than usual. Once dried, store the pasta loosely wrapped in aluminum foil; it will keep for 3 months at room temperature.

7. Never wash the pasta machine. Dust it off after use with a dry pastry brush to remove any dried bits of pasta.

8. Cook the pasta in plenty of water, preferably in a large pasta pot with a drainer insert for lifting the pasta out of the water. Always add at least 1 tablespoon salt per pound of pasta.

9. Do not add oil to the cooking water; it will make the pasta slippery, and it will not hold the sauce very well.

10. Never overcook pasta. Italians like their pasta al dente. This means "to the tooth," or with a little bit of bite left. As it cooks, fish out a piece and break it in half. Look at the center to see if the pasta has cooked through; any remaining uncooked flour means it needs more time. Many people tend to cook pasta until it is soggy.

11. Do not over-sauce pasta. It should be lightly coated, and no puddle of sauce should remain in the base of the serving dish. And pasta is never topped with a snowstorm of grated cheese.

12. Match the right sauce to fit the type of pasta. Thin pasta, like vermicelli, should have a light sauce, like pesto; chunky pasta, like penne, can take a thicker sauce, like a ragù.

No matter what the food police dictate about pasta by calling it a forbidden food, or a carb with consequences, it will always stand the test of time as good and wholesome when prepared correctly in keeping with tradition.

Always a first course, pasta is never the main dish unless it is part of a casserole like a timballo. Consumed in moderation (4 ounces is an average serving), pasta is an important food that is often negatively looked upon, but it has nutrients that are very beneficial. Plain as well as whole-wheat pasta are good sources of selenium, a mineral that activates antioxidant enzymes that protect molecular damage. A 1-cup serving will provide about two-thirds of your recommended daily intake. Pasta also contains manganese, a mineral that helps metabolize carbohydrates and regulates blood sugar.

While interviewing the president of the Barilla pasta company at their headquarters in Parma, Italy, I asked Luca Barilla how many times a week he ate pasta. "Twice a day" was his reply. And this from a man who had a very trim physique!

Pasta Fatta in Casa

Homemade Pasta

5 large eggs

2½ cups unbleached all-purpose flour, plus more as needed

1½ cups semolina flour

⅛ teaspoon salt

When I was a kid, old broom handles propped between kitchen chairs, holding rows of golden yellow pasta in various shapes and sizes, was a familiar sight. Besides spaghetti, there was *farfalle* (butterflies) resting on floured kitchen cloths, as well as plump ravioli filled with ricotta cheese. To make pasta, my mother and grandmothers would put a mound of flour on a large wooden board and make a well in the center. The eggs were broken into the well and beaten with a fork with a pinch of salt. The tricky part came next: moving the flour into the eggs, being careful not to break down the walls of the well—otherwise, the eggs would escape onto the board or, worse, the floor. Admittedly, this method takes a little practice, but once you've got it, it's really easy. Or you can use a food processor or stand mixer. This basic dough can be used for filled pasta, such as tortellini or ravioli. **Makes about 1½ pounds, to serve 6 to 8**

To make the dough in a food processor, put the eggs in the bowl of the processor and process until they are well blended. In a bowl, whisk together the all-purpose flour, semolina flour, and salt. Add the flour mixture to the eggs, 1 cup at a time, and process until a ball of dough starts to form. Add a little water if the dough seems dry, or a little more flour if it seems too wet. The dough should not be so sticky that it clings to your fingers. Turn the dough out onto a floured surface and knead it, adding additional flour as necessary, for about 5 minutes, or until smooth. Cover and let rest for 10 minutes before rolling out and cutting into the desired shape.

To make the dough the traditional way, combine the all-purpose flour, semolina flour, and salt and mound it on a work surface. Make a well in the center of the flour and break the eggs into the well. Beat the eggs with a fork. Then, using the fork, gradually incorporate the flour from the inside walls of the well. When the dough become too firm to mix with the fork, use your hands, incorporating just enough of the flour to make a soft but not sticky dough. You may not need all the flour. Brush the excess flour aside and knead the dough with your hands for about 30 minutes, adding additional flour as necessary to obtain a smooth ball. Cover it with a bowl and let it rest for 10 minutes before rolling out and cutting into the desired shape.

Cut the dough into 4 pieces. Work with one piece at a time, keeping the remaining dough covered. Roll the dough out on a floured surface to the thickness of a sheet of copy paper, or use a pasta machine to roll the dough out to the thinnest machine setting. (All machines are not the same, so you will have to gauge the thinness). Drape the sheets of pasta over dowel rods suspended between 2 chairs to dry slightly, about 5 minutes. Do not let the sheets dry completely or they will be difficult to cut.

If cutting the pasta by hand, roll up each sheet loosely like a jelly roll, then cut it into fettuccine, vermicelli, or lasagna strips with a sharp knife. Or cut the pasta into the desired width with the attachment on the pasta machine. Hang the pasta strips over dowel rods as you cut them, or spread them on floured towels; then cook immediately or dry for storage.

Cook the pasta in a large pot of boiling salted water until al dente, 2 to 3 minutes, drain, sauce, and serve immediately.

To store, leave the strips on the dowel rods for a day. When the ends of the pasta begin to curl, it is dry enough to store. Wrap it loosely in aluminum foil and store in a dark, cool place for up to 3 months.

Francesca Makes Pasta

Bevagna is not to be missed. A little snip of a town in the region of Umbria near the wine center of Montefalco, it still retains its medieval look with its mellow brown stone gates, narrow streets, and beautiful piazza built in the twelfth and thirteenth centuries. Long-standing Roman columns give evidence to its ancient history.

Bevagna is known for its handcrafts and for centuries was an important tile- and cloth-making center. Today it continues the tradition of rope- and basket-making and prized workmanship in wrought iron. Every year toward the end of June, the most important festival takes place: the Mercato delle Gaite, the Market of Gaite, and for a week the town is transformed into a medieval marketplace with its citizens in period costumes practicing old trades: The bakers make bread in open ovens, the basket makers make intricate containers from willow branches, the rope maker turns hemp into cords, and ropes, and the taverns serve food prepared from antique recipes.

In the midst of all this idyllic charm and history lives Francesca Margutti, an accomplished cook to whose home I was headed for lunch one day, thanks to mutual friend and the mayor of the town, Analita Polticcia. Analita's family owns a *pasticceria* (pastry shop) in Bevagna and knows everyone. Because she knew how interested I was in Umbrian cuisine, she wanted me to meet Francesca, who was going to share her pasta making techniques with me. Meeting her in her cheery, lime green–painted kitchen, I was immediately comfortable in the lush surroundings of potted herbs, beautiful roses, cream-colored lilies, and intoxicating lavender plants soaking up the noontime sun on the outdoor terrace.

Francesca is a vigorous woman with short, dark hair and a wide smile. It was evident by witnessing her efficiency in the kitchen with her hands that she has been making good food since she was a young girl.

But before making pasta, there was lunch to consider, and I was ushered outside to the terrace where a pristine table was set with terracotta dishes. The meal started with an antipasto of fresh fava beans dressed in fragrant, deep green Umbrian extra-virgin olive oil served with Pecorino Romano cheese. There were juicy perfumed melon slices, the perfect bed for see-through slices of local prosciutto. There was a plate of attractively arranged spicy salame, dried tomatoes glistening in extra-virgin olive oil, and, of course good, rustic bread. That would have been enough, but it would not have been Italian hospitality at its finest. Fresh, delicate ribbons of fettuccine followed, with a sauce of wild garlic tops, cherry tomatoes, and dried red pepper flakes. I did not leave a trace of that on my plate. Next, an exquisitely prepared *faraona* (guinea hen) seasoned with a mixture of herbs and cooked with wine left me in awe, and I wondered how I would ever get through the afternoon as the wine flowed freely to accompany this *pranzo*. A plate of cavallucci and tozzetti cookies from Analita's pasticceria ended the glorious meal.

Now it was showtime, and Francesca had everything she needed lined up on her wooden board, including her long, thin rolling pin, fresh eggs in a large bowl, and flour. What about salt? No salt until it is time to cook the pasta, then it is added to the cooking water, she explained. I had made pasta hundreds of times, but watching Francesca make it was almost hypnotic as she whipped the eggs around with her hands in a fountain of flour. It took three minutes for her to be happy with the look of the beaten eggs before she blended them with the flour and used every bit of it, leaving not a speck on the board. Now that is planning! She kneaded the dough and told me that this batch will become *pappardelle*, wide ribbon noodles that go so well with wild hare or boar. I loved the way she rolled the dough up onto the rolling pin, wrapping it around the pin and then unwrapping it in such a swift motion that the dough gave a rhythmic slapping sound against the wood. When Francesca was satisfied that the dough was thin enough, she rolled it up gently like a jelly roll and cut it crosswise into ½-inch-wide noodles, then shook out the rolls to uncoil them. Those silky yellow ribbons were perfect, and the smile on her face was her own stamp of approval that here in her cozy kitchen, she had once again made perfect pasta, the badge of honor for any cook—but especially for women of her generation.

Pasta di Spinaci

Spinach Pasta

3 large eggs

2 tablespoons chopped cooked well-squeezed spinach

2 to 2¼ cups unbleached all-purpose flour

½ cup durum semolina flour

⅛ teaspoon salt

Adding a small amount of well-squeezed spinach to pasta dough gives it a vibrant green color. The dough is a little harder to work with because of the added moisture from the spinach, so more flour is necessary per egg to achieve a dough that can be rolled.   **Makes about 1 pound**

Prepare the pasta dough following the directions on page 86, but add the spinach to the food processor bowl with the eggs and process until smooth. Mix 2 cups of the all-purpose flour with all of the durum semolina and add it gradually to the food processor, until a ball of dough forms. Add additional flour if necessary. If making by hand, add the spinach to the well with the eggs and beat with a fork before proceeding as directed.

Roll out the dough, cut into the desired shape, and cook immediately or store as directed.

Pasta al Pomodoro

Tomato Paste Pasta

One of the reasons pasta is such a ubiquitous food is that it can be transformed with so many ingredients. When I make fettuccine, I often add pureed vegetables like carrots or beets to the dough. For tomato fettuccine, a good store-bought tomato paste (such as Mutti brand) turns the dough a vibrant bright orange color.   **Makes about 1½ pounds**

4 large eggs

1½ tablespoons tomato paste

3 cups unbleached all-purpose flour

½ cup durum semolina flour

⅛ teaspoon salt

Prepare the pasta dough following the directions on page 86, adding the tomato paste to the food processor bowl with the eggs and process until well blended. Mix 2½ cups of the all-purpose flour with the durum semolina to start, adding additional flour as necessary. If making by hand, add the tomato paste to the well with the eggs and beat with a fork before proceeding as directed.

Roll out the dough, cut into the desired shape, and cook immediately or store as directed.

Note: Serve with Basil Sauce (page 141). The vibrant green of the pesto contrasts nicely with the reddish-orange pasta. You can use room-temperature pesto or heat it slightly before tossing it with the hot pasta.

Pasta di Pepe Nero

Black Pepper Pasta

4 large eggs

1 tablespoon coarsely ground black pepper

2½ cups unbleached all-purpose flour, plus more as needed

½ cup semolina flour

⅛ teaspoon salt

Cacio e pepe is a popular Roman pasta dish with lots of black pepper and Pecorino Romano cheese. You can get even more black pepper flavor by adding coarsely ground directly to the pasta dough for a nice visual effect as well as a spicy taste. **Makes about 1½ pounds**

Prepare the pasta dough following the directions on page 86, adding the black pepper to the food processor bowl with the eggs, and process until smooth; mix 2½ cups of the all-purpose flour with the semolina to start, adding more flour as necessary. If making the traditional way, add the black pepper to the well with the eggs and beat with a fork before proceeding as directed.

Roll out the dough, cut into the desired shape, and cook immediately or store as directed.

Cappelletti di Nonna Galasso

Nonna Galasso's Little Hats

My Neapolitan Nonna Galasso liked to fill her cappelletti (little pasta hats) with a combination of beef, pork, and veal, but I sometimes prefer a chicken filling. Both are traditional and both are very good. Make these for Cappelletti in Brodo (page 39) or serve them with a light cream sauce or other sauce if you prefer. This recipe makes a lot, so you can use some immediately and freeze the remainder.   **Makes 150 to 200**

In a large sauté pan, heat the olive oil over medium-high heat. Add the meat cubes and brown them on all sides. Remove from the pan and let cool.

In a meat grinder or food processor, finely grind the meats and transfer them to a large bowl. Add the egg, cheese, parsley, lemon zest, and nutmeg, season with salt and pepper, and mix well.

Roll out the dough and fill the cappelletti as directed on page 94. Cook immediately as directed on page 95 or freeze as directed on page 95.

2 tablespoons extra-virgin olive oil

1 (4-ounce) center-cut pork chop, cubed

1 (4-ounce) boneless sirloin steak, cubed

1 (4-ounce) boneless veal roast, cubed

1 large egg

¼ cup grated Parmigiano-Reggiano cheese

2 tablespoons minced fresh flat-leaf parsley

2 teaspoons grated lemon zest

¼ teaspoon grated nutmeg

Salt and freshly ground black pepper to taste

1 recipe Cappelletti Dough (page 94)

Cappelletti di Pollo
Chicken-Filled Cappelletti

FILLING

1 whole bone-in, skin-on chicken breast, about 1¼ pounds

1 large egg, beaten

¼ cup grated Parmigiano-Reggiano cheese

2 tablespoons minced fresh flat-leaf parsley

2 teaspoons grated lemon zest

Dash grated nutmeg

Salt and freshly ground black pepper to taste

CAPPELLETTI DOUGH

4 large eggs

⅛ teaspoon salt

1⅓ cups durum semolina flour

2¾ to 3 cups unbleached all-purpose flour

In Italy, these "little hats" are traditionally served at Christmastime and for other special occasions. They are time-consuming to make, and at my home hundreds of them were made in assembly-line fashion. Nonna Galasso made the dough, Mom rolled it out, and cut the circles, and I put the dab of filling in the center of each circle. Some were cooked immediately in boiling homemade broth and the rest were frozen for future meals.

The dough for cappelletti needs to be softer and wetter than basic pasta dough because if it is too dry, it will be difficult to press the edges closed. You may have to experiment with the recipe below as the proportions are intended as a guideline. Egg size and the absorbency of the flour will determine the dryness of the dough. **Makes 175 to 200**

To make the filling, put the chicken in a saucepan and add cold water to cover. Bring to a boil over medium-high heat, reduce the heat, and simmer until the chicken is tender, 20 to 25 minutes. Remove the chicken and let it cool. Remove the meat from the bones; discard the skin and bones.

In a food processor, finely grind the chicken and transfer it to a bowl. Add all the remaining filling ingredients. Mix well, cover with plastic wrap, and refrigerate.

To make the dough, combine the eggs and salt in a food processor and pulse to blend well. Mix the durum semolina flour and 2¾ cups of the all-purpose flour together and pulse until a ball of dough is formed. If the dough is too sticky, add more flour; if too dry, add a little warm water. Aim for a stretchy, elastic dough that is slightly damp to the touch. On a well-floured surface, knead the dough until smooth, about 5 minutes. Cover the dough with a bowl or damp towel and let it rest for 30 minutes.

Divide the dough into 4 pieces. Work with one piece at a time and keep the rest covered. Flatten the dough slightly with a rolling pin and use a pasta machine to roll it out about ⅛ inch thick. Don't make the dough too thin, or the filling will poke through when the cappelletti are formed. Alternatively, you can roll out each piece of dough on a lightly floured surface with a rolling pin.

Using a l-inch round cookie cutter or a small glass, cut out rounds from each sheet of dough. (Form the scraps into a ball and reroll.) Place a scant teaspoon of the chicken filling in the center of each round. Fold each round in half and pinch the edges together to make a turnover shape. Take the two pointed ends and bring them together to meet; pinch to seal. Place the cappelletti on a floured towel on a baking sheet as you form them.

To cook the cappelletti, bring a large pot of broth or water to a boil. Add about 3 dozen at a time and cook until they bob to the surface. Serve in the broth or in a sauce of your choosing.

To freeze uncooked cappelletti, arrange them in a single layer, without touching, on baking sheets as you form them. Cover with aluminum foil and freeze on the sheets. When they are frozen solid, transfer them to plastic bags. They can be frozen for up to 3 months. Add them frozen directly to boiling broth or water.

Crespelle con Verdure e Formaggio

Crêpes with Vegetables and Cheese

In this version of cannelloni, a *crespella* (crêpe) batter is made for a quicker and more delicate dish than the cannelloni recipe on page 98 that calls for a basic pasta dough. These make a wonderful first course or a light supper with a green salad.   **Serves 8 as a first course**

To make the batter, sift together the flour, salt, and nutmeg into a large bowl. Add the beaten eggs and egg yolk, 1½ cups milk, and the butter. Whisk the mixture until smooth and the consistency of pancake batter. If the batter seems too thin, add a little more flour; if too thick, add a little milk.

Lightly butter a 6- or 8-inch crêpe pan or a nonstick frying pan and heat it over medium heat. When the pan is very hot, add ¼ cup of the batter and swirl the pan to make sure the bottom is evenly coated with a thin layer of batter. Cook for 1 to 2 minutes, or until lightly browned on the underside. Flip the crespella over and cook the other side until lightly browned. Transfer it to a sheet of wax paper. Repeat with the remaining batter, stacking the crespelle between sheets of wax paper as they are made. Lightly grease the pan every so often with butter to prevent the batter from sticking.

Preheat the oven to 350°F. Butter a 9 x 12-inch baking dish.

In a large bowl, combine the ricotta cheese, egg, and 1½ cups of the Parmigiano-Reggiano and mix well. Add the tomatoes, broccoli, parsley, and lemon zest, season with salt and pepper, and mix to combine well.

Spread about ¼ cup of the filling over each crespella and roll up into a cylinder. Place them in a single layer, seam side down, in the buttered dish. Drizzle the melted butter over them and sprinkle with the remaining 1⅓ cups Parmigiano-Reggiano cheese.

Bake for 15 to 20 minutes, or until piping hot. If you wish, run them under the broiler for a few minutes to brown the cheese. Serve immediately, with additional melted butter on the side.

CRESPELLA BATTER

- 1¾ cups all-purpose flour
- ⅛ teaspoon salt
- 1½ teaspoons grated nutmeg
- 2 large eggs, beaten
- 1 large egg yolk, beaten
- 1½ to 1¾ cups milk
- 1 tablespoon unsalted butter, melted, plus more for the pan
- 3 tablespoons grated Parmigiano-Reggiano cheese

FILLING

- 1½ cups whole-milk ricotta cheese homemade (page 332) or store-bought, well drained
- 1 large egg, beaten with a fork
- 1½ cups plus 1⅓ cups grated Parmigiano-Reggiano cheese
- 1 cup seeded and diced fresh plum tomatoes, drained
- 2⅓ cups chopped cooked broccoli
- ¼ cup minced fresh flat-leaf parsley
- Grated zest of 1 lemon
- Salt and freshly ground black pepper to taste
- 8 tablespoons unsalted butter, melted, plus more for serving

Cannelloni Ripieni di Agnello

Lamb-Stuffed Cannelloni

2 tablespoons extra-virgin olive oil

1½ pounds ground lamb

2 teaspoons fennel seeds

2 teaspoons minced fresh mint

Salt and freshly ground black pepper to taste

1½ cups grated Pecorino Romano cheese

4½ cups Fresh Tomato-Basil Sauce (page 141)

1 recipe Tomato Paste Pasta (page 91)

1 cup grated Pecorino Romano cheese

Cannelloni are tubes of fresh pasta stuffed with meat or cheese—and sometimes both. They are a wonderful first course or a meal in themselves. There are two different versions of cannelloni dough used in Italy. One is made with a crêpe-like batter (*Crespelli con Verdure e Formaggio*, page 97); this one is made with a regular pasta dough. **Serves 8 to 10**

Heat the olive oil in a large sauté pan over medium-high heat and cook the lamb until it is browned. Add the fennel seeds, mint, salt, and pepper and cook for 2 minutes. Transfer the lamb to a bowl and stir in the cheese and ½ cup of the tomato-basil sauce. Set aside.

Cut the pasta dough into 4 pieces. Work with one piece at a time, keeping the rest covered. Roll out the dough through a pasta machine to the thinnest setting. Cut each sheet into 5-inch squares, laying the squares on floured cloths in a single layer as you make them.

In a large pot of boiling water, cook the pasta squares a few at a time for 2 to 3 minutes. Remove them with a strainer, drain, and plunge them into a large casserole dish filled with ice water to cool them. Pat them dry on a clean towel before filling them.

Preheat the oven to 350°F.

Butter two 9 x 13-inch baking pans. Spread 3 tablespoons of the lamb filling on each pasta square, roll them into cylinders, and place them in the prepared pans, seam sides down, in a single layer. Cover the cannelloni with the remaining tomato-basil sauce and sprinkle the tops with the Pecorino Romano cheese. Cover the pans with aluminum foil and bake for 30 minutes. Serve immediately.

Frascarelli con Salsa al Burro e Salvia

"Scatters" in Sage Butter Sauce

Frascarelli, a special type of pasta from Umbria, reminds me of the pastina that my grandmothers put in soup. This pasta is made by sprinkling beaten eggs over flour and then gathering the mixture up and sifting it through a sieve or colander to create little beads or "scatters" of dough, which are then served in a simple sage butter sauce.
Serves 4 to 6

10 tablespoons unsalted butter, melted

20 fresh sage leaves, minced

2 cups unbleached all-purpose flour

4 large eggs, beaten with a fork

In a sauté pan, melt the butter over medium-high heat. Add the sage leaves, reduce the heat to medium, and swirl the leaves in the butter for 2 to 3 minutes. Keep the sauce warm over very low heat, allowing the sage leaves to flavor the butter.

Spread the flour in a thin layer on a large work surface. Using your hands, sprinkle the beaten eggs evenly over the flour. Gently gather up the odd-shaped "scatters," or beads, that form and transfer them to a fine-mesh sieve or strainer. Shake the sieve to remove the excess flour. What you are left with are the frascarelli.

In a large pot of boiling water, cook the pasta for 1 minute. Drain well, toss with the warm sauce, and serve.

Fazzoletti di Formaggio
Cheese Folds

In Tuscany, crêpes are called *fazzoletti* ("little hankies") because of how the crêpes are folded). The most memorable ones were served in Torgiano at Tre Vaselle, where Chef Angelo turns them out with lightning speed with all the action centered in the wrist as he flips each one. Serve them as a first course. Fazzoletti can be made and frozen in single layers and filled when ready to use.   **Serves 8 to 10**

To make the filling, melt the butter over low heat in a 6-quart saucepan. Add the flour and whisk to blend well. Slowly add the milk, stirring constantly until smooth. Raise the heat to medium-high and cook, stirring constantly, for about 10 minutes, or until the sauce coats the back of the spoon. Turn off the heat and add all the cheeses and the nutmeg. Season with salt and pepper and stir until smooth. Cover to keep warm and set aside.

To make the batter, sift together the flour, salt, and nutmeg into a large bowl. Add the beaten eggs and egg yolk, 1½ cups milk, and the butter. Whisk the mixture until smooth and the consistency of pancake batter. If the batter seems too thin, add a little more flour; if too thick, add a little milk.

Lightly butter a 6- or 8-inch crêpe pan or a nonstick frying pan and heat it over medium heat. When the pan is hot, add ¼ cup of the batter and swirl the pan to make sure the bottom is evenly coated with a thin layer of batter. Cook for 1 to 2 minutes, or until lightly browned on the underside. Flip the crespella over and cook the other side until lightly browned. Transfer it to a sheet of wax paper.

Repeat with the remaining batter, stacking the crespelle between sheets of wax paper as you make them. Lightly grease the pan every so often with a little butter to prevent the batter from sticking.

Preheat the oven to 350°F. Butter a 9 x 12-inch baking dish.

Spread about 3 tablespoons of the filling over each crespella, making sure to cover the surface evenly. Fold each one in half, then in half again, and place them in the baking dish, slightly overlapping them. Spoon the remaining filling over the crespelle and sprinkle with the Parmigiano-Reggiano cheese.

Bake for 20 minutes, or until piping hot. Run the crespelle under the broiler for 1 to 2 minutes to brown the top, and serve immediately, with additional cheese sprinkled over the top.

FILLING

6 tablespoons unsalted butter

¾ cup unbleached all-purpose flour

6 cups whole milk

½ cup cubed Asiago cheese (about 2 ounces)

½ cup cubed Italian Fontina cheese (about 2 ounces)

½ cup cubed Provolone cheese (about 2 ounces)

⅓ cup grated Parmigiano-Reggiano cheese

1 teaspoon grated nutmeg

Salt and freshly ground black pepper to taste

BATTER

1¾ cups unbleached all-purpose flour

⅛ teaspoon salt

1 teaspoons grated nutmeg

2 large eggs, beaten

1 large egg yolk, beaten

1½ to 1¾ cups whole milk

1 tablespoon unsalted butter, melted, plus more for the pan

3 tablespoons grated Parmigiano-Reggiano cheese, plus more for sprinkling

Rotolo di Pasta al Gorgonzola e Panna

Stuffed Pasta with Gorgonzola and Cream

PASTA DOUGH

1¾ cups unbleached all-purpose flour

¼ cup durum semolina flour

½ teaspoon salt

3 large eggs

FILLING

¼ cup pine nuts

¼ cup extra-virgin olive oil

1 medium onion, peeled and thinly sliced

4 ounces prosciutto di Parma, diced

2½ cups chopped cooked spinach, well drained

1 cup whole-milk ricotta cheese, homemade (page 332) or store-bought, well drained

⅔ cup grated Parmigiano-Reggiano cheese

1 large egg, beaten with a fork

½ teaspoon grated nutmeg

Salt and freshly ground black pepper to taste

While most professional chefs in Italy are men, the one area that remains the domain of women in restaurants (as well as at home) is pasta *fatta a mano* (made by hand). In most Italian restaurant kitchens, it is the *sfoglina* (female artisan pasta maker) who produce the thinnest, sometimes almost translucent, sheets of pasta with only several forceful passes of a *matterello* (rolling pin). It is thin and about two feet long, and the pasta dough yields in elastic submission to its shaping. My friend Maria, who makes all the pasta for Tre Vaselle in Torgiano, taught me how to make this unusual stuffed pasta, which is poached first and then baked. Serve this spectacular dish as a first or main course. To make the job less time-consuming, prepare the filling and sauce a day ahead and refrigerate until ready to use.

Serves 8–10 servings

Preheat the oven to 350°F. Butter a 9 x 13-inch baking dish.

To make the pasta, mix the flours and salt together and mound on a work surface. Make a well in the center of the flour. Crack the eggs into the well. Mix the eggs with your fingers or a fork. Begin by incorporating the flour from the inside of the well into the eggs, taking care not to break through the sides. Add just enough of the flour to make a soft but not sticky dough. Brush away the excess flour and knead the dough until smooth, about 10 minutes. You may need to add a little warm water if the dough seems too dry or a little flour if it is too wet. Cover the dough with a damp towel and let it rest for 30 minutes while you make the filling.

Spread the pine nuts on a rimmed baking sheet and toast them in the oven until lightly browned, about 5 minutes. Watch them carefully, as they burn easily. Set aside to cool.

In a small sauté pan, heat the olive oil over medium heat and cook the onion until soft. Stir in the prosciutto di Parma and pine nuts and cook until the mixture is fairly dry. Stir in the spinach and cook for 1 minute. Transfer the mixture to a bowl and let cool. Add the cheeses, egg, and nutmeg and season with salt and pepper. Mix well. Cover and refrigerate until ready to use.

On a well-floured surface, roll out the dough with a rolling pin into a 22-inch circle. The dough should be very thin, no thicker than a sheet of copy paper. Spread the filling evenly over the dough to within 1½ inches of the edges.

Roll up the dough like a jellyroll. Pinch the seam and both ends of the dough closed to seal it to prevent the filling from coming out. Place the roll, seam side down, along one edge of a large clean cotton kitchen towel. Carefully roll up the pasta in the towel, then tie the ends of the towel with kitchen string.

Bring a large pot of water to a boil. Carefully lower the towel-encased pasta roll into the water, bending it gently to fit. When the water returns to the boil, partially cover the pot and poach the roll for 20 minutes. Use 2 spatulas to carefully transfer the roll to a baking sheet, and let it cool.

Untie and unwrap the towel and carefully transfer the roll to a cutting board. Cut the roll into 1-inch-thick slices and lay them, cut side down, in a single layer in the buttered baking dish.

In a saucepan, combine all the sauce ingredients and bring to a slow boil over medium-high heat, stirring constantly with a wooden spoon. Lower the heat to medium and stir the mixture until smooth. Pour half of the sauce over the rolls.

Bake, uncovered, for 20 to 25 minutes, or until the pasta rolls are hot and the sauce is bubbling. Reheat the remaining sauce to pass at the table, and serve immediately.

CHEESE SAUCE

2 cups heavy cream

½ cup (5 ounces) mascarpone cheese, homemade (page 329) or store-bought, or cream cheese

4 ounces Gorgonzola dolce cheese, crumbled

Spaghetti con Cavolfiore e Acciughe

Spaghetti with Cauliflower and Anchovy

Cauliflower is a vegetable that is greatly admired in Italy. It is a familiar ingredient in frittata, in Sicilian salad, in a variety of soups, and in this pasta dish, where the clever technique of cooking the cauliflower with the pasta not only saves time but adds flavor. Whole-wheat spaghetti bumps up the nutritional value of this dish.   **Serves 4**

Remove the leaves and core of the cauliflower and cut the head into small uniform florets. Set aside.

In a large sauté pan, heat the 3 tablespoons olive oil over medium heat and brown the breadcrumbs. Transfer them to a bowl and set aside.

In the same pan, heat the remaining ⅓ cup olive oil. Add the garlic and cook until softened. Stir in the pepper flakes and cook for 1 minute. Stir in the anchovy paste and 1 teaspoon black pepper and cook for 1 minute longer. Keep the sauce warm over very low heat.

Bring a large pot of salted water to a boil over high heat. Cook the cauliflower with the spaghetti until the cauliflower is crisp-tender and the pasta is al dente; they should be done at the same time. Drain and reserve ½ cup of the cooking water. Add the reserved water and the cauliflower and spaghetti to the sauté pan and toss to coat with the sauce. Transfer the mixture to a shallow serving platter and sprinkle with the cheese, breadcrumbs, and additional salt and black pepper.

1 small head cauliflower

3 tablespoons plus ⅓ cup extra-virgin olive oil

1 cup toasted breadcrumbs

2 cloves garlic, minced

1½ teaspoons red pepper flakes

2 tablespoons anchovy paste

8 ounces whole-wheat spaghetti

Salt and coarsely ground black pepper to taste

½ cup grated Pecorino Romano cheese

Cavatelli con Cime di Rapa e Pangrattati
Little Caves with Broccoli Rapa and Breadcrumbs

CAVATELLI DOUGH

2½ cups fine durum semolina flour

½ teaspoon salt

¾ cup warm water

SAUCE

½ cup fresh breadcrumbs

¼ cup extra-virgin olive oil

3 oil-packed anchovy fillets, drained and coarsely chopped

2 cloves garlic, minced

1 small dried red chile, crumbled

1 tablespoon salt

1 pound broccoli rapa, tough stems trimmed and leaves coarsely chopped

Cavatelli means "little caves" because the dough is shaped similar to gnocchi. There are no eggs in this dough. Water, durum semolina flour (a finer grind of semolina), and a pinch of salt are the sole ingredients. The dough is rolled into long ropes the width of your pinkie finger and traditionally cut into ¼-inch pieces with a small spatula-like tool called a *rasola*, but a butter knife will do. Each piece is rolled under your finger to create an indentation. The little hollows of the cavatelli nicely trap the slightly spicy sauce.   **Serves 6 to 8**

First, make the dough. In a large bowl mix the flour, salt, and enough water to make a dough that is the consistency of bread dough. Add more flour or water as needed. Knead the dough until smooth, then cover the dough and let it rest for 30 minutes.

Cut the dough into 6 pieces and roll each piece under the palm of your hand to create a log that is the thickness of your pinky finger and 14-inches long. Cut each log into ¼-inch-long pieces.

With your finger, draw each piece of dough across a wooden butter paddle, cavarola board, or wooden cutting board, leaving an impression or "little cave," and place them on floured towels. At this point, you can freeze the cavatelli on the trays and then transfer them to plastic bags once hard, or cook them immediately.

To make the sauce, toast the breadcrumbs in a large sauté pan over medium heat until golden, then transfer them to a bowl.

In the same pan, heat the olive oil; add the anchovies, garlic, and dried chile until the anchovies almost dissolve. Cover the pan and keep the sauce warm while the cavatelli cook.

continued on page 108

continued from page 106

Bring 4 quarts of water to a boil over high heat; add the salt, cavatelli, and broccoli rapa and cook until the cavatelli are al dente, about 4 minutes. Drain and reserve 1 cup of the cooking water.

Transfer the cavatelli and broccoli rapa to the sauté pan and combine well over medium heat with the sauce, adding some of the reserved cooking water if the sauce is too dry. Transfer the mixture to a platter and top with the breadcrumbs. Serve hot.

Note: Cavatelli makers can save time; they are available online at Fantes.com.

Rasola tools are available from www.artisanpastatools.com.

Garden in Liguria

Spaghettini in Purgatorio

Spaghettini in Purgatory

Picky eaters? This is a sneaky way to get young children to eat an egg: Mix it with thin strands of pasta and tomato sauce. The dish can be made in 10 minutes. Of course, the recipe can be doubled or quadrupled to serve more. **Serves 1**

Combine the water and tomato sauce in a medium pot. Add the olive oil and salt to taste. Bring to a boil over high heat. Add the spaghettini and cook until almost al dente, 3 to 4 minutes. Lower the heat to a simmer. Add the egg about 1 minute before the spaghettini is cooked and mix until it is well combined.

5 tablespoons water

½ cup tomato sauce

1 teaspoon extra-virgin olive oil

Salt

1 ounce spaghettini or capellini

1 egg, beaten with a fork

Canederli allo Speck

Speck-Flavored Bread Gnocchi

3 cups packed day-old diced bread, crusts trimmed

⅔ cup warm whole milk

2 large eggs, lightly beaten with a fork

¾ cup grated Asiago cheese

2¼ tablespoons unbleached all-purpose flour

2 teaspoons minced fresh flat-leaf parsley

¼ teaspoon grated fresh nutmeg

½ teaspoon salt

Freshly ground black pepper

1 tablespoon unsalted butter

2 slices speck,* finely diced

½ cup finely diced onion

8 cups beef broth, homemade (page 40) or store-bought

Grated Grana Padano or Parmigiano-Reggiano cheese, for sprinkling (optional)

Canederli are the Trentino-Alto Adige region's version of gnocchi. Cousins to the Austrian and German knodel, they are unique bread-based dumplings served in soup or with melted butter and grated cheese. Their origin lies deep in country cooking, when not even a scrap of stale bread was ever wasted. Instead it was combined with other simple ingredients—some herbs, leftover cheese, milk, and bits of meat—and transformed into canederli. Speck, a smoked and air-cured ham from this region, gives added flavor and texture. Today's canederli are sometimes even mixed with fruit and served as dessert. The success of this dish will depend on the quality of the bread. Using spongy, store bought bread would be a sacrilege.

Makes 12 small dumplings, to serve 6

Put the bread in a bowl and add the milk. Mix well and allow the bread to soak in the milk for 30 minutes. The consistency of the bread should be soft but not mushy. Stir in the eggs, cheese, flour, parsley, nutmeg, salt, and a good grinding of black pepper. Set aside.

In a small frying pan, melt the butter over medium heat. Add the speck and onion and sauté until the speck is beginning to brown and the onion is soft; set aside to cool. Add the speck and onion to the bread mixture and mix well. Cover and let rest for 30 minutes.

In a large pot, bring the broth to a boil over medium-high heat. Have a bowl of water handy to wet your hands. Test the dough to make sure you have a mixture that will hold together when boiled: Roll a small amount of dough into a ball and drop it into the boiling broth; if it disintegrates, mix a tablespoon or more of flour into the dough and test again. If the ball does not disintegrate, form 8 golf ball–size canederli. Add them to the boiling broth, reduce the heat to simmer, and cook for about 10 minutes, or until they bob to the top.

Ladle two of the canederli into each of 4 soup bowls and cover them with the broth. Serve hot. Add a sprinkling of cheese over the top if desired.

Another way to serve them is without the broth, with melted butter and fresh sage leaves.

Note: The canederli dough can also be mixed with fresh herbs or cooked spinach.

* Speck Alto Adige is a smoked and dry-cured ham from the South Tyrol region of Italy. It is an artisan product made from quality pork thighs, a little salt, a little smoke, and a lot of fresh air. Speck is seasoned with black pepper, juniper, rosemary, and bay leaf. It is aged slowly for about 22 weeks, depending on size.

Spaghetti alla Puttanesca
Harlot-Style Spaghetti

Spaghetti alla puttanesca is a bold and spicy tomato-laced dish. The term *puttanesca* causes huge arguments among Italian cooks who claim that it was a word in reference to, shall we say, the red-light districts of southern Italy! I leave the discussion to them. What gives this sauce its extra punch is the combination of ingredients that go into it: hot red pepper, salty anchovies, plump olives, and briny capers.
Serves 4

Heat the olive oil in a large sauté pan over medium heat and cook the garlic until it begins to soften. Add the red pepper flakes and cook for 1 minute. Stir in the anchovies and tomato paste and cook for 2 minutes. Stir in the green and black olives, capers, and tomatoes and cook for 2 to 3 minutes, until the tomatoes start to shrivel. Raise the heat to high and add the wine, allowing it to reduce for a couple of minutes. Stir in the parsley, lemon zest and juice. Season with salt and pepper and keep warm while the spaghetti cooks.

Bring a large pot of water to a boil over high heat. Add the spaghetti and 1 tablespoon salt and cook until the spaghetti is al dente. Drain, reserving ¼ cup of the pasta water. Add the reserved water to the sauce and stir over low heat to blend. Add the spaghetti and toss well with the sauce. Garnish with whole olives and serve in bowls with Pecorino Romano cheese sprinkled on top.

2 tablespoons extra-virgin olive oil

2 tablespoons minced garlic

1 teaspoon red pepper flakes *or* ½ teaspoon red pepper paste

2 heaping tablespoons chopped anchovies in olive oil or anchovy paste

1 tablespoon tomato paste

½ cup coarsely chopped green olives (10 to 12), plus a few whole for garnish

⅓ cup pitted oil-cured black olives (8 to 10), cut in half, plus a few whole for garnish

2 tablespoons capers in brine, drained

2 cups halved cherry tomatoes or coarsely chopped canned plum tomatoes

⅔ cup dry red wine

2 tablespoons chopped fresh flat-leaf parsley

Grated zest and juice of 1 large lemon

Salt and freshly ground black pepper to taste

8 ounces plain or whole-wheat spaghetti or chickpea pasta

Grated Pecorino Romano cheese, for sprinkling

Farfalle con Salsa di Cavolo Nero

Butterflies with Kale Sauce

There are so many sauces for pasta; some are smooth and some are chunky. Ragù, tomato, and pesto are some of the more common ones. In today's Italian kitchen, clever cooks are thinking up all kinds of sauces. From my garden comes this inspiration for kale sauce. In Tuscany, kale is called *cavolo nero*, or black cabbage, because of its dark green leaves. It is the perfect sauce for short cuts of pasta like farfalle, rigatoni, or fusilli. Did I mention it's healthy, too? **Serves 4**

In a medium sauté pan, heat the olive oil over medium heat. Stir in the leeks and cook just until they begin to wilt, then stir in the garlic and continue cooking just until it softens. Cover and keep warm.

Bring a large pot of water to a boil over high heat. Add the kale and 1 tablespoon salt and cook just until the kale wilts. Use a slotted spoon or spider to drain and transfer the kale to the sauté pan. Mix it well with the leek mixture. Transfer the mixture to a blender or food processor. Add the pasta to the same pot and cook until al dente. Drain the pasta, reserving ¼ cup of the cooking water, then return the pasta to the pot.

Process the kale mixture, adding 2 tablespoons of the reserved pasta cooking water. The sauce should have a smooth but not too thin consistency. If the sauce is too thick, add a little more water. It should have the consistency of heavy cream.

Add the sauce to the pot with the pasta; stir well to combine over low heat until it is hot. Add the lemon zest and cheese and mix well. Salt to taste.

Serve hot.

¼ cup extra-virgin olive oil

½ cup thinly sliced leeks, white part only

2 cloves garlic, minced

1 pound kale, stems removed and leaves shredded

Salt to taste

8 ounces rigatoni, farfalle, or fusilli

Grated zest of 1 large lemon

¾ cup grated Pecorino Romano cheese

Frittata Bianca

White Frittata

8 ounces vermicelli, spaghetti or linguine

Salt and freshly ground black pepper to taste

6 tablespoons unsalted butter

1 cup grated Parmigiano-Reggiano cheese

4 large eggs

½ cup minced fresh basil

¼ cup minced fresh flat-leaf parsley

Neapolitans love their frittata, known to the rest of the world as an omelet. Made with eggs and whatever else comes to mind like leftover vegetables, cooked meat, and even pasta, it can be a picnic food, lunch, or easy supper. This so-called white frittata comes from the fact that there is little color to the dish, but the taste more than makes up for it!   **Serves 6 to 8**

Bring a large pot of water to a boil over high heat. Add the vermicelli and 1 tablespoon salt and cook until the vermicelli is al dente. Drain and transfer the pasta to a large bowl. Stir in 4 tablespoons of the butter and the cheese, and season with salt and pepper. Set aside.

In a separate bowl, beat the eggs, basil, and parsley with a fork until foamy; add salt and pepper to taste. Pour the eggs over the pasta and stir to combine well. Set aside.

In a 12-inch nonstick frying pan, melt the remaining 2 tablespoons butter over medium heat. Add the vermicelli mixture, smoothing it out with a wooden spoon so it is an even thickness. Cook until the mixture holds together as one piece when the pan is shaken, about 5 minutes. It should look golden brown. Place a plate larger than the diameter of the pan over the top of the vermicelli and flip it out onto the plate. Return the vermicelli to the pan to finish cooking the underside, about 5 more minutes.

Cut into wedges and serve hot or cold.

Cena di Pasta in Una Pentola

Pasta Dinner in One Pot

Now we are getting somewhere with the no-time-to-cook dilemma. This unconventional way to cook pasta would startle most Italians, but honestly, it is a great way to get dinner on the table in short order. One pot and all the ingredients, including the raw pasta, get cooked together—and there is no end to the variety of ingredients one can use. **Serves 4**

Heat the oil in a large saucepan over medium heat. Cook the onion until it softens. Stir in the garlic and cook for a couple of minutes. Add the tomato paste and anchovy paste, if using, and coat the onion and garlic well. Lower the heat to medium-low and cook for a couple of minutes. Add the tomatoes, wine, penne, and salt to taste. Push the penne under the liquid to make sure all is covered with the sauce. Bring the ingredients to a boil, cover, and cook over medium heat until the penne is al dente. Uncover and add the Swiss chard; mix it in and cook just until the leaves wilt.

Serve in bowls and pass the grated cheese for garnishing.

1 tablespoon extra-virgin olive oil

1 medium onion, diced

2 cloves garlic, minced

2 tablespoons tomato paste

1 teaspoon anchovy paste (optional)

1 (28-ounce) can chopped plum tomatoes, undrained

¼ cup dry red wine

8 ounces penne

Salt to taste

1 cup shredded Swiss chard leaves

Grated Parmigiano-Reggiano cheese, for garnishing

Scialatielli all'Amalfitana

Amalfi-Style Pasta with Seafood

1 extra large egg

⅓ to ½ cup whole milk

4 tablespoons extra-virgin olive oil

Salt and freshly ground black pepper to taste

2½ cups unbleached all-purpose flour

2 tablespoons grated Pecorino Romano cheese

2 tablespoons minced fresh basil

1 clove garlic, finely minced

¼ cup minced fresh flat-leaf parsley

3 pounds clams or mussels, scrubbed

1 cup dry white wine

2 cups halved fresh cherry tomatoes

Scialatielli, from the region of Campania, are short, stubby fresh pasta that are very popular in Amalfi and Naples. The dough is unusual in that it contains not just flour and eggs but milk, grated Pecorino Romano cheese, and flecks of parsley or basil. In Amalfi, it is common to have it with a seafood sauce, while in Sorrento, it is served with tomatoes and fresh mozzarella. The word *scialatielli* is said to come from the Neapolitan dialect word *scialare*, meaning "to enjoy," and *tiella*, meaning "pan." **Serves 4**

Combine the egg, ⅓ cup milk, 2 tablespoons of the olive oil, and ½ teaspoon salt in a bowl or a food processor and mix or pulse until smooth. Add the flour and cheese and mix or pulse until the mixture is grainy looking. Add the basil and mix or pulse just until the dough begins to leave the sides of bowl. If the dough seems too dry, add a little of the remaining milk until you can pinch a piece of dough between your fingers and it does not crumble.

Transfer the dough to a floured surface and knead for 3 to 4 minutes into a smooth ball. Place a bowl over the dough to cover it and allow it to rest for 30 minutes to relax the gluten and make it easier to roll.

Meanwhile, heat the remaining 2 tablespoons olive oil in a 12-inch or larger sauté pan; add the garlic, parsley, and clams and toss for a couple of minutes. Add the wine, cover the pan, and cook until the clams open; discard any that do not open.

When cool enough to handle, remove the clams from their shells (save a few in their shells for garnish), catching any juices over a bowl. Set the clams aside. Strain the liquid and set aside.

Return the clams to the sauté pan along with the cherry tomatoes. Add the strained liquid. Taste and add salt and pepper as needed. Cover and keep warm while the pasta cooks.

continued on page 120

continued from page 118

Divide the dough into quarters and keep the rest covered while working the first piece. Flatten the dough into a 4-inch-wide piece. Place it through the rollers of a hand-crank pasta machine set to the thickest setting (#1). Set the rollers to the next thickest setting down (#2) and run the dough through again. Use a small knife to cut ⅛-inch-wide strips and place the strips on a clean towel. Repeat with the remaining dough.

Bring a large pot of water to a boil over high heat. Add the scialatielli and 1 tablespoon salt and cook for 2 to 3 minutes. The pasta should be cooked through but not mushy. Drain, reserving ¼ cup of the cooking water. Add the scialatielli and cooking water to the pan with the clam mixture and toss well. Serve hot.

Note: Traditionally, cheese is not served with seafood dishes, but given that there is cheese in the dough, sprinkling some on top for serving would not be frowned upon.

Ziti con Pomodori e Melanzane alla Siciliana

Ziti with Tomatoes and Eggplant, Sicilian Style

The Planeta winery near Vittoria, Sicily, was my destination for a tour of what many consider to be the most visionary winery in Sicily. After the tour, lunch was offered, starting with ziti in a fresh cherry tomato sauce with bits of eggplant. The sauce was light and beautifully balanced, and the technique of cooking the onion in water first to soften the taste was sheer genius! **Serves 4 to 6**

In a medium saucepan, heat 4 tablespoons of the olive oil over medium heat; add the eggplant cubes and cook until they are golden brown. Transfer to a bowl and set aside.

Pour the water into the saucepan. Add the onion and cook until it softens. Add the tomatoes and remaining 2 tablespoons olive oil, season with salt, and cook until the tomatoes collapse and are very soft.

Transfer the mixture to a food processor and puree all the ingredients until smooth. Return to the saucepan and stir in the eggplant. Reheat until hot. Keep the sauce warm while the pasta cooks.

Bring a large pot of water to a boil over high heat. Add the ziti and 1 tablespoon salt and cook until al dente. Drain, reserving 2 tablespoons of the cooking water. Add the ziti and cooking water to the sauce and toss well to coat the pasta. Transfer the ziti to a heated serving bowl or platter. Sprinkle with grated cheese and the toasted breadcrumbs. Serve immediately.

6 tablespoons extra-virgin olive oil

1 medium eggplant, cut into ½-inch cubes

½ cup water

1 large onion, diced

2 pounds ripe cherry tomatoes, cut in half

Salt to taste

1 pound short cut pasta such as ziti or penne

Grated Parmigiano-Reggiano cheese

½ cup toasted breadcrumbs

Spaetzle allo Speck e Cipolla Rossa

Spaetzle with Speck and Red Onion

Spaetzle is a rustic pasta most commonly associated with Germany, but it is also part of the cuisine of the northern South Tyrol region of Italy. It is made with eggs, flour, salt, and milk or water. The dough is shaped by hand or with a spoon by scraping it off a wooden cutting board directly into boiling water. The shape resembles small birds; the word *spaetzle* means "little sparrow." Spaetzle is served as a first course, here flavored with a sauce made from onion and speck, a local air-cured, smoked, and spice-seasoned ham. The fastest way to make spaetzle is with a spaetzle maker, available in kitchen stores and online. **Serves 4 to 6**

In a large bowl, whisk together the eggs, water, 1 teaspoon salt, and the nutmeg; stir in enough flour to make a loose batter and refrigerate for at least 1 hour.

To make the sauce, melt the butter over medium heat and cook the onion until it begins to soften. Add the speck and continue cooking until the speck begins to brown. Keep warm while you cook the spaetzle.

To cook the spaetzle, bring a large pot of water to a boil over high heat. Add 1 tablespoon salt. Place a spaetzle maker over the top of the pot and fill the spaetzle cup with some of the dough. Move the cup back and forth across the pot; as you do this, the dough will fall into the water, cook in a minute or two, and bob to the top. Continue making spaetzle until all the dough is used. Drain them well, using a slotted spoon or long-handled sieve. Toss them in the sauce and serve.

SPAETZLE DOUGH

4 large eggs

⅓ cup water or milk

Salt

¼ teaspoon grated nutmeg

2 cups unbleached all-purpose flour

SAUCE

4 tablespoons (½ stick) unsalted butter

1 medium red onion, large dice

4 ounces speck, diced

Spaghetti alla Chitarra con Ragù di Agnello

Spaghetti with Lamb Ragù

DOUGH

3 cups durum semolina flour

⅛ teaspoon salt

4 large eggs, beaten with a fork

LAMB RAGÙ

½ cup extra-virgin olive oil

1 pound ground lamb

3 whole bay leaves

3 cloves garlic, minced

Kosher salt and freshly ground black pepper to taste

½ cup dry white wine

1½ cups chicken broth, homemade (page 38) or store-bought

1 (15-ounce) can whole peeled plum tomatoes, undrained

2 large red bell peppers, cored, seeded, and sliced ¼ inch thick

1 large yellow bell pepper, cored, seeded, and sliced ¼ inch thick

1 pound spaghetti

Grated Pecorino Romano cheese to garnish

The *chitarra* is a rectangular wooden instrument with thin, taut wire strings pulled lengthwise across it and used to make spaghetti alla chitarra. I inherited my Sicilian grandmother's handmade chitarra, and it brings back a flood of memories of her every time I use it. The name comes from the musical sounds that the form makes (like a guitar) when a sheet of pasta dough is laid over it and rolled over with a rolling pin. This cuts the pasta into thin spaghetti. The recipe can also be made using store-bought spaghetti, but will not be as light and delicate—note that it will also take longer to cook. **Serves 4 to 6**

On a wooden board, combine the flour and salt. Make a hole in the center of the flour with your hands to form a well and add the eggs. Whisk the eggs with a fork to break them up. Use your hands to bring the flour into the well, mixing with the eggs until a dough forms. It will look rough at first. Add just enough flour to make a soft dough; knead it with your hands until it is smooth and not sticky. This step can also be done in a food processor by whirling the eggs first, then adding the flour and salt and pulsing until the dough begins to form around the blade. Carefully remove it and knead it into a ball of dough as described above.

Cover the dough and let it rest on a floured surface for 30 minutes. This will relax the gluten in the dough and make it easier to roll out.

Cut the dough into quarters. Work with one piece at a time, keeping the rest covered. Flatten each quarter with a rolling pin. Thin each piece in a hand-crank pasta machine, using the settings on your machine; the dough should be just a bit thicker than a sheet of copy paper. Or use a rolling pin to thin the dough if you do not have a pasta machine. Place each piece one at a time, laying it flat lengthwise on top of the chitarra, and roll over it with a rolling pin to create spaghetti. As you make it, place the spaghetti on lightly flour-dusted towels.

To make the ragù, heat the oil over medium-high heat in a 6-quart saucepan until it begins to shimmer, then lower the heat to medium. Add the lamb and cook until browned, 6 to 8 minutes. Add the bay leaves and garlic and season with salt and pepper; cook until the garlic softens. Stir in the wine and cook for 2 to 3 minutes. Add the broth and tomatoes (breaking them up with a spoon), season with salt and pepper, and bring everything to a boil. Reduce the heat to medium-low and cook, stirring occasionally, until the sauce is slightly thickened, 35 to 40 minutes. Stir in the peppers and cook until they are tender but not falling apart. Discard the bay leaves.

When the ragù is ready, bring a large pot of water to a boil over high heat. Add 1 tablespoon salt and the spaghetti. Cook the spaghetti for not more than 4 minutes. Drain, reserving ¼ cup of the cooking water. Transfer the spaghetti to pan with the ragù and add the reserved water. Add salt and pepper and, using tongs, toss the spaghetti in the sauce. Serve hot.

Rigatoni al Pesto di Pomodoro

Rigatoni with Dried Tomato Pesto

1 cup Dried Tomatoes
in Olive Oil
(page 132)

1 clove garlic, minced

1 pound rigatoni

1 tablespoon salt

3 tablespoons
minced fresh basil

⅓ cup grated
Parmigiano-
Reggiano cheese

At the Regaleali wine estate in Vallelunge, Sicily, I learned the art of making *estrattu*, a very dense and concentrated tomato paste that no Sicilian cook of any merit would be without. Making the handmade paste is a hot, backbreaking summer job. First, you must start with fresh plum tomatoes with skins and seeds removed. The tomatoes are cooked into a sauce with the addition of onions, local herbs like oregano and basil, and salt and spices. There is no standard recipe, since the method varies from place to place, and every cook will tell you that his or her method is the tried and true one. The sauce is spread on long boards or placed in shallow tin pans, topped with screens to keep bugs away, and placed in the searing Sicilian sun, where it is frequently moved back and forth by hand with small implements resembling paddles to help it dry and remove the excess liquid.

To dehydrate and concentrate enough tomatoes to make estrattu to fill one jar takes about 10 pounds of tomato sauce! Not surprisingly, the flavor is very intense. Think of it as tomato pesto with attitude.

This process takes days, though there is a way to make something similar by using a dehydrator. It is not exactly the same taste as estrattu, but it makes a really good substitute. To do it, use ripe plum tomatoes that have been washed, dried, and cored. Cut them in half lengthwise and place them, cut side down, on the dehydrator and dry them according to the manufacturer's instructions. Remove the tomatoes when they are the consistency of dried apricots. This could take a day or two depending on the dehydrator and the size of the tomatoes. No dehydrator? Place the cut tomatoes on racks placed over baking sheets and dry them in a 250°F oven. This could take even longer.

Place the dried tomatoes in a food processor and puree them into a paste. Through the feed tube add just enough extra-virgin olive oil to smooth out the tomatoes, but don't add too much. The mixture should remain thick like the consistency of peanut butter.

Transfer the paste to a bowl and add salt and a grinding of black pepper to taste. Fill jars with the paste, cap, and refrigerate or freeze. To use, add it to your recipes in small amounts to really beef up the cooking flavors. A little goes a long way in soups, stews, pasta, and sauces. **Serves 6**

Drain the tomatoes, reserving 2 tablespoons of their oil. Put the tomatoes and the reserved oil in a food processor or blender and pulse until coarsely ground. (Alternatively, you can chop the tomatoes very fine by hand.) Transfer the tomatoes to a saucepan, stir in the garlic, and cook over medium heat for 2 to 3 minutes. Remove from the heat and set aside.

Bring a large pot of water to a boil over high heat. Add the rigatoni and salt and cook the rigatoni until al dente. Drain, reserving ⅓ cup of the cooking water. Add the rigatoni and reserved water to the saucepan with the tomato pesto and toss over low heat to coat the rigatoni. Add the basil and cheese and toss again. Serve immediately.

Note: A generous grinding of fresh black pepper adds to the spiciness of this dish.

Tortelli di Zucca di Raffaella

Raffaella's Squash-Filled Tortelli

FILLING

1 pound butternut
  squash

½ cup water

¼ cup crushed
  amaretti cookies

½ teaspoon grated
  nutmeg

½ teaspoon salt

2 tablespoons grated
  Parmigiano-
  Reggiano cheese

TORTELLI DOUGH

4 large eggs

3 cups unbleached
  all-purpose flour

¼ teaspoon salt

SAUCE

12 tablespoons
  (1½ sticks)
  unsalted butter

½ cup grated
  Parmigiano-
  Reggiano cheese

Raffaella Neviani is a dear friend who lives in Cavriago, in the region of Emilia-Romagna, where fresh filled pasta is legendary—like her recipe for squash-filled tortelli. Crushed amaretti cookies (small almond cookies) added to the filling provide just a hint of sweetness; you can find them in some grocery stores and online. The recipe makes a lot, so you can freeze some for later use. **Makes about 100**

Preheat the oven to 350°F.

To make the filling, cut the squash in half, scoop out the seeds, and discard them. Place the squash, cut side down, in a small baking dish, add the water, and cover the dish with aluminum foil. Bake for 35 minutes, or until the squash is easily pierced with a fork. Let cool. With a spoon, scoop the flesh into a colander and let it drain for 45 minutes to remove excess liquid.

Transfer the squash to a bowl and mash it well. Add the amaretti cookies, nutmeg, salt, and Parmigiano-Reggiano cheese and mix well. Cover and refrigerate until ready to use.

To make the pasta, combine the eggs, flour, and salt following the directions for Homemade Pasta (page 86). Cover the dough and let it rest for 30 minutes.

Knead the dough for about 5 minutes; cut it into 4 pieces. Work with one piece at a time, keeping the rest covered. Roll each piece out to the next-to-the-last thinnest setting on a hand-crank pasta machine, or roll it out with a rolling pin on a floured surface to a thickness of ⅛ inch.

Cut 4 x 2½-inch rectangles from the sheets of dough. Place a generous teaspoon of the squash filling in the center of each rectangle; fold the rectangles in half lengthwise, making sure to pinch and seal the edges well. Place the tortelli on a floured towel. Gather the dough scraps into a ball and reroll them to make more tortelli. (To freeze, arrange uncooked tortelli in a single layer on floured baking sheets, cover with aluminum foil, and freeze until hard. Transfer them to plastic bags and freeze for up to 3 months. Do not defrost them before boiling; they will take a little longer to cook.)

When you are just about ready to cook the pasta, make the sauce. Melt the butter in a medium sauté pan over medium heat, stir in the cheese, and mix well. Keep warm while the tortelli are cooking.

Bring a large pot of salted water to a boil over high heat. Cook two dozen tortelli at a time, for 1 to 2 minutes, or until they rise to the surface. Drain them carefully, using a slotted spoon or colander. Place them in a shallow serving bowl and toss them with the melted butter and cheese sauce.

Note: Tortelli are also good with sage butter sauce. Add a small handful of fresh sage leaves to the melted butter and press on them in the butter with a wooden spoon to release their flavor.

Lasagne Bianche con Pinoli

White Lasagne with Pine Nuts

FILLING

½ cup pine nuts

6 (10-ounce) packages fresh or frozen (thawed) spinach

5 large eggs

6 cups whole-milk ricotta cheese, homemade (page 332) or store-bought

3 cups diced mozzarella cheese (about 12 ounces)

4 tablespoons (½ stick) unsalted butter, at room temperature

8 ounces prosciutto di Parma, diced

6 tablespoons minced fresh flat-leaf parsley

2 teaspoons grated nutmeg

2 teaspoons salt

2 teaspoons ground white pepper

Lasagne doesn't always sport a red sauce. There are many regional variations, including this lasagne made with a simple white sauce. This recipe makes enough to feed a crowd and can be made a couple of days ahead. It is a delicious departure from its tomato-based cousin. **Serves 16**

Preheat the oven to 350°F.

To make the filling, spread the pine nuts on a rimmed baking sheet and toast them until lightly browned, about 5 minutes. Set aside to cool, but leave the oven on.

If using fresh spinach, discard the stems and wash the leaves well. Place them in a large dry pot, cover, and cook over medium heat until the leaves wilt, about 4 minutes. Drain the leaves in a colander. Squeeze out the excess moisture and finely chop them. If using frozen spinach, squeeze out the excess moisture and finely chop it.

In a large bowl, combine the spinach and pine nuts. Beat in the eggs. Then add all the remaining filling ingredients, mixing well. Cover and refrigerate until ready to use.

To make the sauce, in a large saucepan, heat the milk over medium heat to just under a boil. Remove from the heat and set aside. In another large heavy saucepan, melt the butter over medium-high heat. Add the flour and whisk it into the butter until a paste-like mixture forms. Whisk in the warm milk, salt, and nutmeg and whisk until the mixture comes to a boil. Lower the heat to medium and continue whisking until the sauce thickens, 5 to 10 minutes. Remove the sauce from the heat and stir in the sage. Cover and keep warm while you get the pasta ready.

Cut the pasta dough into 4 pieces. Work with one piece at a time, keeping the rest covered with a damp towel. Roll out the dough through a hand-crank pasta machine to the second-finest setting, or roll it out by hand on a floured surface to a thickness of ⅛ inch. Cut the sheets of dough into 3 x 6-inch strips and lay them flat on clean towels.

Bring a large pot of water to a boil over high heat. Add the salt and lasagne strips, a few at a time, and cook for 2 to 3 minutes. Drain them and lay them flat on clean cotton towels.

To assemble, the lasagne, spread ½ cup of the white sauce over the bottom of a 9 x 13-inch casserole dish. Cover the sauce with a layer of lasagne strips, then spread about 2 cups of the spinach filling over the lasagne. Spoon a thin layer of sauce over the filling. Repeat two more times, ending with a top layer of lasagne strips. Spread 1 cup of white sauce over the lasagne, sprinkle with ½ cup of the Parmigiano-Reggiano cheese, and cover the casserole tightly with aluminum foil.

Repeat with the remaining ingredients to fill another pan. Bake for 30 minutes. Let stand for 10 minutes before cutting and serving.

WHITE SAUCE

8 cups whole milk

16 tablespoons (2 sticks) unsalted butter

1 cup unbleached all-purpose flour, sifted

2 teaspoons salt

1 teaspoon grated nutmeg

3 tablespoons finely minced fresh sage

Assembly

1 recipe Homemade Pasta (page 86)

1 tablespoon salt

1 cup grated Parmigiano-Reggiano cheese

Pomodori Secchi Sott'Olio

Dried Tomatoes in Olive Oil

14 meaty plum tomatoes

3 cups red wine vinegar

8 fresh basil leaves, washed and dried

3 tablespoons capers in brine, drained

2 tablespoons whole black peppercorns

2 teaspoons fine sea salt

3 cups extra-virgin olive oil

To make dried tomatoes, you will need fresh plum tomatoes free of any blemishes or bruises and a dehydrator, plus several small sterilized jars. Once you make your own, there is no going back to store-bought varieties that are often too salty and costly. Double or triple the recipe below to make more.   **Makes about 3 cups**

Wash and dry the tomatoes. Core them and cut them in half lengthwise. Place the tomatoes, cut side down, on the racks of a dehydrator and dry according to the manufacturer's instructions until they are shriveled but still bendable, like a dried apricot.

Heat the vinegar in a large noncorrosive saucepan and bring to a boil over medium-high heat. Add the dried tomatoes and boil them for 2 minutes. Use a slotted spoon to remove them and place them in a colander.

Layer the tomatoes into the jars and divide the basil, capers, peppercorns, and salt evenly among the jars. Slowly add the olive oil to each jar and fill to the top.

With a wooden spoon, press down on the tomatoes, submerging them under the oil. **This is a critical step!** No tomatoes should be above the olive oil. This prevents air from getting into the jars. Add more olive oil if necessary.

Cap the jars and allow them to sit on your counter for a day. Then open the jars to see if more oil is needed. Top off with oil if necessary. Cap the jars again and store them in the refrigerator. They will keep for several weeks. Bring to room temperature when needed. Return what you do not use to the refrigerator.

Pasta Sauces

Sauces make many foods appealing, adding flavor and moistness. The Romans were geniuses at this, and one of their most important sauces was garum, an anchovy-based sauce that was used on many foods and frequently on not-so-fresh food. In fact, garum sauce was so popular that it was factory-produced in many areas of the Roman Empire.

Sauces are flavor enhancers that unify a dish and make it complete, and pasta epitomizes the need for sauces because without them, pasta would be dead on a plate. There are hundreds of sauces, some as uncomplicated as the classic *aglio e olio* (garlic and oil) and some as complex and intense as a Bolognese *ragù* (meat sauce). Differences in sauces for pasta vary from town to town and region to region, with the raw products cultivated from north to south providing the ingredients for them. But the one sauce that the world defines as pasta's permanent partner is simply tomato sauce. Its place in the history of Italian gastronomy took hold in the nineteenth century in Naples, where the process of drying pasta also began. Combining the two was the perfect marriage. Then, when the waves of southern Italians came to America's shores in the 1890s and early 1900s, they brought with them the art of creating what would become recognized here as their national dish, *maccheroni al pummarola* (macaroni with tomato sauce).

But long before the tomato was considered safe to eat and embraced by southern Italians, pasta was often combined with sugar, breadcrumbs, cheese, olive oil, or nut-based sauces. Consider a recipe from the manuscript *Libro di Cucina del Secolo XIV*, translated by Ludovico Frati, in which a lasagne layered with a pesto of almonds was sprinkled with spices and sugar before serving. Or the old culinary tradition still practiced today in Salemi, Sicily, for the feast of Saint Joseph on March 19 (page 340), in which spaghetti is tossed with olive oil and sprinkled with toasted breadcrumbs and sugar. Some say that the breadcrumb topping is symbolic of wood shavings because Joseph was a carpenter.

The point is that there are no standard sauces in Italian cuisine; they are as individual as the circumstances and people who create them. This was also true for my immigrant ancestors. My mother and grandmothers made tomato sauce with cuts of meats like chuck roast, spareribs, and sausages that needed simmering for a long time to tenderize them and add flavor to the sauce. This type of tomato sauce is a ragù and was served with pasta as a first course, while the meats were removed and reserved as a second course. When a tomato sauce is made

without meat, it is simply called a *salsa di pomodoro*. (Some regions use the terms *salsa* and *sugo* interchangeably, adding more confusion. A sugo is really just the pan juices that have accumulated from cooked meats, such as roast lamb, that are spooned over portions when serving.)

In dairy-rich Lombardia and Emilia-Romagna, wonderful butter and cheese sauces as well as long-simmered ragù are common. In Liguria, the classic sauce is pesto, made from delicate basil leaves, nuts, cheese, and extra-virgin olive oil. The rich volcanic ash offered up by Mount Vesuvius in Naples, in the region of Campania, yields juicy plum tomatoes, sturdy eggplant, sweet and hot peppers, and other vegetables, all used to make various types of sauces.

Nontraditional sauces began to take their place in Italy as *alta cucina* (gourmet cooking), developed to meet the expectations of the sophisticated tourist. Wine sauces flavored with herbs and spices and citrus-based sauces using blood orange and lemon are combined with vegetables such as broccoli and arugula to bring something new to the table. Even legumes like cannellini beans and chickpeas are pureed and blended into sauces.

Though there are no rules for making sauces, there are guidelines for how to dress different types of pasta with them. For example, if the pasta is a thin, long type like vermicelli or spaghetti, the best option is a light, smooth sauce like garlic and oil, or a meatless tomato sauce that evenly coats the strands of pasta. On the other hand, a short, chunky pasta like fusilli or rigatoni calls for a heavier sauce like a ragù or a vegetable or nut sauce, so that bits and chunks of the ingredients can cling to and invade all the little crevices of the pasta (which is why macaroni shapes were created in the first place).

Some sauces can be prepared ahead and frozen successfully. This is especially true for tomato sauces—both meat and meatless—as well as vegetable sauces. Freezing pesto is not recommended. Some people make and freeze it without the cheese, then add the cheese after the pesto defrosts, but I find that the texture and taste are a bit off, with the basil becoming too sharp and watery. Instead of freezing pesto, try storing it in jars in your refrigerator (see page 145). Pesto sauce will keep refrigerated for up to a month if topped with a thin layer of olive oil.

This chapter focuses on sauces for all types of pasta. When Italians dress pasta, the sauce amount is in balance with the amount of pasta. The sauce does not weigh down or drown it but clings to it and lightly coats it. No sauce should remain as a puddle in the bottom of the bowl. In other words, the pasta should be the star.

Real Neapolitan Tomato Sauce

Striano may not be a destination for many, but for me it was a trip of a lifetime to see how San Marzano DOP plum tomatoes are processed for sale. Striano is in the province of Naples, close to where my maternal grandmother was born. She would always talk about Italian tomatoes being so much more flavorful than our own. I wanted to visit the Strianese Conserve to get a better understanding of why these tomatoes are so outstanding and deserving of the DOP (Denominazione di Origine Protetta, or denomination of protected origin) label. Only the tomatoes grown in the Sarnese-Nocerino area are considered the best because they are grown within the shadow of Mount Vesuvius in extraordinary fertile soil that is perfect for growing. The farmers who grow them are lucky enough to have nearby water for irrigation. This makes for a win-win situation all around. The European Union recognized the importance of these tomatoes from the provinces of Naples, Salerno, and Avellino and bestowed the coveted DOP standard. But it wasn't until the manufacturing and processing of these tomatoes became an industry in the mid-1960s that awareness of the San Marzano tomato became well known.

Today, touring the huge, modern, gleaming tomato-processing plant in Striano is a tribute to Italian ingenuity and mechanized machinery that is all about precision. A sea of the red fruit running along conveyor belts is scrutinized along the way by an army of red-uniformed women, who inspect and remove any tomatoes that are not up to standards, and they do this all day, every day in tomato season. A complicated mechanization process takes place that washes, cooks, and cans the tomatoes.

It is no surprise that the tomato put southern Italian food on the American map and created a love affair for all things tomato-based, including pizza and spaghetti. But we have compromised what those foods are really like at their Italian source. Tomato sauce

is a case in point. There is a dizzying number of ways to make tomato sauce. Some use onions and garlic, some add tomato paste, some add carrots and celery, and some add meat, in which case it is no longer a simple *salsa di pomodoro* but a *ragù*.

Real Neapolitan tomato sauce was and still is made with nothing more that plum tomatoes peeled and crushed between your hands, whole cloves of garlic warmed in a couple tablespoons of lard or olive oil, and a fistful of basil leaves, all cooked for about ten minutes. Salt was added for taste, and that is tomato sauce in its purest form.

When tomatoes are in season in my home garden, I make tomato sauce and passata (page 215). Some of the harvest is bagged and frozen for winter use. When defrosted, the tomatoes become the basis for ragù.

Note: Strianese DOP tomatoes from the Agro Sarnese-Nocerino are available in some grocery stores, Italian specialty stores, and online.

Salsa Fresca di Pomodoro Napoletano

Fresh Neapolitan Tomato Sauce

12 to 14 in-season, large, meaty, ripe plum tomatoes

2 tablespoons extra-virgin olive oil

6 or 7 cloves garlic, peeled

6 or 7 fresh basil leaves, torn into pieces

Salt to taste

Makes about 4 cups

Bring a large pot of water to a boil over medium-high heat and add the tomatoes. Boil for just a couple of minutes, until the skin begins to blister. Drain, cool, peel, and core the tomatoes; transfer to a bowl and set aside.

Heat the olive oil in a soup pot over medium heat. Add the garlic cloves and press on them with a wooden spoon. Let the garlic cook until it softens, begins to turn golden, and give off its aroma.

Take the tomatoes by the handful and crush them between your fingers right into the garlic in the pot. Cook, stirring occasionally, for 10 minutes. Add the basil leaves and cook for 3 to 4 more minutes. Add salt to taste. Done.

At this point you have a choice: Leave the tomato sauce chunky and use as is or puree it into a smooth sauce. To do this, transfer the sauce to a fine-mesh sieve placed over a large bowl. Use a spoon to stir and press the sauce through, leaving the seeds behind.

The tomato sauce can be kept in the refrigerator for up to 1 week or in the freezer for up to 3 months.

Note: Another technique for removing tomato skins is to microwave instead of boiling them. Pierce the skin in a couple of places with a small knife. Microwave on high power for 30 seconds to shrink the skin; cool and peel.

Salsa Fresca di Pomodoro e Basilico Con Vino

Fresh Tomato-Basil Sauce with Wine

Tomato sauce put Naples on a course to worldwide culinary fame. There are many versions like this one, made with the addition of red wine.   **Makes 9 to 10 cups**

If using fresh tomatoes, core them, cut them into chunks, and puree them in a food processor until smooth. Strain the fresh or canned tomatoes through a fine-mesh sieve to remove the seeds. Set aside.

In a deep, heavy pot, heat the olive oil over medium heat. Add the onion and cook until it softens. Add the garlic and cook until soft. Add the tomatoes and stir to blend. Add the wine and basil, season with salt and pepper, and stir well. Bring to a boil, lower the heat, and simmer for 25 minutes. The sauce is ready to use, or it can be refrigerated for up to 1 week or frozen for up to 3 months.

5 pounds fresh, ripe plum tomatoes *or* 3 (28-ounce) cans crushed plum tomatoes

½ cup extra-virgin olive oil

½ cup diced onion

3 cloves garlic, minced

1½ cups dry red wine

4 or 5 large fresh sprigs basil

Coarse salt and freshly ground black pepper to taste

Ragù Napoletano
Neapolitan Meat Sauce

3 tablespoons extra-virgin olive oil

1 clove garlic, chopped

1 onion, coarsely chopped

1 rib celery, coarsely chopped

1 large carrot, coarsely chopped

1 pound beef round or chuck steak, cut into ½-inch cubes

½ cup dry red wine

2 (28-ounce) cans plum tomatoes, undrained

1 bay leaf

1 tablespoon coarse salt

A ragù starts life with a *soffritto*, a sauté of aromatic vegetables like onions, carrots, and celery, to which other ingredients are added. It is a thick sauce that is perfect over chunky types of pasta as well as over slices of polenta. Years ago, lard was the cooking fat of choice, but today olive oil has replaced it.   **Makes about 8 cups**

In a large saucepan, heat 2 tablespoons of the oil over medium heat. Add the garlic and cook until it softens. Add the onion, celery, and carrot and cook for 5 to 7 minutes, or until soft. Using a slotted spoon, remove the vegetables from the pan; set aside.

Add the remaining 1 tablespoon olive oil to the saucepan. Pat the meat cubes dry with paper towels and add them to the pan. Brown the pieces well.

Add the wine, lower the heat, and simmer for 5 minutes. Add the tomatoes, bay leaf, and salt. Return the vegetables to the pan. Simmer the ragù, covered, over low heat until the meat is tender, about 45 minutes. Discard the bay leaf. Transfer the sauce to a food processor and process until smooth.

Use immediately or store in the refrigerator for up to 3 days or in the freezer for up to 3 months.

Spaghetti con Salsa di Aglio e Olio

Spaghetti with Garlic and Oil Sauce

Aglio e olio (garlic and oil) is one of those bedrock sauces that could be made in minutes and often was the answer to what's for supper. Just two staples of the Mediterranean diet, garlic and olive oil, blend together to provide simple flavor for a plate of pasta. Sometimes toasted breadcrumbs are sprinkled over the top.   **Serves 4**

8 ounces spaghetti

Salt

½ cup extra-virgin olive oil

2 medium cloves garlic, finely minced

1 teaspoon coarsely ground black pepper

Bring a large pot of water to a boil over high heat. Add the spaghetti and 1 tablespoon salt and cook until the spaghetti is al dente. Drain, reserving ⅓ cup of the pasta water.

   In a medium sauté pan, warm the oil over medium heat. Add the garlic and cook until it softens. Add 1 teaspoon salt and the pepper. Add the reserved pasta cooking water and mix well. Cook over low heat for 1 minute. Add the spaghetti to the sauce and toss to coat. Serve immediately.

Pesto Genovese

Pesto Sauce

2 cloves garlic, peeled

½ teaspoon coarse sea salt

1 tablespoon pine nuts or walnuts

2 cups packed fresh, young basil leaves (no stems)

6 tablespoons mild extra-virgin olive oil

6 tablespoons grated Parmigiano-Reggiano or Grana Padano cheese

2 tablespoons grated Pecorino Romano cheese

Mention of the first time that pesto was made is up for grabs all over the culinary map. Some claim that the crusaders brought basil seeds from the Holy Land to Genoa. Others claim that it is an offspring of the herbal sauces that the ancient Romans made. But what is certain is that pesto sauce is to the region of Liguria what tomato sauce is to the region of Campania.

To make pesto Genovese according to rules laid out by the Consorzio del Pesto Genovese, (the organization that oversees the traditional way to make it), the basil must be cultivated in and around Genoa, and only tender, young, small leaves can be used. Other ingredients include Ligurian extra-virgin olive oil and fresh, mild-tasting garlic. The grated cheese must be either Parmigiano-Reggiano or Grana Padano in combination with Pecorino Romano cheese from Lazio, Tuscany, Sicily, or Sardinia. The pine nuts must be from Liguria, but walnuts are sometimes substituted. The salt must be coarse sea salt. Only then are you good to go and can make authentic pesto as the Genovese do so well.

To make pesto in the traditional way, a mortar—preferably made with Carrara marble from Tuscany—and a wooden pestle are used. The basil leaves are washed in cold water and dried. For every 30 leaves of basil, one clove of mild garlic should be used. The olive oil should also be mild, not spicy. The garlic is added first to the mortar and gently mashed down with a few grains of the salt, using the pestle in a circular motion and against the sides of the mortar; then the nuts are added and mashed down so they are amalgamated into the sauce. Next the leaves are added, a handful at a time, along with a few more grains of salt, and gently mashed down in a rotating manner. This is important because the essential oils in basil leaves need to be released as gently as possible.

When the pesto is a brilliant green liquid, the cheeses are mixed in. Then the olive oil is dribbled in, a little at a time, and mixed with the ingredients until a fluid, not paste-like sauce is obtained.

Pesto sauce is used on trenette or trofie, two classic Ligurian pastas. It is the last thing added to minestrone soup and is the sauce favored by Ligurians for potato gnocchi. Of course, there are many other uses for it—it is perfect mixed into risotto, adds flavor to cooked vegetables, and finds its way as a topping for pizza and focaccia.

Given the constraints of time today, pesto can be made using a food processor, but the taste and texture will not be the same as that made by hand, and it will oxidize more quickly due to the bruising of the leaves by the steel blade and the residual heat from the processor. There are two things that basil dislikes: water on its leaves, which turns them black, and being refrigerated. Basil—like the translation of its name, meaning "kingly"—needs to be treated with care and respect. **Makes enough to dress 1½ pounds pasta**

Using a mortar and pestle, mince the garlic with the salt using a rotating motion. Add the nuts and a few additional grains of salt and continue to mash down the ingredients. Add a small handful of basil at a time and continue rotating and mashing the mixture until it is has broken down and is a vibrant green color. Begin adding the olive oil a few drops at a time until a fluid, sauce-like consistency is obtained. Stir in the cheeses. Use immediately or transfer to an airtight jar and put a thin film of olive oil over the top of the pesto sauce to prevent it from turning brown. Refrigerate for up to 1 week.

If using a food processor, pulse the garlic, salt, and nuts a few times to break them down. Add the basil leaves and gently pulse until they are reduced to a mash, then drizzle in the olive oil through the feed tube while the motor is running. Stir in the cheeses.

Salsa di Pomodoro Giallo

Yellow Tomato Sauce

Did you know that tomatoes were originally yellow? *Pomodoro* means "apple of gold," referring to tomatoes. It seemed appropriate to include a yellow tomato sauce made from the Sun Gold cherry tomato variety grown in my garden. Sweet as sugar and plump with a mild flavor, this sauce comes together in minutes and is best made in season. Use the sauce for pasta, fish, or risotto.   **Makes about 2½ cups**

Heat the olive oil in a medium saucepan over medium heat. Add the garlic and cook until soft. Stir in the red pepper flakes, if using. Add the yellow tomatoes and sugar, season with salt and pepper, and stir well. Increase the heat to medium-high and cook, stirring occasionally for 5 minutes. Off the heat, stir in the basil. The sauce is best when freshly made but can be refrigerated for up to 1 week.

3 tablespoons extra-virgin olive oil

1 large clove garlic, chopped

1 teaspoon red pepper flakes (optional)

2 cups coarsely chopped yellow cherry tomatoes

1 teaspoon sugar

Salt and freshly ground black pepper to taste

2 tablespoons chopped fresh basil

Salsa Arrabbiata

Oven-Roasted "Mad" Tomato Sauce

3 pounds fresh plum tomatoes

3 tablespoons extra-virgin olive oil

3 large cloves garlic, finely chopped

1½ teaspoons red pepper flakes

1½ teaspoons salt

1½ teaspoons freshly ground black pepper

1⅓ cups minced fresh basil

This zippy tomato sauce starts out in the oven. Called *arrabbiata* ("mad"), it gets its kick from hot red pepper flakes. Add as much as you can tolerate!   **Makes 3½ cups**

Preheat the oven to 400°F.

Cut the tomatoes in half. Place them, cut side down, on a nonstick baking sheet and roast for 10 to 15 minutes, or until they are just slightly soft. Transfer the tomatoes to a food processor or blender and pulse until very smooth. Set aside.

In a medium saucepan, heat the olive oil over medium heat. Add the garlic and red pepper flakes and cook until the garlic softens. Add the pureed tomatoes and cook for 10 minutes.

Pour the mixture into a cheesecloth-lined sieve set over a bowl. Strain the tomatoes, using a wooden spoon to press on the solids to extract as much liquid as possible. Discard the solids. Add the salt, pepper, and basil; stir to blend. The sauce is best when freshly made but can be refrigerated for up to 1 week.

Salsa di Gorgonzola

Gorgonzola Cheese Sauce

This sauce made with Gorgonzola dolce is assertive, elegant, creamy, and perfect for the Rotolo di Pasta on page 102. Gorgonzola, a blue-veined cow's milk cheese, is made in the town of the same name, in the region of Lombardia in northern Italy. There is also Gorgonzola forte, a sharper and drier type of this cheese. For this recipe, Gorgonzola dolce is used in combination with mascarpone cheese, a full-fat soft cheese also from northern Italy. These two ingredients in combination create an unforgettable sauce. **Makes about 3 cups**

2 cups heavy cream

½ cup (5 ounces) mascarpone cheese, homemade (page 329) or store-bought

4 ounces Gorgonzola dolce cheese

In a medium saucepan, combine the ingredients. Bring to just below the boil, and stir with a wooden spoon over low heat until the cheeses are smooth and well combined. Use immediately or refrigerate for up to 5 days. Reheat slowly.

Salsa di Peperono Rosso

Red Bell Pepper Sauce

4 large red bell peppers

4 tablespoons (½ stick) unsalted butter

2 cloves garlic, minced

1 cup heavy cream or half-and-half

1 teaspoon grated nutmeg

1 teaspoon salt

¼ teaspoon freshly ground black pepper

¼ cup minced fresh basil or thyme

Peperoni means "peppers," not the dried sausage used on pizza. Peppers are everywhere in Italian cuisine—stuffed, fried, baked, and marinated. In the summer, when my garden is overflowing with them, I make this sauce for dressing butterfly pasta because the sauce clings to every nook and cranny. Sometimes I really indulge and add shrimp or lobster with the pasta. It is not a traditional dish, but cooks must always stay ahead of the curve.   **Makes about 3½ cups**

Preheat the broiler. Lightly grease a rimmed baking sheet.

Place the peppers on the baking sheet and broil them, turning them occasionally, until blackened all over, about 15 minutes. Transfer them to a large paper bag, close the bag tightly, and let the peppers cool for 20 minutes.

Working over a bowl to catch any juices, peel away the blackened skins. Do not be tempted to rinse the peppers, as the valuable juices will be lost. Remove the ribs and seeds, using a paper towel to wipe away the seeds. Transfer the peppers and any accumulated juices to a food processor or blender and puree them until smooth. Set aside.

In a large sauté pan, melt the butter over medium heat. Add the garlic and cook until it softens. Add the pepper puree and mix well. Lower the heat and gradually stir in the heavy cream. Add the nutmeg, salt, black pepper and cook, stirring, for 5 minutes. Remove from the heat and stir in the basil or thyme. Toss immediately with hot pasta or refrigerate for up to 3 days.

Real Italian Tomatoes

There are two classes of Italian tomatoes: those used in cooking, called *da salsa*, and those used for salads, called *insalatari*.

The da salsa type includes the famous San Marzano DOP, a meaty, sweet plum tomato grown in the area around Mount Vesuvius, where the volcanic ash is part of the reason for the tomato's great taste. The San Marzano is, by law, the only tomato that can be used on *la vera pizza Napoletana*, authentic Neapolitan pizza. Other types of plum tomatoes, like Redorta and Roma, are also good for sauce, as long as they are meaty, sweet, and low in acid.

The insalatari salad tomatoes are juicer and less pulpy than the da salsa type and have more seeds. Italians prefer their salad tomatoes a little on the greenish side. Costoluto Genovese, Pantano Romanesco, and Cuore di Bue are perfect salad tomatoes.

Sweet-as-sugar tomatoes, like Piennolo del Vesuvio, Pendolino, the ciliegini of Puglia, Basilicata, and Calabria, and the Sicilian Pachino are good as both salad and sauce tomatoes.

When the harvest is at its peak, that's when it is time to make *la salsa di pomodoro* (tomato sauce), but it's also time to think ahead and dry and preserve plum and cherry tomatoes in jars *sott'olio* (in olive oil, page 132) for the long winter ahead, or to use as part of an antipasto, or as a topping for bruschetta, or ground up as a quick pesto-type sauce for short cuts of pasta like ziti and farfalle. Dried plum tomatoes in olive oil have exquisite flavor and make a great gift to give to yourself or someone else. With a little planning, you can have the taste of fresh tomatoes all year long. Besides making batches of tomato sauce and drying some for preserving in olive oil, why not try freezing them whole for use in soups, stews, and sauces? One way to do this is to blanch whole plum tomatoes in boiling water for a minute or two, then drain and cool them. The skin should peel off easily. Pop them into freezer bags and use them in the winter to add flavor to all kinds of dishes.

For cherry tomatoes, wash and dry them, then put them into freezer bags. In the winter, cook them until they start to shrivel, then puree them to make a delicious tomato soup or add them whole to stews.

Using a dehydrator or your oven is another way to dry tomatoes. Choose tomatoes that are unblemished; core and cut them in half lengthwise. Place them, cut side down, in a single layer on lightly oiled baking sheets and roast them at 350°F for 35 to 45 minutes, or until they are shriveled looking and the consistency of dried apricots. They should be bendable, not roasted to a crisp. Let them cool, then layer the slices in sterilized pint-size jars. Cover the tomatoes with extra-virgin olive oil and make sure that no tomatoes are poking out of the oil. Add 1 tablespoon salt to each jar. Cap tightly and place the jars in a canner rack. Fill the pot with water to cover the tops of the jars. Cover and bring the water to a boil, then lower the heat to medium and gently process them for 2 hours. Allow the jars to cool in the canner; remove them and cool to room temperature. Store for future use. The uses are endless but here are nine of my favorite ways to enjoy them . . . until next summer:

1 As a topping for crostini

2 Ground up as a quick sauce for pasta

3 As a side dish to meat, fish, or poultry

4 As an ingredient for beef stew

5 As a filler for sandwiches

6 As part of an antipasto

7 As a topping for pizza or focaccia

8 Mixed into risotto

9 As a gift from your kitchen

Salsa di Ricotta

Ricotta Cheese Sauce

Have you ever thought of using ricotta cheese as a sauce for pasta? It is one of my favorites, and the key is to use fresh, thick whole-milk ricotta because the skim-milk variety is too thin and watery. Lots of grated lemon zest gives this sauce a very clean taste. This sauce makes enough to dress 1 pound of pasta, such as linguine or spaghetti.

Serves 4 to 6

In a large bowl whisk together the ricotta cheese, 1 teaspoon salt, and pepper until well blended. Set aside.

Bring a large pot of pasta to a boil over high heat. Add 1 tablespoon salt and the pasta and cook until al dente. Drain the pasta, reserving ¼ cup of the cooking water.

Return the pasta to the pot and add the ricotta cheese mixture, the reserved pasta cooking water, lemon zest, and grated cheese. Mix everything well over low heat and serve when hot.

1½ cups whole-milk ricotta cheese, homemade (page 332) or store-bought, well drained

Fine sea salt

½ teaspoon freshly ground black pepper

1 pound pasta of your choice

2 tablespoons grated lemon zest (from 2 large lemons)

½ cup grated Parmigiano-Reggiano cheese

Sugo Finto
False Sauce

1 small onion, cut into chunks

1 rib celery with leaves, cut into chunks

1 medium carrot, peeled and cut into chunks

1 clove garlic, peeled

2 sprigs fresh flat-leaf parsley

2 tablespoons extra-virgin olive oil

2 tablespoons diced pancetta

2½ pounds fresh or canned plum tomatoes, chopped

Salt and freshly ground black pepper to taste

Sugo finto is a tomato sauce that is well known in many regions of Italy. It is considered a mock or false sauce because it is simmered like a ragù but contains little or no meat. Its origin is part of the *contadina* (farmer) tradition, where meat was unaffordable to the lower classes.
Makes about 3 cups

Combine the onion, celery, carrot, garlic, and parsley in a food processor and pulse several times to reduce everything to a paste consistency. Set aside.

Heat the oil in a large soup pot over medium heat. Add the pancetta and fry for a few minutes, until it begins to give up its fat. Add the vegetable mixture from the food processor and cook, stirring, until it softens.

Add the tomatoes; season with salt and pepper. Partially cover the pot and cook for about 35 minutes, stirring occasionally. The sauce should be slightly thickened and is ready to use on any type of short cut pasta like ziti, rigatoni, or gemelli. Or you can store it in the refrigerator for up to a week.

Salsa di Domenica

Sunday Sauce

Sunday Sauce . . . for many of us, it brings back memories of a rich meat and tomato sauce simmering on the stovetop early on Sunday morning. While it cooked, the spiritual side of Sunday took over as many attended Mass. I know I was always distracted in prayer, just anticipating that first forkful of tomato sauce and pasta. This is a long-simmered sauce that combines a variety of meats for flavor. Beef and pork and chicken were favorite combinations, but whatever the cook used, it was always delicious.   **Serves 6**

In a large pot, heat the olive oil over medium heat. Add all but ½ cup of the onions and wilt them down, then stir in the tomato paste, coating the onions well, and continue cooking until they are almost a deep brown color. Stir in all but 1 tablespoon of the garlic and cook until it softens. Transfer the onions to a bowl. Add additional oil if the saucepan seems dry. Add the sausages and brown them; transfer to a dish. Add the steak and brown well.

Return the sausages and onion mixture to the pot. Stir in the tomato puree, wine, and sugar; season with salt and pepper. Mix well, cover, and simmer for 30 minutes.

Tie the parsley and basil sprigs together with kitchen string and add them to the sauce. Continue cooking over low heat for 2 to 3 hours.

Preheat the oven to 350°F.

In a large bowl, combine the ground beef, pork, and veal with the egg, ½ cup reserved onion, 1 tablespoon reserved garlic, minced parsley, cheese, and moist breadcrumbs. Mix well with your hands.

With wet hands, form golf ball–size meatballs. Place them on a nonstick baking sheet and bake them for 20 minutes. Drain off any excess fat and transfer the meatballs to a bowl.

About 30 minutes before the sauce is done, add the meatballs to the sauce. (The meatballs will be kept warm and served as a second course.)

Bring a large pot of water to a boil over high heat. Add 1 tablespoon salt and the pasta and cook until al dente; drain and transfer the pasta to a serving bowl. Add the sauce (without the meatballs) and toss to combine; serve as a first course.

2 tablespoons extra-virgin olive oil

3 medium onions, minced

¼ cup tomato paste

4 cloves garlic, chopped

4 sweet Italian sausages

1 pound round steak

10 cups Fresh Tomato Puree (page 215)

1 cup dry red wine

1 tablespoon sugar

Salt and freshly ground black pepper to taste

4 sprigs fresh flat-leaf parsley plus 2 tablespoons minced flat-leaf parsley

4 sprigs fresh basil

⅓ pound ground beef

⅓ pound ground pork

⅓ pound ground veal

1 large egg

¼ cup grated Pecorino Romano cheese

½ cup fresh breadcrumbs soaked in ⅓ cup milk

1 pound ziti or penne

La Genovese

Neapolitan Onion Sauce

2¼ pounds chuck or bottom round roast, tied with kitchen string

Salt and freshly ground black pepper to taste

2 tablespoons extra-virgin olive oil

4 ounces prosciutto or pancetta, diced

1 rib celery, diced

1 carrot, diced

4 pounds mild yellow onions, thinly sliced

¾ cup dry red wine

Water as needed

1 pound candele or ziti

Grated Pecorino Romano cheese

Pasta and pizza with tomato sauce may define Neapolitan cooking in many people's minds, but la Genovese is really considered one of the gems in the arsenal of Neapolitan sauces—and it has nothing to do with the city of Genoa in the northern region of Liguria from which it takes its name. So why the name? We will never know for sure, but as with so many classic dishes, this one has several stories to support the name.

The most logical one centers on the port of Naples and its trade with other parts of Italy as well as with other cultures. Since Genovese merchants often spent long periods of time in Naples, they brought their own chefs with them, who cooked with local ingredients like onions, celery, carrots, and whatever scraps of meat could be had like a prosciutto bone or bits of local salame, to create a long-simmered sauce that is now known as la Genovese and to this day is unknown in Genoa and in many parts of Italy.

The first printed recipe for the sauce is nothing like it is today. In 1837, Ippolito Cavalcanti published a recipe in his *Cucina casarinola co la lengua napolitana* (*Home Cooking in the Neapolitan Language*) that is more of a French preparation for a long-simmered meat stock.

It starts out with what Italians would call *gli odori*, the flavoring agents for a sauce or stew. This was a combination of diced onion, carrot, and celery and less-desirable cuts of meat that required a long cooking time, like stew beef or pork or a combination of meats. The onions became the major player in the sauce, but they had to be sweet onions, not too strong since the sheer amount of them seemed as if they would overwhelm the finished product. The sweet red Tropea onion of Calabria is said to be the favorite when making this sauce today.

Some cooks add tomato paste with the onions, which is not traditional but helps with the color. Purists say that the long cooking of the onions turns them velvety and creates the sauce's burnt-reddish color.

continued on page 160

continued from page 158

When the meat is cooked, it is saved for the second course, and the sauce is used to dress pasta like ziti, mezzani, or candele, long tubular pasta that is broken into thirds before being boiled.

There is also a version of this sauce called *finta Genovese* ("fake Genovese") that is made without meat, for when it was forbidden by the Catholic Church to eat meat on fast days. **Serves 6**

Dry the meat with paper towels. Generously salt and pepper the chuck roast.

In a Dutch oven or other large, high-sided pot, heat the olive oil over medium-high heat; add the chuck roast and pancetta and brown the roast slowly on all sides. Add the celery and carrot and cook for a couple of minutes. Add the onions and the wine and cook, allowing the wine to evaporate.

Cover and cook for 2 hours over very low heat, stirring occasionally. Add water as needed to keep the roast from sticking to the bottom of the pan. Check the meat for tenderness; if it needs more time, continue cooking until it is tender and the onions have been reduced to a very creamy consistency.

Remove the meat from the pot and set aside. Slice and serve it as a second course or refrigerate and serve it for another meal.

Bring a large pot of water to a boil over high heat. Add 1 tablespoon salt and pasta and cook until al dente. Drain the pasta and add it to the pot with the onion sauce. Mix well. Serve with grated cheese.

Salsa Verde

Green Sauce

This creamy broccoli and spinach sauce takes advantage of the broccoli stems as well as the florets. Serve it over a short cut of pasta like rigatoni, ziti, or penne. **Serves 8**

Use a vegetable peeler to shave off the outer layer of the thick broccoli stem. Cut the stem into 1-inch pieces. Cut the broccoli florets into ½-inch pieces to make 2 cups.

Bring a large pot of water to a boil over high heat. Boil the broccoli florets until a knife easily pierces them. Scoop the florets out of the water to drain and transfer them to a bowl. Add the stems to the same pot and boil until tender. Scoop the stems out of the water. Save the water to boil the rigatoni. Drain and transfer the stems to a blender. Add the spinach to the blender and puree the mixture until it is very smooth. (Alternatively, use an immersion blender to puree the ingredients.) Transfer to a bowl and set aside.

In a large sauté pan, heat the olive oil over medium heat; add the garlic and cook until it softens. Stir in the red pepper flakes and continue cooking for a couple of minutes. Add the reserved broccoli florets and toss to combine. Off the heat, stir in the cream and thyme leaves. Stir in the broccoli-spinach sauce, season with salt and pepper, and keep partially covered and warm.

Bring a pot of rinsed water to a boil again. Add 1 tablespoon salt and the rigatoni and cook until al dente. Drain, reserving ¼ cup of the cooking water. Add the rigatoni and reserved cooking water to the sauce and mix well. Serve sprinkled with grated cheese.

1 small head broccoli

1 cup well-squeezed cooked spinach *or* 1 (10-ounce) package frozen spinach, thawed and well squeezed

2 tablespoons extra-virgin olive oil

1 clove garlic, minced

¼ teaspoon red pepper flakes or red pepper paste

Grated zest and juice of 1 lemon

½ cup light cream

2 tablespoons fresh thyme leaves

Salt and freshly ground black pepper to taste

1 pound rigatoni

Grated Pecorino Romano cheese

Bread

As I approached Altamura in the region of Puglia (Italy's heel), a sign along the highway that read *Città del Pane* ("city of bread") reminded me why I had come here. Altamura, whose name means "high walls," was named for the ancient walls outside the city. Pane di Altamura, made in antiquity, continues to be made today by generations of bakers like the Di Gesu family, who proudly gave me a lesson on how the bread is made and baked in a hundred-year-old oven with a stone floor fired by oak wood. The unique flour used to make the golden loaves of Altamura is known as *farina di semola rimacinata*, a hard wheat flour ground to a silky consistency that gives the crumb its mellow yellow color. The other ingredients, water and natural yeast made from yogurt, are used in place of commercially prepared dried yeast. After rising, the bread is shaped into a round with one side higher than the other to symbolize those ancient high walls. Cracking open the crusty hot loaf with your hands and tasting its moist and slightly tangy crumb gives credence to the words of the Latin poet Horace who proclaimed it "the best bread in the world."

Pane di Altamura was granted DOP (protected designation of origin) status by the European Union in 2003 because of the careful attention paid to using the unique, local raw materials within the boundaries of Altamura.

Bread has long been the main sustenance for people around the world. In Italy, there are hundreds of regional breads. Some of the best known are *panettone*, the famous sweet Christmas bread studded with golden raisins, citron, and other candied fruits from Milan; *pane Toscano*, the saltless bread of Tuscany; *rosetta* ("little rose"), the crusty, hollow rolls of Rome; *carta di musica* ("music bread") from Sardinia, so called because the cracker-like bread is as thin as a sheet of music; *piadina*, the flat bread of Romagna; *ciabatta* ("slipper bread"), the flat bread created in Verona; and *pane Siciliano*, Sicilian bread made with golden durum semolina flour that is encrusted with sesame seeds. Many other regional types are made to commemorate festivals, feast days, and holidays.

It would take a separate volume to give justice to the breads of Italy, and I realize that not everyone has time to make bread, but here are some favorites. I hope they may tease you enough to give them a try.

Tips for Bread Baking

1 Unless otherwise stated, all ingredients should be at room temperature. Do not add cold flour stored in the refrigerator or freezer to a yeast mixture, as it will impair the yeast.

2 Unbleached all-purpose flour has a higher gluten content than bleached flour. Gluten is wheat protein, and it is what gives elasticity to dough, enabling it to be kneaded without resistance and to retain its shape when baking.

3 Semolina, the central core of the hard wheat berry, is a coarse, golden-yellow flour used to make breads and dry pasta.

4 Semola di grano duro rimacinata is a finer grind of semolina flour used for making such things as semolina gnocchi, fresh pasta, pastries, and Sicilian Bread (page 182).

5 Some breads, like Pane Toscano (page 188) and Panettone (page 170), require a *cresciuta*, or "mother" dough (also known as a sponge or starter) made from yeast, water, flour, and sometimes a little sugar. The mother must be made in advance and left to brew and bubble for 8 to 24 hours. Using a mother dough produces a definite tang, a result of long and slow fermenting, and allows the dough to rise impressively and still hold its shape.

6 To simulate the stone ovens of Italy, bake bread on baking stones. They are available online or in kitchenware stores.

7 Yeast dough is very forgiving. If you prepare the dough but cannot bake it the same day, lightly coat it with olive oil or a little butter, put it in a plastic bag, seal it, and refrigerate. When you are ready to proceed, remove it from the bag, put it in a lightly oiled bowl, cover with a towel, let rise until doubled in size, and then continue with the recipe. It will take a little longer to rise since it is cold.

8 A baker's peel is very useful for bread making. This wood or metal paddle with a long handle allows you to transfer the risen dough to a hot baking stone. Use it for bread, pizza, focaccia and rolls as well. Baker's peels are available online or in kitchenware stores.

9 Successful bread making depends in large part on using the right ratio of flour to liquid. Too much liquid will produce a sticky affair; too little liquid and a crumbly mess will result. It also depends on how the ingredients are measured; in Italy ingredients are weighed. I am a firm believer of using a scale to weigh out ingredients, but I realize that most cooks use measuring cups, so these recipes have been formulated using standard volume measurements—metal or plastic measuring cups for dry ingredients and glass measuring cups for liquids. I recommend using the "sprinkle and sweep" method for measuring dry ingredients like flour and sugar. This calls for lightly sprinkling the dry ingredient with a spoon into the measuring cup until it is over the rim and sweeping off the excess from the top of the cup with the flat edge of a butter knife.

Yeast

In my bread book, *What You Knead*, I commented that many people have told me that they would not dare attempt to make a yeast dough because of fear of killing the yeast! Too bad, because this is an unnecessary worry; if they could overcome it, they would be introduced to the wonderful world of making not just bread, but savory and sweet rolls, pizza, focaccia, and a host of other yeast-based foods.

Yeast is nothing more than a single-cell fungus that ferments sugar to produce alcohol and carbon dioxide. In baking, it is the catalyst that allows dough to rise.

In years past, it was easy to find 2-ounce blocks of moist cake yeast (also called compressed yeast), but it was very perishable, needed to be refrigerated, and eventually was replaced with active dry yeast. Sold in sealed packets, in jars, and in bulk, active dry yeast has a long shelf life and is much more convenient to use. Adding liquid to active dry yeast wakes up the dormant cells. Instant yeast (also known as rapid rise yeast), as its name suggests, can be added directly to dry ingredients.

So where does the fear come in? Worries that the yeast will be killed due to the temperature of the water are unfounded if you get in the habit of using an instant-read thermometer to check the temperature. I find that the sweet spot for fermenting cake yeast in water is 95°F and 110°F for active dry yeast. There are many recipes today that skip this step for cake, dry, and instant yeast, adding it directly to liquid and dry ingredients simultaneously.

I love cake yeast and use it every chance I get; in my opinion it gives a much better flavor to the dough. But for convenience, active dry yeast is used in the recipes in this book. But just in case you are adventuresome and want to try using cake yeast, just remember that one-third of a 2-ounce cake yeast is equal to one packet (2¼ teaspoons) of active dry yeast.

Impasto Base
Basic Bread Dough

The beauty of this dough is that you can easily double or triple the recipe, and it freezes well, too.   **Makes 1¾ pounds dough**

In a large bowl, dissolve the yeast in ¼ cup of the warm water. Allow the yeast to proof (get foamy), about 5 minutes. Add the remaining water and the salt. Add the flour, 1 cup at a time, working the mixture until it comes together in a ball. You may not need all the flour. Transfer the dough to a floured work surface and knead it for 5 to 10 minutes, folding the dough over on itself several times, until it is shiny and elastic.

Grease a bowl generously with olive oil. Put the dough in it and turn the dough a few times to coat with the oil. Cover the bowl tightly with plastic wrap, place it in a warm place away from drafts, and let the dough rise for 3 to 4 hours, or until doubled in size. The more slowly and longer the dough ferments and rises, the tangier the flavor will be. Punch the dough down, turn it out onto a floured surface, and knead a few times. Shape it into a loaf of bread, small rolls, breadsticks, or filled calzones, or make the focaccia on page 177.

1 package active dry yeast

1¾ cups warm (110°F) water

2 teaspoons salt

4 to 5 cups unbleached all-purpose flour

Extra-virgin olive oil, for greasing the bowl

Panettone

Milan's Christmas Bread

SPONGE

1 package active dry yeast

½ cup warm (110°F) water

¼ cup unbleached all-purpose flour

PANETTONE

⅔ cup golden raisins

¼ cup grappa or brandy

5 tablespoons unsalted butter, at room temperature, plus more greasing for the bowl

2 large eggs

4 large egg yolks

¾ cup sugar

¼ cup warm (110°F) water

1 tablespoon vanilla extract

4½ to 5 cups unbleached all-purpose flour

Grated zest of 1 medium orange

Grated zest of 1 medium lemon

½ cup chopped candied citron

During the Middle Ages, at Christmastime, people often ate a bread that was a little richer and more refined than their daily dose of coarse bread. Panettone, that tall cylinder of sweetness, is mentioned in documents as far back as the 1200s, when it was referred to as *pane di tono*, meaning "bread of the rich" in Milanese dialect. Studded with candied orange and lemon peel, citron, and golden raisins, and rich with eggs and butter in the dough, it was far too expensive to be something that country folk enjoyed. A fifteenth-century manuscript written by George Valagussa, a tutor to the powerful Sforza family, mentions such a bread being given by the head of a household to guests in a gesture of peace and friendship.

Italians consume an estimated 5½ pounds of panettone per family each Christmas season. Panettone used to be baked without a mold and thus did not reach such tall heights. Then, in 1919, it was commercially produced by Angelo Motta, who is credited with the technique of allowing the dough to rise three times before baking it in paper molds that in turn gave it its distinctive domed top.

Most Italians buy panettone today from large-scale producers like Bauli, but homemade is still the best and requires a bit of time to make, since you must start by making a "mother" dough, or sponge. This recipe has been streamlined to cut down on the preparation time with good results. Panettone is a good keeper; it can be made ahead and frozen for up to 2 months.   **Makes 1 large loaf or 2 small loaves**

To make the mother, dissolve the yeast in the warm water in a medium bowl. Stir in the flour with a spoon. The mixture will be loose. Cover the bowl with plastic wrap and let rise in a warm place for at least 6 hours, or overnight.

In a small bowl, combine the raisins and grappa and let soak for at least 4 hours, or overnight.

When you are ready to start, stir the butter, eggs, egg yolks, sugar, warm water, and vanilla together in a large bowl, or in the bowl of a stand mixer. Drain the raisins into a small strainer set over a bowl and press on the raisins with a spoon to extract as much liquid as possible. Set the raisins aside and add the liquid to the egg mixture. Add the sponge and mix well with your hands. Add the flour, about 2 cups at a time, mixing with your hands, or in a mixer, until a soft ball of dough forms.

Turn the dough out onto a floured work surface and knead for 5 to 10 minutes with your hands, or until it is smooth and elastic, adding additional flour as needed.

Butter a large bowl, place the dough in the bowl, and turn to coat the dough with the butter. Cover with a clean cloth and let rise for 6 hours in a warm place.

Butter and flour a paper panettone mold (available at Fantes.com) or other deep mold at least 6 inches tall and 7 to 8 inches wide. Alternatively, you can use 2 (2-pound) coffee cans and make 2 smaller loaves.

Punch down the dough and turn it out onto a floured surface. Flatten the dough with your hands and sprinkle it with the lemon and orange zest. In a small bowl, mix the raisins and citron with 1 tablespoon flour and sprinkle the mixture over the dough. Fold the dough in half, press the edges together, and knead by hand to distribute the fruits. Continue to knead for 5 to 10 minutes, or until the dough is smooth, adding additional flour if necessary. Place the dough in the mold, cover with a clean cloth, and let rise for 35 minutes in a warm place.

Preheat the oven to 400°F.

Cut an X in the top center of the panettone with a kitchen scissors. Bake for 5 minutes, reduce the heat to 375°F, and bake for 10 minutes. Reduce the heat to 350°F, and bake for 30 to 35 minutes longer, or until a skewer inserted into the center comes out clean. If the top begins to brown too much, cover it loosely with a piece of aluminum foil.

Cool the panettone on a rack for about 30 minutes before removing it from the mold.

Note: There are many versions of panettone. Some use Vin Santo, a sweet dessert wine, instead of grappa. Some are made with olive oil instead of butter, some include pine nuts and anise seed instead of raisins and citron, and some are filled with figs, chestnuts, and even chocolate.

Scaccia

Sicilian Pizza Bread Loaf

1 pound Basic Pizza Dough (page 174) or store-bought pizza dough, at room temperature

1½ cups tomato sauce

8 ounces caciocavallo cheese, thinly sliced and slices cut in half

Scaccia is an unusual rustic Sicilian pizza bread loaf that is quick to make from ready-made or homemade dough.   **Makes 1 loaf**

Preheat the oven to 450° F. Grease a 9 x 5-inch loaf pan, then line it with parchment paper.

Roll the dough on a floured surface into a 26 x 18-inch rectangle, with the long side facing you. Spread half of the sauce over the center of the dough. Lay half of the cheese slices over the sauce. Fold the left and right sides of the dough over the sauce, overlapping each other by 2 inches.

Spread the remaining sauce over the right side of the dough, then fold the left side over the sauce and pinch the ends closed.

Fold the dough in half from top to bottom and place it in the prepared loaf pan. Cover with a towel and let rise for 30 minutes.

Uncover and pierce the top of the dough with the tines of a fork. Bake until the bread is dark brown, about 30-35 minutes.

Invert the loaf onto a cooling rack, then turn it upright. Let cool for 5 minutes. Cut crosswise into thick slices and serve warm.

Impasto Base per la Pizza

Basic Pizza Dough

1½ cups warm (110°F) water, preferably filtered

1 teaspoon active dry yeast

3 to 3¼ cups Caputo or King Arthur 00 flour

1 teaspoon salt

Extra-virgin olive oil, for greasing the bowl

TOPPING FOR PIZZA MARGHERITA

1 cup tomato sauce or 12 thin slices fresh plum tomatoes

2 cups fresh mozzarella cheese, chopped

8 fresh basil leaves

Extra-virgin olive oil, for drizzling

There is no question that the right flour makes the best pizza. Caputo flour, the very same flour used in Naples to make their famous pizza, is a high-gluten flour, 12 to 14 percent protein. The traditional pizza Napoletana has a thin, soft middle and a *cornicione* (crust rim) that balloons up in the oven with charring on the edges. Caputo flour is available online, or you can substitute 00 flour, which is Italian all-purpose flour and available online from King Arthur Flour or Brick Oven Baker. (Unbleached all-purpose flour will also give good results.) This recipe was developed using Caputo flour, so you may find yourself needing to adjust the amount of water depending on what type of flour you use. This dough is made very quickly in a food processor. You will note that only 1 teaspoon of yeast is used, resulting in a slow rise, giving much better flavor to the dough. Make a classic pizza margherita, topping the dough with tomato, mozzarella cheese and fresh basil.
Makes 2 pizza crusts

Pour the water into the bowl of a food processor fitted with the steel blade. Add the yeast and whirl to blend. Let stand for 10 minutes, until chalky and bubbles begin to appear. Add 2½ cups of the flour and the salt; whirl to combine and form a ball of dough that moves away from the sides of the bowl and is not tacky to the touch. Add more flour if the dough is very wet, but be careful not to add too much flour or it will result in a dry, hard texture. The dough should be soft but not gooey.

Grease a large bowl with olive oil and coat the dough in the oil. Cover the bowl with plastic wrap and allow the dough to rise until doubled in size, about 2 hours. The dough can be made a day ahead; after the rising step, punch it down and place it in a plastic bag in the refrigerator until needed, then transfer the dough to a large bowl and allow it to stand for several hours at room temperature before forming the pizza.

When ready to form the pizza, punch down the dough and divide it in half. Stretch each half with your hands into a 10-inch circle. Place each piece on a lightly oiled sheet of parchment paper.

Preheat the oven to 450°F at least 30 minutes before baking; heating a baking stone in the oven is ideal for a great crust but, lacking that, you can place the pizza with the parchment paper on a rimless baking sheet.

Divide the tomato sauce or tomatoes equally between the two pieces of dough. Scatter the mozzarella on top. Bake until the bottom and edges turn golden brown, about 15–20 minutes minutes. Remove the pizza from the oven and scatter the basil leaves over the top. Cut in wedges and serve hot, with a drizzle of olive oil over each slice.

Focaccia al Rosmarino, Pepe Nero e Aglio

Focaccia with Rosemary, Black Pepper, and Garlic

A straightforward focaccia is a flat bread usually made in a rectangular pan and flavored with simple ingredients like a brushing of olive oil, a few olives, a sprinkling of cheese, and some fresh herbs like rosemary or oregano. Depending on the region of Italy, the toppings can change like a chameleon. The word *focaccia* comes from *focolare*, meaning "hearth," because these flatbreads were originally made in stone ovens.   **Makes 2 focacce**

If using a baking stone, place it on the middle rack of the oven and preheat the oven to 500° F. If using baking sheets, preheat the oven to 450° F and lightly brush 2 (18 x 13-inch) baking pans with olive oil.

Heat the olive oil over medium heat in a small sauté pan. When it begins to shimmer, turn it off and add the garlic and 4 tablespoons of the rosemary, pressing on the mixture to infuse the oil. Set aside.

If using baking sheets, divide the dough in half and roll out each piece on a lightly floured surface into an 18 x 13-inch rectangle. Place the pieces on the oiled baking sheets and brush the dough with half of the garlic-rosemary oil. Sprinkle each one evenly with the remaining 1 tablespoon rosemary, black pepper, and half of the grated cheese. Bake for 15 to 20 minutes, or until the bottoms are crisp and the tops golden brown. Cut into squares and serve hot.

If using a baking stone, divide the dough in half and set one half aside. Roll out the dough on a lightly floured surface to a 15 x13-inch circle and place on a baker's peel dusted with cornmeal. Brush the dough with half of the garlic-rosemary oil and sprinkle with 1 tablespoon rosemary, black pepper, and half of the grated cheese. Transfer the dough from the peel to the stone using a jerking motion of the wrist. Bake for 10 to 12 minutes, or until the bottom is crisp and the top is golden brown. While the first focaccia is baking, prepare the second one and have it ready on the baker's peel. Cut each focaccia into squares and serve warm or at room temperature.

Note: Throw away your pizza wheel! Use kitchen shears to cut focaccia and even pizza. No struggling, just nice even slices.

3 tablespoons extra-virgin olive oil, plus more for greasing the baking sheets if necessary

3 large cloves garlic, minced

6 tablespoons fresh rosemary needles

1 recipe Basic Pizza Dough (page 174)

Cornmeal (if using a baking stone)

Coarsely ground black pepper to taste

½ cup grated Pecorino Romano cheese

La Vera Focaccia col Formaggio di Recco

Recco's Famous Cheese-Filled Flatbread

3 cups unbleached all-purpose flour

¼ teaspoon salt, plus additional coarse salt for sprinkling

¼ cup extra-virgin olive oil, plus more for greasing the pan and brushing the focaccia

½ to ¾ cup cold water.

12 ounces crescenza or stracchino cheese, broken into small clumps

La vera focaccia col formaggio di Recco is a classic dish from the town of the same name near Genoa. A non-yeast dough is made and rolled so thin that it could double as a tablecloth for a card table! The dough is dotted with stracchino, or crescenza, a creamy cow's milk cheese that is the consistency of a full-fat cream cheese. Like other classic recipes, this focaccia has its own story authenticated by the Consorzio Recco Gastronomica. During the era of the third crusade in the twelfth century, in the chapel of the abbey of Saint Fruttuoso, a blessing was given to the crusaders who were about to depart for the Holy Land. To send them on their way, tables were laden with bread made with farro, a type of wheat, as well as figs, grapes, fish stew, olives, and flatbread made from semolina flour and giuncata, a creamy cheese made in a rush basket that became the famous focaccia made in Recco.

Fast-forward to a visit I made to Recco and to Il Ristorante Manuelina, which is famous for the tradition of making la vera focaccia col formaggio di Recco. There the pride of this native dish is all too evident, as I was shown the technique for stretching the dough over your knuckles so as not to tear it. The ingredients are simple enough—flour, olive oil, salt, and cheese—but what makes this focaccia so special is the quality of those ingredients and the baking of the focaccia in a really hot oven. Crescenza Vaschetta (Mauri brand) cheese was used for this recipe; it is available in Italian specialty stores and online. A perforated (13-inch or larger) pizza pan works well for even browning, but any large pan will do. **Serves 6 to 8**

continued on page 180

continued from page 178

Mix the flour, salt, olive oil, and cold water in a bowl until a ball is formed. Transfer the dough to a floured surface and knead it until smooth and soft. Cover and allow it to rest for 30 minutes.

Preheat the oven to 450°F. Brush a 13-inch perforated pizza pan with olive oil.

Divide the dough in half and roll each into a 14-inch circle. Lift the dough with your hands and stretch it using your knuckles and rotating the dough clockwise as you stretch it. It should be thin enough to see through.

Line the pan with one sheet of dough and allow the excess to overhang the edges. Scatter tablespoon-size dabs of cheese evenly all over the dough.

Repeat the rolling and stretching of the second half of dough. Place it over the cheese-covered dough, allowing the excess to overhang the pan. Trim the edges of the dough so there is just about a 1-inch overhang.* Pinch the two dough edges together to seal them. Make random small cuts in the top dough with kitchen scissors to allow steam to escape. Brush the top with olive oil and sprinkle evenly with coarse salt.

Bake until golden brown and puffed about 20-25 minutes. Transfer the focaccia to a cooling rack. Cool slightly before cutting into wedges. Serve warm.

*Use the leftover dough to make wine crackers. Roll the dough into a thin rectangle, brush it with olive oil, and sprinkle coarse salt over the top. Cut into small squares, place on a lightly oiled baking sheet, and bake for 5 to 8 minutes, or until golden brown. Cool the crackers on a wire rack.

Focaccia alla Molisana

Focaccia, Molise Style

Focaccia has been around since the days of ancient Rome, when it was served as a street food. Still in vogue, focaccia has morphed into many different shapes and is called by many different dialect names. In the region of Molise, focaccia is a two-crusted pie with a multilayered, complex flavor.   **Serves 8**

Preheat the oven to 350° F. Grease a 9- or 10-inch cake pan and line the bottom with parchment paper.

In a food processor or bowl, combine the flour, ¼ cup of the olive oil, the white wine, and 1 teaspoon salt and form a soft, smooth dough. Set aside while you make the filling.

In a large sauté pan, sweat the escarole leaves in a little water over medium heat until they are wilted; drain them and squeeze them very dry. Finely chop the leaves. Heat 2 tablespoons of the olive oil in the same sauté pan; add the escarole, garlic, olives, capers, raisins, pine nuts, and anchovies (if using), mixing well. Stir in the grated cheese. Cool the mixture to room temperature.

Divide the dough in half and roll each half into a 12-inch circle. Place one piece in the prepared cake pan. Spread the cooled filling over the dough and top with the second dough circle. Brush the top with the beaten egg and bake for 30 to 35 minutes, or until golden brown. Cut into wedges and serve warm.

3 cups or more unbleached all-purpose flour

½ cup extra-virgin olive oil

½ cup dry white wine

Coarse sea salt and freshly ground black pepper to taste

2 medium heads escarole, leaves separated and cleaned

2 cloves garlic, minced

10 black olives, pitted and chopped

1 tablespoon capers in salt, well rinsed

2 tablespoons raisins

¼ cup pine nuts

8 anchovies in oil, chopped (optional)

½ cup grated Pecorino Romano or Parmigiano-Reggiano cheese

1 large egg beaten with 2 teaspoons water

Pane Siciliano con Semi di Sesamo

Sicilian Bread with Sesame Seeds

CRESCIUTA

¼ teaspoon active dry yeast

½ cup warm (110°F) water

½ cup unbleached all-purpose flour

DOUGH

1 teaspoon active dry yeast

2 cups warm (110°F) water

4 to 5 cups durum semolina flour

2 teaspoons fine sea salt

1 teaspoon wheat gluten (optional)

Cornmeal, for sprinkling (optional)

⅓ cup sesame seeds

I learned the art of Sicilian bread making from Carmelo di Martino, the resident bread maker at the Regaleali winery near Vallelunga. We started with what seemed like a mountain of *farina di semola di grano duro rimacinata* (golden yellow durum flour) that was dumped into a wooden trough and mixed with a *cresciuta* ("mother" dough), water, and salt. Carmelo showed me how to use my knuckles, not my hands, to knead the dough. Later, after it had risen, he showed me how he formed the dough into an S shape. The loaves were baked in an old stone oven fired by pruned olive tree branches. The finished loaves had a golden crumb and a nutty-tasting sesame crust. **Makes 1 large loaf or 2 small loaves**

To make the cresciuta, dissolve the ¼ teaspoon yeast in the water in a small bowl and let stand for 10 minutes, or until foamy. Stir in the flour, cover the bowl, and let the mixture sit in a warm place for at least 4 hours or overnight.

When you are ready to make the dough, in a large bowl, dissolve the 1 teaspoon of yeast in the warm water in a large bowl. Cover and let stand for 5 minutes, or until foamy.

Stir the cresciuta into the yeast and water mixture and blend well. Add 2 cups of the semolina flour, the salt, and wheat gluten (if using) and mix until a pancake-like batter forms. Add additional flour a little at a time until you have a smooth ball of dough that is soft but not sticking to your hands.

Turn the dough out onto a floured surface and knead it with your hands for about 20 minutes. Place the dough in a large bowl and cover with plastic wrap. Let it rise until doubled in size, about 1½ hours.

Punch down the dough with your hands, divide it in half, and roll each half into a 30-inch-long rope. Curl each rope back and forth into a serpentine shape, leaving a 6- or 7-inch-long tail at the end. Lay the tail over the middle of the loaf; do not tuck it under. This form is called *mafalda*. Place the dough on a baker's peel sprinkled with cornmeal or just line the peel with parchment paper. Cover and let rise in a warm place for about 2 hours, until doubled in size.

Place a baking stone on the middle rack over the oven and preheat the oven to 425°F.

Brush the top of the dough with water and sprinkle with sesame seeds, pressing them in slightly.

If using cornmeal, sprinkle it on the baking stone just before baking the bread. Slide the loaf from the peel onto the baking stone. Bake the bread for about 30 minutes, or until an instant-read thermometer inserted into the middle of the loaf registers between 195°F and 210°F. The bread should be golden brown and hollow sounding when tapped on the bottom. Let the bread cool on a rack before slicing. Alternatively, bake the bread on a parchment lined baking sheet.

Piadina Romagnola

Romagna's Classic Flatbread

3 cups unbleached all-purpose flour

¼ teaspoon salt

3 tablespoons lard or extra-virgin olive oil

1 cup water or milk

Casa Artusi in Forlimpopoli is a splendid cooking school dedicated to Pellegrino Artusi, gourmand and author of the celebrated book *Science in the Kitchen and the Art of Eating Well*. I had the privilege of teaching there with the Mariette, instructors (all women) who are experts in the field of local cooking. Together we made *piadina*, flatbread that has been a symbol of Romagna, the eastern part of the region of Emilia-Romagna, since the Middle Ages, when various types of grains like oats, were ground into flour, mixed with water, and cooked over hot coals. This was peasant food. For the people of Romagna, piadina is their identification. Giovanni Pascoli, a poet and native son of Romagna, once said, "Nothing speaks more of Romagna than this bread of ours . . . it is a symbol that speaks of devotion to our land."

Also known as *piada* or *pié*, the word *piadina* (from *piadena*) means "flat" or "low." The rustic rounds of flatbread are made from unleavened dough that today is baked on a *tiella* or *piastra* (flat clay griddle), though originally they were baked on round clay *testo* over hot coals. You can use a griddle, electric frying pan, or cast iron pan to make them.

In Romagna, piadina is sold from brightly *baracchini* (kiosks) and are a much-loved street food. Rules dictate their thickness, so that the farther north one travels, the thicker the piadina becomes. Recipes for the dough vary from place to place, with some cooks preferring to mix the flour with milk instead of water. Piadina is not only served with traditional ingredients such as prosciutto di Parma, other cured meats, cheese, olives, and marinated vegetables but with jam and Nutella. **Makes 8**

In a bowl, combine the flour and salt. Add the lard and enough of the water to make a soft dough. Turn the dough out onto a floured work surface and knead it until smooth. Cover it and let it rest for 30 minutes.

continued on page 186

continued from page 184

Heat a 12-inch nonstick pan (or a tiella or piastra if you have one) over medium heat for about 5 minutes.

Roll the dough on a lightly floured surface into an 18-inch-long rope and cut 9 (2-inch) pieces. Roll each piece into a 9-inch circle and poke holes on the surface with the tines of a fork. Place them in the pan one at a time and cook until they begin to puff just a bit. Flip them over and cook the other side. Little brown spots will appear on them; this is part of the look of the piadina.

As they cook, transfer them to a cooling rack. They should be thin and soft. When cool, they can be served with a variety of cured meats like prosciutto di Parma, culatello, and other salumi. They are also good with squacquerone cheese, a soft cow's milk cheese from the region.

The Mareiette, Casa Artusi, Romagna

Lo Sfincione alla Palermitano

Pizza, Palermo Style

Sfincione (Sicilian pizza) is found in the province of Palermo and in particular in the town of Bagheria, where it is a staple of the Christmas season. It has always been considered a peasant dish and is about an inch thicker than Neapolitan pizza. The dough begins with a *cresciuta* ("mother" dough) that helps enhance the flavor and rise of the dough, and more yeast is used in this recipe than for Basic Pizza Dough (page 174). The topping is a very bold flavor combination of anchovies, cheese and breadcrumbs.   **Makes 2 thick 9-inch pizze**

To make the cresciuta, in a medium bowl, dissolve the yeast in the water; stir in the flour and mix well. Cover and allow to rest for 30 minutes.

To make the dough, pour the flour and salt onto a work surface and make a well in the center. Add the cresciuta and work the flour into it. Add as much of the water as needed to make a dough that is soft and elastic and not sticking to your hands. Add the olive oil to the dough and work it in with your hands until it is completely absorbed. Cover and allow the dough to rise until doubled in size, about 2 hours.

Meanwhile, in a sauté pan, simmer the onion in the water over medium heat until soft. Drain and blot the onion dry. Add the olive oil to the pan; when it is hot, add the onion and sauté until golden brown. Stir in the tomato sauce and simmer for 10 minutes. Season with salt and pepper.

Liberally oil two 9-inch cake pans. After the dough rises, punch it down with your fists and divide it in half. Spread each half in a cake pan, stretching it out with your fingers so it covers the bottom in an even layer. Sprinkle the anchovies over each half, pushing them down into the dough as far as they will go. Scatter the cheese over the dough, then spread the tomato and onion sauce evenly over the cheese. Mix the breadcrumbs and oregano together and sprinkle in an even layer over the sauce. Cover the pans and allow them to rise for 2 hours. Meanwhile, preheat the oven to 425°F.

Bake the sfincione for 30 to 35 minutes, or until the crust is golden brown. Drizzle the tops with olive oil and cut into pieces. Serve hot.

CRESCIUTA

1 teaspoon active dry yeast

½ cup warm (110°F) water

¾ cup unbleached all-purpose flour

DOUGH

5¼ cups unbleached all-purpose flour

2 teaspoons coarse sea salt

2 cups warm (110°F) water

3 tablespoons extra-virgin olive oil

TOPPING

1 large onion, peeled and thinly sliced

1 cup water

½ cup extra-virgin olive oil, plus more for greasing pans

1½ cups tomato sauce

Coarse sea salt and coarsely ground black pepper to taste

8 anchovy fillets in oil, drained and cut into small pieces

8 ounces provolone or fresh mozzarella cheese, cut into bits

1 cup toasted breadcrumbs

2 tablespoons dried oregano

2 tablespoons extra-virgin olive oil, for drizzling

Pane Toscano

Tuscan Bread

STARTER

½ teaspoon active dry yeast

½ cup warm (110°F) water

1 cup unbleached all-purpose flour

DOUGH

1½ teaspoons active dry yeast

1¼ cups warm (110°F) water

4 to 4½ cups unbleached all-purpose flour

Cornmeal, for sprinkling (optional)

Bread has always had historical and symbolic meaning. Somewhere in antiquity the idea of combining coarse grains and water took hold and literally changed the way in which people interacted with one another. Human suffering, wars, and the course of history have been determined by whether or not there was bread to eat.

One of the many breads that has its roots in historical events is Tuscan bread. Its main characteristic is that it has always been made without salt because of a salt tax imposed by the popes in the thirteenth and fourteenth centuries. To show their displeasure, Tuscans went without salt, and bakers refused to put it in their bread. To this day, this saltless bread is eaten daily in Tuscany and is a reminder of the steadfastness of a proud people. Some people say that the saltless bread is the perfect foil for the many kinds of flavorful foods traditionally eaten with it. Cooked cannellini beans, flavored with dark green Tuscan olive oil, is a triumph on this bread. Slices of it become *fettunta*, grilled Tuscan bread rubbed with a fresh garlic clove and drizzled with peppery extra-virgin olive oil. Making Tuscan bread requires a starter dough and needs at least a day to develop its sour tang. **Makes 1 large loaf**

To make the starter, sprinkle the yeast over the warm water in a small bowl. Let it proof until foamy, about 10 minutes. Stir in the flour and mix well. It should have the consistency of a soft dough. Cover the bowl with plastic wrap and allow the dough to rise in a warm draft-free place overnight.

The next day, make the dough. In the bowl of a stand mixer or food processor, sprinkle the yeast over ¼ cup of the water and proof it until foamy, about 10 minutes. Add the remaining 1 cup water. Add the starter and mix well. Add 3½ cups of the flour and mix well. Add enough of the remaining flour to make a soft ball of dough. Turn the dough out onto a floured surface and knead it with your hands until smooth and not sticky. Place the dough in a lightly greased bowl; cover with plastic wrap, and let it rise for 3 to 4 hours, or until doubled in size.

If using a baking stone, set it on the middle rack of the oven. Preheat the oven to 450°F.

Turn the dough out onto a floured surface and gently form it into a rectangular or round loaf. If using a baking stone, place the loaf on a baker's peel dusted with cornmeal, or place the dough on a greased baking sheet. Cover and let rise for about 35 minutes, or until doubled in size.

Carefully slide the bread onto the stone from the peel, or place the baking sheet in the oven. Bake for 30 to 35 minutes if using a stone or 45 minutes if using a baking sheet. The bread should be nicely browned and hollow sounding when tapped on the bottom, and an instant-read thermometer inserted into the middle of the loaf should register between 195°F and 210°F. Cool the bread on a cooling rack.

Pane con Fichi e Zucca

Fig and Zucchini Bread

Butter, for greasing the pans

3 large eggs

1½ cups sugar

¾ cup extra-virgin olive oil or sunflower oil

1 tablespoon vanilla or Fiori di Sicilia extract*

2 cups well-dried shredded zucchini

2 cups unbleached all-purpose flour, plus more for dusting the pans

2 teaspoons ground cinnamon

¼ teaspoon ground cloves

2 teaspoons baking soda

1 teaspoon salt

½ teaspoon baking powder

1 cup chopped walnuts

1 cup diced fresh or dried figs

Grated zest of 1 large lemon

My love for this quick bread/tea cake is based on two fig trees that I have babied for years. Because I live in a cold climate where they would not survive a harsh winter, their large terracotta pots are hoisted every fall onto a dolly and reside in the garage for the long winter months. Every spring, they are ceremoniously rolled out again, and come September, they reward me with beautiful figs that are not just for eating but for making pies, jams cookies, and this fig bread. It is perfect with tea or when you have too much zucchini! **Makes 2 loaves**

Preheat the oven to 350° F. Grease two 8 x 4-inch loaf pans with butter and dust the pans with flour, shaking out any excess. Set aside.

In a large bowl, beat the eggs with a mixer until light and fluffy looking. Beat in the sugar a little at a time. Beat in the oil and extract. Stir in the zucchini.

In a separate bowl, sift together the flour, cinnamon, cloves, baking soda, salt, and baking powder. Add flour mixture to the egg mixture and mix until well blended. Gently stir in the nuts, figs, and lemon zest. Divide the batter between the loaf pans, filling them three-quarters of the way full.

Bake for 45 minutes to 1 hour, or until a cake tester comes out clean and the tops are firm to the touch. Cool to room temperature before removing from the pans.

*Fiori di Sicilia extract is available from King Arthur Flour company. It has a concentrated citrus flavor.

Pampepato
Ferrara's Christmas Bread

Created at the monastery of Corpus Domini in Ferrara during the fifteenth century, pampepato (or pampapato) is a Christmas bread that is rich with chocolate, nuts, spices and fruit. The name, depending on who you ask and how it is spelled, can mean "peppered bread" (pan pepato) or "bread of the pope" (pan del pappa). In Ferrara, Duke Borso d'Este served pampepati at a banquet in 1456 and inserted a gold coin in each loaf. In the Middle Ages the loaves were sent as gifts to the pope. Ferrara even gave an 11-pound pampepato to General Dwight D. Eisenhower during the war.   **Makes 2 round loaves**

Preheat the oven to 350°F.

Spread the almonds on a rimmed baking sheet and toast for 5 minutes, watching carefully to prevent them from burning. Transfer the almonds to a bowl and set aside. Line the baking sheet with parchment paper and set aside.

Blend the flour, baking powder, baking soda, salt, cinnamon, cloves, ginger, nutmeg, and a grinding of black pepper together in a large stand mixer. Stir in the orange, lemon, and citron rind. Set aside.

Combine the sugar, cocoas, and water in a saucepan and stir the ingredients over medium heat for about 10 minutes. Cool for 5 minutes, then stir in the vanilla and pour the mixture into the flour mixture to combine well. Stir in the almonds. Remove the dough from the mixer; divide it in half and form 2 domed rounds, each about 6 inches in diameter. Set them on the baking sheet several inches apart.

Bake for 30 to 35 minutes, or until a cake skewer inserted in the middle comes out clean. Cool the breads on a rack.

Melt the chocolate in a heat-proof bowl set over a pan of simmering water. Stir in the olive oil. Brush the bottom of the breads with the melted chocolate and allow them to dry before turning them over and brushing the top and sides. Allow the breads to dry completely. Cut into thin slices and serve with a dessert wine such as Vin Santo.

¾ cup slivered almonds

4 cups unbleached all-purpose flour

1 tablespoon baking powder

½ teaspoon baking soda

¼ teaspoon salt

1 teaspoon ground cinnamon

¼ teaspoon ground cloves

¼ teaspoon ground ginger

½ teaspoon ground nutmeg

Coarsely ground black pepper

½ cup diced candied orange rind

½ cup diced candied lemon rind

½ cup diced candied citron

1½ cups sugar

¾ cup unsweetened cocoa powder

½ cup sweetened cocoa powder (also sold as "sweet ground chocolate")

1 cup water

1 tablespoon vanilla extract

8 ounces bittersweet chocolate

1 tablespoon extra-virgin olive oil

Casatiello Napoletano

Neapolitan Stuffed Easter Bread

1 package active dry yeast

2 cups warm (110°F) water

4 cups unbleached all-purpose flour

⅓ cup grated Pecorino Romano cheese

⅓ cup extra-virgin olive oil

1 teaspoon salt, plus more to taste

1 teaspoon coarsely ground black pepper, plus more to taste

8-ounce chunk provolone or scamorza cheese, cut into ½-inch cubes

8-ounce chunk salame, mortadella, or ham, cut into ½-inch cubes

4 large eggs

Casatiello is an impressive-looking savory filled Neapolitan Easter bread that symbolizes faith and the message of Easter. The word *casatiello* in the Neapolitan dialect means "cheese" because of the use of cheese in the dough and in the filling. For Easter, the rising dough meant the promise of new life, the shape of the bread symbolized a crown, and the eggs meant rebirth. There are many variations of this stuffed bread, but it is one of those antique recipes not made much at home anymore.   **Makes 1 large (10½-inch) round loaf**

Dissolve the yeast in ½ cup of the water and allow it to proof and get foamy, about 10 minutes. Heap the flour on a work surface or put it in the bowl of a stand mixer.

Add the yeast mixture, olive oil, salt, and pepper and work it into the flour; add the Pecorino Romano cheese and enough additional warm water to make a soft ball of dough. Cover and let it rise in a warm place for 1½ hours, or until it doubles in size.

Preheat the oven to 375°F. Grease a 10-inch tube pan with a removable bottom and set aside.

Punch down the dough and break off a large orange-size piece and set it aside. Knead the remaining dough for a few minutes and roll it out into an 18 x 14-inch rectangle and scatter the provolone and salame cubes over the surface to within 1 inch of the edges. Sprinkle with salt and pepper.

Starting at the longest side, roll up the dough up as for a jelly roll, then tuck in the ends. Place the roll in the tube pan, seam side down. Bring the two ends together and fold them under. Cover and allow to rise for about 1 hour, or until the dough is three-quarters of the way up the sides of the pan.

continued on page 194

continued from page 192

Place three of the eggs randomly on the top of the dough, pressing them in to anchor them.

Divide the reserved piece of dough into 6 equal pieces and roll each piece into a 4-inch-long length. Use two pieces to a make a cross over each egg. Beat the remaining egg with a fork and brush it all over the surface of the dough.

Bake for 45 minutes, or until the casatiello is golden brown. Let cool on a rack, then run a butter knife along the inside edges of the pan to loosen the bottom and remove it. Turn the bread out. Cut into wedges and serve warm.

Positano

Breadcrumbs

Stale bread was never wasted at home when I was growing up. Even the smallest piece could be used for something, and when there was enough to make *pangrattati* (breadcrumbs), it was toasted in a 300°F oven to dry it out slowly without burning it. The dry pieces were placed in paper bags and smashed into fine crumbs with a rolling pin. These days this can be done quickly in a food processor.

Fine crumbs are used to bind fillings for stuffing vegetables, added to meatballs, used as a coating for frying fish, and incorporated into cake batters.

Coarse crumbs often take the place of cheese for pasta dishes. The crumbs are sprinkled over the pasta before being served, as in the recipe for Spaghetti with Cauliflower and Anchovy (page 105). Breadcrumbs keep well in jars in the refrigerator or freezer.

Table Set for a Saint

March 19 is no ordinary day in Sicily; it is the traditional feast day of Saint Joseph, Father of the Holy Family, patron of carpenters and pastry chefs, and protector of the poor and the dying. On that day towns and villages prepare what is known as *le tavole di San Giuseppe* (the tables of Saint Joseph), a gastronomic display of more than a hundred dishes in his honor. Why all the fuss? Because Saint Joseph is credited with delivering Sicily from famine during the Middle Ages; in gratitude for being spared, families of farmers and fishermen built altars in their homes and opened their doors to friends and strangers to share what abundance they had.

Salemi, Sicily, a small town in the Belice Valley, celebrates in a big way. Weeks before the feast, the women of the town begin food preparations. Because the feast day usually occurs during Lent, only meatless dishes are permitted. Bread is the most important component; one specialty is a type of sourdough left to rise for hours before being shaped into intricately sculpted designs of Saint Joseph's beard, his sandals, carpenter tools, and staff. Letters of the alphabet, stars, birds, flowers, and crosses are carved from the dough using ordinary implements like a pasta wheel, hair combs, sewing needles, and thimbles. The entire town is covered in these bread ornaments, along with oranges and lemons, and foliage strung over elaborate outdoor altars, lampposts, and doorways and in shop windows.

Busloads of worshippers arrive on the day to partake in the blessing of the tables and to view the altars set up in private homes, where Saint Joseph is the guest of honor. In front of him is a groaning board of foods ranging from pasta with breadcrumbs to symbolize the wood shavings of a carpenter, to fava beans, fried cardoons, fish dishes, arancine, and *bigne* (filled cream puffs). Fava beans are of great significance on this day because during Sicily's most severe famine, this crop thrived while others failed. That is why it is often referred to as the lucky bean.

Before anyone can eat these foods, the clergy comes to offer prayers and bless the tables. The Holy Family, represented by children, are the first to eat, and they must taste each of the multitude of dishes with a pause in between each one for a drumbeat sound as the crowd roars "Viva San Giuseppe!" By tradition the Holy Family cuts into a large loaf of bread and gives out pieces to all assembled. Eating this bread will ensure good luck in the coming year.

When waves of Sicilian immigrants arrived in America, many continued the tradition of the tables, preparing them in thanksgiving for favors received through prayers to Saint Joseph. In New Orleans, the tradition is especially strong since many Sicilian immigrants settled there, as well as in my hometown of Buffalo, New York, where my maternal grandmother prepared elaborate dishes after Saint Joseph granted her wish of having my grandfather cured of a serious illness. Viva San Giuseppe!

MELENZANINA
SENZA SEMI
ORI- Sicilia
€ 3.50 AL·K?

FAGIOLINI
ORI:- ITALIA
€ 4.50 AL·K?

Prodotto: FAGIOLINI
Cat:'I'
Origine:ITALIA
Lotto: 246

Vegetables

Google the Mediterranean Diet, and a nifty-looking pyramid will pop up, illustrating food groups divided into categories like grains, vegetables, fish, meat, poultry, and fruit. What this pyramid shows is that the best foods for a healthy lifestyle start at the bottom of the pyramid, with a heavy focus on whole grains and lots of vegetables. Move up the pyramid and fish, olive oil, and fruits are important. Move up farther and meat and poultry are recommended occasionally, and at the top point of the pyramid, desserts are a once-in-a-while treat. Italians have lived this diet for centuries, with olive oil being a common denominator in cooking. The olive's historic significance in antiquity and as a food is well noted from its biblical mention in the Old Testament to the work of wealthy Roman merchant and gourmand, Marcus Gavius Apicius, who wrote one of the earliest surviving cookbooks, *De Re Coquinaria (The Art of Cooking)* during the reign of Tiberius (14 to 37 CE). A rare copy exists in the library of the New York Academy of Medicine.

From their long history, Italians have lived the concept of farm to table from cultivating to planting and harvesting vegetables. As I was driving through the town of Branca on my way to Gubbio, in Umbria, a beautiful patchwork quilt of a vegetable garden, complete with an elderly gentleman vigorously hoeing the rows and sporting a tweed beret came into view. I stopped the car, got out, and in my best Italian said, "Buongiorno, sono Marianna." Pietro Cardoni, leaning on his rake, seemed bewildered at first to see an American in his backyard! He was mild mannered, soft spoken, and meditative in his demeanor. I asked if I could see his garden. He motioned me toward a luscious carpet of green plants all happily thriving under the Umbrian sun. One by one, he pointed out the names of the plants. "What do you do with all these vegetables?" I asked. "Pirarina, my sister-in-law, cooks them," he laughed. "I just plant them for

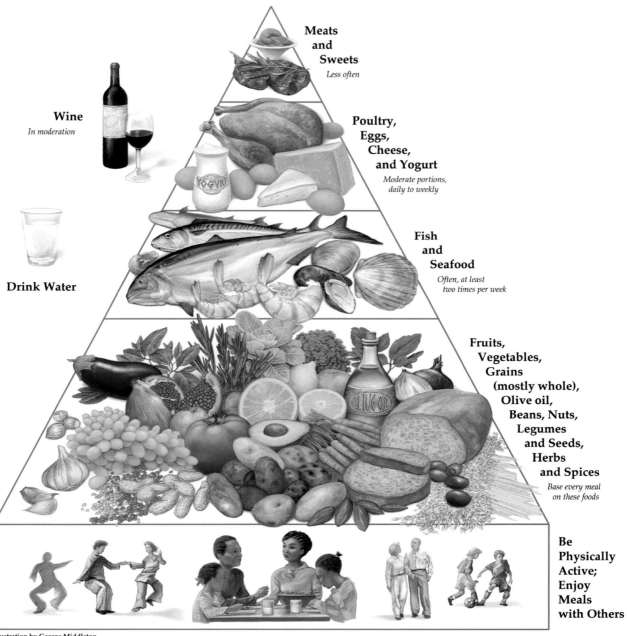

Mediterranean Diet Pyramid

A contemporary approach to delicious, healthy eating

Meats and Sweets
Less often

Wine
In moderation

Poultry, Eggs, Cheese, and Yogurt
Moderate portions, daily to weekly

Drink Water

Fish and Seafood
Often, at least two times per week

Fruits, Vegetables, Grains (mostly whole), Olive oil, Beans, Nuts, Legumes and Seeds, Herbs and Spices
Base every meal on these foods

Be Physically Active; Enjoy Meals with Others

Illustration by George Middleton

Market in Sicily

the table and for the fun of it." I then asked if it was true that most
Italians have gardens. He said it was—wherever there is a patch
of land, the Italians will plant, because not everyone lives near a
city where they can go to the markets to get vegetables: "Most of
us live in small towns, so we must think of ourselves." I wanted
to know what vegetables were his favorites and how they were
cooked. With a conductor's wave of the hand he replied: "Basta, le
verdure miste, olio di oliva, prezzemolo, aglio e cosi si fa qualcosa

da mangiare"—"A variety of vegetables cooked simply with olive oil, parsley, and garlic is all one needs."

Italian gardens, whether large or small, require imagination in order to use every available speck of land. Some are tucked beside railroad tracks, others ring the Autostrada, and still others are wedged in next to bridges and factories. In crowded cities, apartment balconies tell stories of the occupants, with the daily display of laundry flapping in the breeze right alongside terracotta pots of basil, tomatoes, peppers, and eggplants.

Wander through the narrow streets of any town and outdoor vegetable stands will be on display with what is *della stagione* (in season), along with a sign politely telling you "Non tocare" (do not touch). It is customary to ask the vendor to select what you want, and he or she might even strike up a conversation about how you are going to cook them.

Many regions are famous for certain kinds of vegetables, like the sweet spring peas that are mixed into the classic Risi e Bisi (page 69) in Venice. In Florence, spinach is popular in stuffings, while in Rome, artichokes—roasted, fried, or stuffed—are a must. Tomatoes, eggplant, and squash rule the regions of Campania and Sicily. Sweet and hot peppers and the onions of Tropea are the foundation of Calabrian cooking.

Art of the Artichoke

Nasty. That's how many people describe artichokes. They are all thumbs when it comes to knowing how to cook them—and speaking of thumbs and fingers, they are afraid of those thorny, tough leaves that, if one is not careful when handling them, could require a Band-Aid or two. But artichokes are one of the glories of spring and fall. Their hues range from delightful purples to all shades of green. They are members of the thistle family, and there are many varieties. Our most common here is the globe artichoke, big, meaty and thorny. Artichokes were introduced to America by way of California and Italian immigrant farmers who settled there and planted the first commercial crop. Today Castroville, California, is the artichoke capital and main source for artichokes sold nationwide.

Here's what to look for when buying them. The leaves should be closed, not fanned open; tight leaves means they're fresh. They should feel heavy in your hand, and the stem end should not be soft or bendable. They should have a uniform color, and aficionados agree that artichokes that have been nipped by frost and have tinges of brown on their leaves taste even better.

Preparation takes many forms, including stuffing them whole, or using only the hearts and stuffing their cavities, or marinating them as part of a salad, or cutting them in wedges and stewing them. They are exquisite steamed and served plain with melted butter. Bump up the wow factor and stuff them with spicy Italian sausage, or stew them with tomatoes and wine for cold weather eating.

Getting to the most tender part of the artichoke seems to require the fortitude of an archaeologist scraping away layers of leaves and struggling to remove that hairy choke at the very bottom before the big payoff, the tender heart. But there is an easier way: Strip away the tough outer leaves (and this could mean a couple of layers) with your fingers by bending the leaves backward or cut them off with scissors. A good way to know if you have taken off enough tough leaves is to stop when the color of the leaves turns from dark to pale green. Cut off about ¼ inch down from the top with a sharp knife and scrape the stem end with a vegetable peeler. Cut the artichokes in half lengthwise and place them, cut side down, in a large saucepan. Cover them with water and the juice of several lemons and bring them to a boil. Lower the heat to medium-low, cover the pot, and cook until you can easily pull off one of the leaves without any effort. Drain and cool. Use a small spoon or a melon baller to easily remove the hairy choke and pale yellow leaves. Prepared this way, artichokes become edible containers that can be filled with cheese, meat, rice, or vegetables or served as is with melted butter, which is my favorite way to have them. Nutty and mild with a slightly sweet taste, the artichoke is art itself.

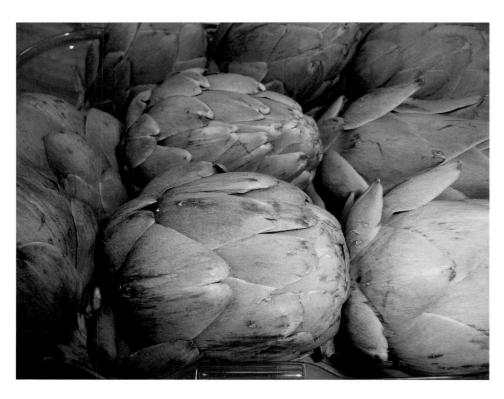

Cruschi e Patate

Crunchy Peppers and Potatoes

A few years ago, while traveling in the region of Basilicata in the south of Italy, I was introduced to the most amazing dried sweet red peppers called peperoni Senise and often referred to as Basilicata's red gold. They are named after the agricultural area where they are grown between the Agri and Simi Rivers near the city of Senise They are a cornerstone of Basilicata cooking. These thin-skinned, pointed peppers are prized for a local dish called *patate e cruschi* (pronounced "cruise-key"). *Cruschi* means "crispy" or "crunchy," and these flash-in-the-pan, crisp-as-potato-chip peppers deliver in every sense of the word.

Senise peppers are harvested in early August and enjoy IGP (Indicazione Geografica Protetta) status. This means that only peppers grown in the Basilicata region can be called peperone di Senise. If you travel in this region, you will see these peppers strung up like Christmas garlands on strings called *serte* and dried in the sun. They are shipped worldwide and are utilized both fresh and dried. But there is something wonderful that happens when they are dried; their flavor intensifies. Cooking them in their dried form requires the cook to pay attention, since they can burn in the blink of an eye. They are available online and in Italian specialty food stores. **Serves 4**

¼ cup extra-virgin olive oil

4 to 6 whole peperoni di Senise

4 Yukon Gold potatoes

1 large garlic clove, sliced

Salt and freshly ground black pepper to taste

Wash and dry the potatoes and poke them in several places with a small knife. Microwave or boil them until tender. Once they are cool enough to handle, peel and dice them. Set aside.

Heat the oil in a sauté pan over medium heat and fry the peppers, one at a time, for about 30 seconds, or until they swell and take on a bright red color. Do not overcook them or they will turn black. Add more oil to the pan as needed.

Drain the peppers on absorbent paper; when cool, cut them into 1-inch pieces and set aside.

In the same pan, fry the potatoes until they are golden brown. Season with salt and pepper. Carefully combine the peppers with the potatoes and serve.

Decostruito Parmigiana di Melanzane

Deconstructed Eggplant Parmigiana

Extra-virgin olive oil, for greasing the pan

3 large eggs

Salt and freshly ground black pepper to taste

1 cup sliced almonds

1½ to 2 cups panko breadcrumbs

2 medium eggplants, trimmed and each cut into eight ¼-inch thick round slices

16 thick slices fresh mozzarella or provolone cheese

2 cups tomato sauce

Fresh basil leaves, for garnish

For all the eggplant lovers, here is a new way to prepare eggplant parmigiana without having to fry anything and without a lot of unnecessary fillings, like meats, veggies, eggs, olives, and mushrooms. Small, round, violet-colored eggplant called Violetta grow in my garden, but any type is fine for this dish. The beauty of it all is that it is baked and delivers great taste and a nice crunch from the almond and breadcrumb mixture. A little unconventional, yes, but that is how recipes develop. **Serves 4**

Lightly oil a rimmed baking sheet.

Beat the eggs with a fork in a shallow bowl; season with salt and pepper to taste. In another bowl, combine the almonds and breadcrumbs.

Coat both sides of each slice of eggplant in the beaten egg and then coat and press both sides in the almond mixture. Lay the slices on the lightly oiled baking sheet in a single layer. Refrigerate, uncovered, for 30 minutes.

Preheat the oven to 350°F.

Bake the eggplant for about 12 minutes, or until nicely browned on the underside, then carefully turn the slices over and bake the other side. Top each slice with a slice of the cheese and allow it to melt. Remove them from oven and stack 4 slices on top of each other on each plate; top each one with some of the tomato sauce and serve hot, garnished with basil leaves.

Funghi Misti Sott'Olio

Marinated Mixed Mushrooms

2 pounds mixed mushrooms, such as porcini, button, cremini, and shiitake

3 cups red wine vinegar

extra-virgin olive oil

Coarse sea salt to taste

4 small dried hot chili peppers, split lengthwise

1 tablespoon dried oregano

1 tablespoon toasted fennel seeds

1 tablespoon black peppercorns, slightly crushed

Making your own marinated mushrooms is easy and the payoff is so delicious. Use a variety of mushrooms for added texture and taste or use all one kind if you prefer. A dehydrator is an indispensible kitchen tool for drying the mushrooms, but placing them on a rack over a baking sheet and oven-drying them is a good alternative. Use the mushrooms as part of an antipasto or serve them on top of grilled bread. **Makes about 3 cups**

Wipe the mushrooms with damp paper towels or use a mushroom brush to remove excess dirt. Trim the ends and cut the mushrooms into thick slices. Place them on dehydrator racks and dry them until they are the texture of a dried apricot, bendable but not crispy. Put a handful of mushroom slices on a piece of cheesecloth and tie with kitchen string. Repeat to fill and make other cheese-cloth bags.

In a large pot, bring the vinegar to a rolling boil. Lower the heat to medium; add the mushrooms and cook for 4 minutes. Fish out the cheesecloth bags and drain; untie the cheesecloth and transfer the mushrooms to clean towels and let dry. In a medium bowl, mix the olive oil with the salt, hot peppers, oregano, fennel seeds, and peppercorns. Add the mushrooms and toss well to combine.

Transfer the mushroom mixture to small sterilized jars. Fill each jar with enough olive oil to completely cover the mushrooms. Cover the jars and refrigerate for up to 2 weeks.

Polpetti di Funghi

Mushroom Meatballs

Mushroom meatballs from Sicily are made from pinolini, mushrooms that are similar to the meaty and woodsy-tasting porcini. They grow at the base of pine trees and have a hint of a pine taste. If you can find fresh porcini, use them, otherwise substitute cremini, shiitake, or button mushrooms.   **Makes 16 to 18 (1-inch) meatballs**

Wipe the mushrooms with damp paper towels and trim the stems if they are tough. Put the mushrooms in a saucepan and cover with water. Bring the water to a boil, reduce the heat to a simmer, and cook for 2 to 3 minutes. Drain, cool, and finely mince the mushrooms. Transfer them to a bowl. Stir in the eggs, garlic, parsley, cheese, and breadcrumbs and mix well. Season with salt and pepper. Use your hands to form the mixture into 1-inch balls.

In a large sauté pan, heat the peanut oil over medium heat. Fry the meatballs until they are browned and crusty. Drain them on paper towels and serve warm as an antipasto.

10 ounces fresh mushrooms

1 large egg, slightly beaten

3 cloves garlic, minced

¼ cup minced fresh flat-leaf parsley

¼ cup grated Pecorino Romano cheese

⅔ cup fresh breadcrumbs

Salt and freshly ground black pepper to taste

¼ cup peanut oil

Il Gattò Napoletano

Neapolitan Potato Cake

12 tablespoons (1½ sticks) unsalted butter, at room temperature, plus more for greasing the pan

1 cup dry breadcrumbs

2 pounds Yukon Gold potatoes

6 tablespoons grated Parmigiano-Reggiano cheese

⅔ cup whole milk

2 large eggs, lightly beaten with a fork

¼ teaspoon ground nutmeg

Salt and freshly ground black pepper to taste

4 ounces boiled ham, diced

1 fresh mozzarella ball (about 5 ounces), diced

Naples is the ancestral home of common foods such as pizza and pasta, but more elegant Neapolitan dishes like gattò are based on French and Spanish influences. *Gattò*, from the French word *gateau*, means cake. But Neapolitan gattò is not a sweet cake, but rather a rich potato and cheese casserole that was served at the royal court. It was created in Naples in 1768 for the marriage of Queen Maria Carolina of Austria and King Ferdinand IV. The queen had great influence on the types of food served, and she brought French aristocratic cooking to Naples. **Serves 8**

Preheat the oven to 350°F. Lightly grease a 9-inch round cake or pie pan with butter. Coat the pan with ¼ cup of the breadcrumbs. Set aside.

Microwave the potatoes until soft. Let them cool, then peel them. In a large bowl, mash or rice the potatoes until smooth. Add the Parmigiano-Reggiano cheese, milk, eggs, 4 tablespoons of the butter, and nutmeg. Season with salt and pepper. Combine the ingredients well.

Spread half of the potato mixture in the prepared pan. Scatter the ham and mozzarella cheese over the potatoes. Dot with 4 tablespoons butter. Spread the remaining potato mixture over the ham and cheese. Dot with the top with the remaining 4 tablespoons butter. Spread the remaining ¾ cup breadcrumbs over the top.

Bake the gattò for 40 to 50 minutes, or until it is firm to the touch. Cool slightly. Cut into wedges and serve hot directly from the pan.

Finocchio Cremoso Cotto in Padella

Creamy Pan-Cooked Fennel

What is the hesitation about eating fennel? Many people shy away from this gorgeous vegetable because, in their words, "It tastes like licorice." Italians have been eating it for years, mainly consuming it raw as a crunchy *digestivo* after a meal. Fennel, affectionately known as finocchio, is great in garden salads, but it truly shows off its versatility in this creamy, nutmeg-flavored side dish. Try it roasted and grilled, too. **Serves 4**

2 large fennel bulbs, white part only

4 tablespoons (½ stick) unsalted butter

⅔ cup light cream

Salt and freshly ground black pepper to taste

Grated fresh nutmeg, for sprinkling

½ cup grated Parmigiano-Reggiano cheese

Cut each bulb in half and then into quarters, leaving the core attached to keep the layers together.

Melt the butter in a sauté pan large enough to hold the fennel in one layer. When the butter is hot, add the fennel pieces and cook over medium heat without disturbing them for 5 minutes. Turn the pieces over, reduce the heat to low, and pour in the cream around the edge of the pan. Cover and cook until the fennel is knife-tender and almost all the cream has evaporated.

Season with salt and pepper. Transfer the fennel to a serving dish. Dust with grated nutmeg, sprinkle with the cheese, and serve as a side dish.

Passata di Pomodoro

Fresh Tomato Puree

Passata di pomodoro is a smooth tomato puree made from ripe plum tomatoes that have been passed through a food mill or tomato press to remove the skin and seeds. The pulp becomes the base for making tomato sauce. **Makes about 4 cups**

5 pounds plum tomatoes

Salt

2 tablespoons bottled lemon juice*

Microwave the tomatoes in batches just until the skins begin to blister; cool, core and peel away the skin. Place the tomatoes, a few at a time, in a tomato press or a food mill and extract the pulp. This is now the passata. Discard the seeds and skin.

Transfer the passata to a bowl. Add salt to taste. Fill a sterilized quart-size jar with the passata and add 2 tablespoons bottled lemon juice to help raise the pH level, which is necessary to prevent bacteria from growing. Cap and place it in a large canning pot with a rack. Fill the pot with cold water to completely submerge the jar by 1 inch. Bring to a boil and then simmer gently for 40 minutes. Turn off the heat and allow the jar to cool completely in the pot before removing and storing it. Alternatively, you can fill a quart-size plastic bag with the passata and freeze; this eliminates the need to process it in a water bath.

*Bottled—*not* fresh—lemon juice is used because it has been acidified so it has a consistent acid level; the acidity can vary with fresh lemon juice.

Vignarola

Roman-Style Spring Vegetables

8 baby artichokes
   or 1 (9-ounce)
   package frozen
   artichoke hearts,
   thawed

Juice of 2 lemons

2 tablespoons
   extra-virgin olive
   oil

1 small bunch
   scallions, trimmed
   and thinly sliced

4 ounces pancetta
   or prosciutto di
   Parma, minced

½ cup chicken
   broth, homemade
   (page 38) or
   store-bought

2 cups fresh or frozen
   fava beans

2 cups fresh or frozen
   peas, thawed

1 cup hearts of
   romaine lettuce,
   torn into small
   pieces

Salt and freshly
   ground black
   pepper to taste

¼ cup minced fresh
   mint

Vignarola is a Roman dish to welcome spring, made with in-season peas, beans, and artichokes. The word *vignarola* comes from *vigneto*, meaning "vineyard," and is an old practice of planting vegetables between grapevines. Vignarola can be more than just a vegetable side dish with lamb chops; offer it as crostini with crusty bread or use it as a sauce for a short cut of pasta like rigatoni or fusilli.   **Serves 6**

Trim the stem ends of the artichokes and remove any tough outer leaves. Cut them in half lengthwise and scrape out any hairy choke; for baby artichokes, this may not be necessary. Cut the artichoke halves crosswise into thin slices and place them in a bowl of cold water. Add the lemon juice and toss the pieces in the water. Set aside until ready to cook, then drain the slices well.

Heat the olive oil in a large sauté pan over medium heat; add the scallions and pancetta and cook until the scallions soften. Add the artichokes and broth, cover, and cook for 10 minutes. Add the fava beans and cook for 3 minutes, then add the peas and lettuce and cook for 5 minutes. Mix well. Season with salt and pepper. Add the mint just before serving

Cavolo Nero con Uvette e Semi di Sesamo

Kale with Raisins and Toasted Sesame Seeds

In Tuscany, kale is known as *cavolo nero* ("black cabbage"). The sturdy, quilted-looking leaves are part of a traditional soup called *ribollita* ("reboiled"). There are many ways to cook kale, from steaming and serving with cannellini beans to mixing it into frittata and making a sort of pesto out of it for pasta. Or cook it with raisins, toasted sesame seeds, and a splash of balsamic vinegar glaze.   **Serves 4**

Put the raisins in a bowl of warm water to soak for 30 minutes.

In a small nonstick sauté pan, toast the sesame seeds over medium heat until golden brown; transfer them to a small bowl and set aside.

Place a steamer basket in a large pot and pour in water to just below the bottom of the steamer basket. Bring the water to a boil over high heat, add the kale, and cover. Steam the kale just until it wilts. Drain and squeeze the kale dry.

Heat the olive oil in a medium sauté pan over medium heat; add the garlic and cook until it softens. Add the kale and cook for a few minutes. Drain the raisins and stir into the kale mixture. Season with salt and pepper. Stir in the balsamic glaze. Serve hot, topped with the toasted sesame seeds.

½ cup golden raisins

2 tablespoons sesame seeds

1 large bunch kale, stems removed and leaves coarsely chopped

2 tablespoons extra-virgin olive oil

2 cloves garlic, thinly sliced

Salt and freshly ground black pepper to taste

2 tablespoons Balsamic Glaze (page 30)

Carciofi Ripieni alla Romana

Roman-Style Stuffed Artichokes

2 large artichokes

2½ cups chicken broth, homemade (page 38) or store-bought, or vegetable broth

1 cup farro

2 tablespoons minced fresh flat-leaf parsley

2 tablespoons minced fresh mint

½ cup grated Pecorino Romano cheese

Salt and freshly ground black pepper to taste

Extra-virgin olive oil, for drizzling

To eat in Rome and not have artichokes would be a gastronomic gaffe. Artichokes are beloved by Romans, thanks to the Jewish population that lived in a restricted part of the city and worked in the food sector, where they adopted the artichoke as part of their local cuisine. Artichokes were prepared in a number of ways, most famously deep-fried whole for a dish called *carciofi alla giudia*, or Jewish-style artichoke. Deep-frying the whole artichoke is art itself, as the leaves open like a huge flower, which indeed they are as members of the thistle family. The Roman artichoke variety is called cimaroli, a thornless variety without any hairy choke, so the entire thing is edible. Our globe variety has none of these characteristics. To make deep-fried globe artichokes, you must trim the leaves of their thorns and scrape out the choke with a small spoon. This makes for tedious work but can be done. A good substitute would be to use baby artichokes. Another way to prepare artichokes is to stuff them with seasoned fresh breadcrumbs, mint, and garlic. They take on even more goodness when stuffed with farro, a nutritious wheat grain. **Serves 4**

Rinse and dry the artichokes; use a vegetable peeler to peel away the outer layer of the stem. Remove the tough outer leaves. With a sharp knife, cut off ¼ inch from the top. Using scissors, clip off the thorny tips of all the remaining leaves. Cut the artichokes in half lengthwise right through the stems. Place the halves, cut side down, in a sauté pan large enough to hold them in a single layer. Cover them with water and bring to a boil. Cover the pan, lower the heat to medium, and cook until you can easily pull away a leaf, about 45 minutes.

Meanwhile, bring the broth to a boil in a saucepan and stir in the farro; lower the heat to medium-low, cover, and cook until the farro is tender, 5 to 7 minutes. Drain and transfer to a bowl. Mix in the parsley, mint, and cheese. Season with salt and pepper. Set aside.

Preheat the oven to 350°F. Brush a baking dish with olive oil.

When the artichokes are tender, drain them carefully and cool slightly. Use a small spoon to remove the pale green hairy choke just above the stem area. Fill each artichoke half with the farro mixture, packing it in and mounding it slightly. Drizzle the tops with olive oil. Cover and bake for 15 to 20 minutes, or until heated through. Drizzle the tops with more olive oil just before serving.

Gratin di Pomodoro
Tomato Gratin

3 to 4 tablespoons extra-virgin olive oil

4 cups (1-inch) ciabatta bread cubes

2 cloves garlic, minced

5 cups halved cherry tomatoes

1 tablespoon sugar

1 teaspoon salt

Freshly ground black pepper

1 cup diced Montasio, or Italian Fontina cheese

2 tablespoons chopped fresh basil

A tomato gratin makes a great side dish and is a delicious way to use up extra summer tomatoes. **Serves 4**

Preheat the oven to 350°F.

Heat 2 tablespoons of the olive oil in a stovetop-to-oven casserole dish over medium heat. Brown the bread cubes in batches, then transfer them to a bowl; add more oil as needed to brown the remaining cubes.

Add 1 tablespoon olive oil to the same pan. Cook the garlic over medium heat until it softens; stir in the tomatoes, sugar, salt and a grinding of pepper and cook until the tomatoes exude their juices. Return the bread cubes to the pan and press them down into the tomatoes. Sprinkle the cheese on top and bake until the casserole is set and nicely browned, 12 to 15 minutes. Sprinkle basil over the top and scoop from the pan to serve.

Polpette di Zucchine

Zucchini Meatballs

If you plant zucchini, you know how it can divide and conquer a garden. When that happens, the urge is to give them away, make zucchini soup, fry it, pickle it, sauté it, and the list goes on. My advice is to make these delicious and light-tasting meatballs. Serve them plain or with a light tomato sauce. They are perfect as an appetizer when made mini size. Change the texture by adding pine nuts or raisins, or come up with your own additions. Cooked rice or quinoa can be substituted for the breadcrumbs.   **Serves 8 to 10**

Preheat the oven to 350°F.

Spread out the zucchini on 2 nonstick baking sheets and place them in the oven. Turn off the heat and let the zucchini dry out for a couple of hours to remove excess water. This step can be done a day ahead. Refrigerate the zucchini until ready to use.

In a large bowl, combine the breadcrumbs, eggs, cheese, parsley, oregano, and salt. Coarsely chop the zucchini and add it to the bowl; mix well. Refrigerate the mixture for 20 minutes.

Scoop small amounts of the mixture into your hands and form meatballs the size of a small egg (to make about 18), or make them larger if you prefer. Put the flour in a shallow dish and roll the balls in the flour.

Heat the vegetable oil in a large sauté pan over medium-high heat and fry the meatballs, turning them occasionally so they brown evenly. (Alternatively, you can bake them in an oiled casserole dish in a 350°F oven for 20 to 25 minutes.) Transfer the meatballs to a serving dish; serve hot with tomato sauce, if desired.

2 medium zucchini, shredded

3 tablespoons extra-virgin olive

3 cloves garlic, minced

1¼ cups fresh breadcrumbs

2 large eggs, lightly beaten with a fork

⅔ cup grated Pecorino Romano cheese

½ cup minced fresh flat-leaf parsley

1½ teaspoons dried oregano

1 teaspoon fine sea salt

All-purpose flour, for dusting

¼ cup vegetable oil

Tomato sauce, for serving (optional)

Bistecca di Cavolfiore con Cime di Rapa e Formaggio

Cauliflower Steak with Broccoli Rapa and Cheese

⅓ cup extra-virgin olive oil, plus more for greasing the pan

Grated zest and juice of 1 large lemon

Salt and freshly ground black pepper to taste

1 large head cauliflower (or 2 medium heads), lower leaves removed and head cut from top to bottom into 4 (½-inch-thick) slices

2 cups cooked broccoli rapa

2 cups grated Asiago cheese

Roasting a whole head of cauliflower is popular, but cauliflower steak brings this vegetable to a new visual and taste level. Imagine thick slices slow-roasting in the oven until the edges are slightly caramelized—and to gild the lily for extra nutrition and a completely balanced meal, top it with cooked broccoli rapa and melting cheese. You could also use spinach or Swiss chard, or any other green vegetable you choose. **Serves 4**

Preheat the oven to 400°F. Brush a large nonstick baking sheet with olive oil.

In a bowl, whisk together the olive oil and lemon juice and season with salt and pepper. Brush both sides of each slice of cauliflower with the mixture and place them in a single layer on the baking sheet.

Roast for 25 minutes, then lower the heat to 325°F and carefully turn the slices over using two wide metal spatulas. Continue roasting until the cauliflower is fork-tender, about 15 minutes more. About 5 minutes before taking the cauliflower out of the oven, spread each slice with ½ cup of the broccoli rapa and sprinkle each one with ½ cup of the cheese Return to the oven until the cheese is melted. Serve hot.

My Italian Garden

On a misty Sunday morning, long before my neighbors have sipped their first cup of coffee, I make my way up the hill to work magic. I have everything I need: gloves, tools, water, dirt, and a plan.

My husband, Guy, is the master gardener and mastermind of the plan, conceived many years ago when he was a medical student. I am just the helper, and we have performed this ritual together for many years. Standing at the top of the hill, we survey the expanse of land before us and know what we have to do. We are about to create our Italian vegetable garden.

We have tender seedlings ready to go into their new home after spending some weeks under grow lights in the basement, where Guy has coaxed them from dormancy into life. And we have seeds that will be sown directly into the ground. It always amazes me how something as tiny as a peppercorn, placed in the ground, can come crashing through the earth's crust and claim its place as a living plant in the garden.

I have learned so much about growing vegetables from Guy, who aside from having a busy life as a physician, has maintained our garden since we have been married. Each year the garden has grown in size from just a small plot behind our apartment complex to a 60-by-30-foot garden that supplies us with enough vegetables to literally feed the neighborhood.

I want to be truthful: Our garden has ruined us. It has made us aware of the quality of homegrown produce and acutely aware of how lucky we are to be able to grow our own vegetables. Yes, we have become food snobs. We demand fresh, pesticide-free foods and, like so many others these days, we want to know what is in our food. This attitude is not without sacrifice, because organizing, planting, maintaining, harvesting, and putting food by is not for those without dedication or ambition. In a word, a vegetable garden is *work*. And don't think that it is cheaper to have a garden than spend

money at the grocery store. It is more expensive when you add up the hours, cost of equipment, plants and seeds, along with fertilizer, black plastic to keep out the weeds . . . you get the picture.

So why do it? Because we know better. We know that our food supply has been tinkered with by giant agribusinesses whose goal is to make money at the expense of our wellbeing. Genetically modified foods (GMOs) are now the norm. If you don't believe me, just look at the number of farmers' markets that have exploded across the country. People know that eating local is better, and they trust their local farmers to provide honest food that they are willing to pay a little more for. I realize that not everyone has a garden, but farmers' markets can fill that void—and so can your local supermarket if you choose wisely and buy as locally as possible.

As the daily gifts from my garden make their way into my kitchen, I think ahead to the long winter months when the garden rests and I get to work preserving as many vegetables as I can. Swiss chard, zucchini, beans, tomatoes, squash, and many others are turned into soup or blanched, canned, or frozen and when the first blast of cold arrives, all those efforts from the day that the first seedling was planted begin to repay us in a big way.

Fish

Fish and seafood, Amalfi coast

It's the eyes. That is what some travelers have a hard time with when they see whole fish being served in Italy. I try to get them to understand that one of the best things about eating in Italy is knowing that the ingredients are fresh, and whole fish means not only fresh but local.

Given that Italy is surrounded by water on three sides, it is easy to understand why seafood is a big part of the diet. To really get to know Italy's rich variety of fish and shellfish, take a walk through a local fish market, like the colorful and boisterous Ballarò market in Palermo, Sicily, or the fish market in the Trastevere neighborhood of Rome, or the more reserved Rialto fish market in Venice. A dizzying selection of octopus, squid, swordfish, tuna, shrimp, baccala, rombo, eel, anchovy, dentice, scorpion, orata, branzino, trout, scallops, clams, and sea urchins would just be the beginning of what you would see.

Fish can be boiled, baked, fried, breaded, stuffed, stewed, or grilled. For me there is nothing more delicious than grilled delicate branzino, served with juicy lemon wedges and a drizzle of extra-virgin olive oil. It is what I order in Italy each chance I get. The classic *fritto misto di pesce* (fish fry) gives the hungry fish lover an opportunity to try different kinds of fish that are dusted in flour, quickly fried in olive oil, and served with tangy lemon wedges. Marinated cold fish dishes like anchovy and sardines are an integral part of antipasti.

Fish stews that go by names like *brodetto, cacciucco*, and *zuppa di pesce* are popular as a first or main course. The type of fish used varies from place to place, but one thing is for sure: A fish stew will contain more than one type of fish. We can thank the fisherman and shrewd cooks of a bygone era for this because nothing went to waste; the trimmings, including the heads, were cooked together with a few herbs and maybe some wine and water to create a tasty stew. In Livorno, Tuscany a fish stew must contain at least five different kinds, one for every letter c in the dialect word *cacciucco*, meaning "stew." That makes cacciucco alla Livornese a pretty expensive dish by today's standards, but it is up to the cook to decide how many fish to use; some use only one or two. The history of this dish involves a story that dates back almost five hundred years. It seems that a poor fisherman lost his life in a shipwreck, leaving his children with no one, so neighboring fishermen took pity on them, gathering what fish they had and turning it into stew. The more realistic reason is that whatever fishermen did not sell was thrown into the pot and became stew or soup.

The best brodetto that I have ever had was in Porto Recanati in the Marche region, where cooks rigidly adhere to tradition like using saffron and being very picky about the freshness of the fish.

Fish Market, Palermo, Sicily

Ippoglosso al Burro e Dragoncello

Pan-Grilled Halibut with Tarragon Butter Sauce

8 tablespoons unsalted butter

4 tablespoons minced fresh tarragon

Grated zest and juice of 1 large lemon

2¼ tablespoons lemon pepper seasoning

1 tablespoon fine sea salt

4 (6-ounce) halibut steaks

Halibut has a dense texture, making it suitable for grilling, baking, or pan-frying. Its delicate taste makes it a candidate for a variety of seasonings and sauces but butter and fresh tarragon sauce with a squeeze of fresh lemon juice gets my vote every time. For frying, the important thing is to get a well-seasoned cast iron pan smoking hot before adding the fish. This will prevent it from sticking and will result in a beautiful crust. How will you know when it is cooked? Use a trusty instant-read thermometer—the fish is cooked at 140°F.   **Serves 4**

Melt the butter in a small saucepan over very low heat. Stir in the tarragon, lemon zest, and juice and keep the sauce warm while the fish cooks.

Place a well-seasoned cast iron pan over very high heat until it is smoking hot, then lower the heat to medium-high. (Alternatively, you can place the cast iron pan directly on a preheated grill until it is very hot.)

Meanwhile, mix the lemon pepper and salt together in a small bowl and spread it out on a sheet of wax paper. Place the halibut pieces on top of the seasoning mixture and press it into the fish. Turn the fish over and do the same on the other side. Rub the mixture evenly on both sides.

Place the fish in the hot pan and watch it cook, taking on great color in no time with no sticking whatsoever. Cook for about 6 minutes on each side, depending on the thickness of the fish. The fish is cooked when an instant-read thermometer inserted in the center of each steak registers 140°F.

Transfer the halibut steaks to 4 dinner plates and pour the warm sauce over the top. Serve immediately.

Venerdì Torte di Pesce

Friday Fish Cakes

My mother was a firm believer in the health benefits of fish, serving it too often for my taste when I was a child. That was one reason why I dreaded the season of Lent, a time when every Friday meant some sort of fish would be on my plate, when all I really wanted was a hamburger and French fries! And as if that were not enough, Mom also made my siblings and me swallow a tablespoon of fish oil every night after supper, Lent or no Lent. When I look back on those days, I can see that Mom was way ahead of her time if you consider all the prodding we get these days about how good fish and fish oil is for our health. One of Mom's stand-by recipes for Lent was fish cakes, formed like meatballs and then slightly flattened so that they resembled round disks.   **Serves 4**

1½ cups soft fresh breadcrumbs

¼ cup milk

3 large eggs

2 tablespoons minced fresh flat-leaf parsley

Salt and coarsely ground black pepper

1 pound fresh monkfish, haddock, flounder, or cod fillets, cut into 4-inch pieces

3 cups water

1 small carrot, peeled and cut in half

1 small onion, peeled and quartered

¼ to ⅓ cup unbleached all-purpose flour

¾ cup dry breadcrumbs

2 to 3 cups vegetable oil, for frying

Lemon wedges, for serving

Whisk together the fresh breadcrumbs, milk, 1 egg, parsley, 1 teaspoon salt, and ¼ teaspoon pepper in a small bowl. Set aside.

In a shallow sauté pan, combine the fish, water, carrot, onion, and salt to taste; simmer until the fish easily flakes, 8 to 10 minutes, depending on the type and thickness of the fish.

Carefully lift the fish out of the water with a slotted metal spatula or strainer and transfer it to a bowl to cool to room temperature. Dice the carrot and add it to the breadcrumb mixture. Discard the cooking water and onion. Flake the fish with a fork, then add it to the breadcrumb mixture; season with salt and pepper and combine well.

Put the flour on one plate and the dry breadcrumbs on another. In a shallow bowl, beat the remaining 2 eggs lightly with a fork.

With wet hands, divide the fish mixture evenly into 8 balls. Roll each ball in the flour and shake off the excess. Coat the balls in the beaten egg, then roll them in the breadcrumbs, coating them evenly. Place the balls on a plate and press down slightly on them with your hand to flatten them a little.

In a deep pot or deep-fryer, heat the vegetable oil to 375°F. Fry the fish cakes in the oil until golden brown, 4 to 5 minutes. Drain on absorbent paper and serve hot, accompanied by lemon wedges.

Pesce al Forno al Limone, Pomodori e Olive

Baked Fish with Lemon, Tomatoes, and Olives

Italian cooks do not like to tinker too much with fresh fish. Their reasoning is that the freshness speaks for itself and needs only the right cooking treatment, either grilled or baked, and just a touch of seasonings.   **Serves 4**

Preheat the oven to 400°F. Lightly brush a casserole dish with olive oil.

Lay the fillets in a single layer in the casserole. Alternate laying tomato slices and lemon slices over the fillets. Scatter the olives around the dish. Season with salt and pepper and drizzle all with olive oil.

Bake for 8 to 10 minutes, or until an instant read thermometer registers between 140°F and 145°F and the fish flakes easily when poked with a fork. Serve immediately.

Extra-virgin olive oil, for greasing the pan and drizzling

4 (6-ounce) fish fillets, such as cod, haddock, or sea bass

2 large beefsteak tomatoes, sliced into ¼-inch-thick rounds

2 lemons, cut into thin rounds

½ cup pitted black oil-cured olives

Salt and freshly ground black pepper to taste

Pesce Misto al Bricole

Mixed Fish Casserole with Buttery Cracker Crumbs

This quick stovetop chowder uses a mixture of fish, and the cracker crumb topping gives an added texture. Be sure all the fish pieces are cut to uniform size (about 2 inches) to ensure even cooking.   **Serves 4**

CRACKER TOPPING

5 tablespoons unsalted butter

1½ cups Ritz crackers, finely crushed

FISH

2 pounds mixed cut-up chowder fish, such as haddock, cod, halibut, and monkfish

Grated zest of 1 lemon plus 2 tablespoons lemon juice

1 small onion, finely minced

SAUCE

2 tablespoons unsalted butter

2 tablespoons unbleached all-purpose flour

1 fish bouillon cube dissolved in 1¼ cups boiling water

Salt to taste

2 tablespoons minced fresh tarragon

2 tablespoons minced fresh thyme

To make the cracker topping, melt the butter in a 9-inch stovetop casserole dish or cast iron skillet. Stir in the cracker crumbs and coat them well. Transfer them to a bowl and set aside.

Toss the fish pieces, lemon zest, and juice and together in a large bowl. Set aside.

To make the sauce, melt the butter over medium heat in the same casserole used to brown the breadcrumbs; whisk in the flour and continue whisking until a smooth paste is formed. Slowly pour in the hot fish bouillon and continue to whisk until the mixture begins to thicken; keep the consistency loose. Season with salt. Stir in the tarragon and thyme.

Transfer the fish mixture to the casserole dish and gently combine it with the sauce. Cover and cook the casserole for 6 to 8 minutes, or just until the fish easily flakes with a fork. Sprinkle the cracker topping over the top of the casserole and serve hot.

Spaghetti e Calamari della Vigilia di Natale

Christmas Eve Spaghetti and Squid

This colorful spaghetti and squid dish was served every Christmas Eve when I was growing up. It was brought to the table on a platter with great ceremony by my mother, who somehow seemed to disappear in a cloud of fog created by the hot spaghetti.   **Serves 6**

Bring a large pot of water to a boil over high heat. Stir in 1 tablespoon salt, lower the heat to a simmer, and add the squid. Cover the pot and cook the squid until fork tender, 15 to 20 minutes. Remove the squid with a slotted spoon or strainer and transfer to a bowl.

In a large sauté pan, heat the olive oil over medium heat. Add the garlic cloves and cook for 2 to 3 minutes, just to flavor the oil. As soon as the garlic turns golden, remove and discard it. Add the red pepper flakes and cook for 1 minute, being careful not to burn them. Add the squid, cover, and keep warm over low heat.

Return the pot of water to a boil and cook the broccoli florets until crisp-tender, about 5 minutes. Scoop the broccoli out of the water with a strainer and add them to the squid; cover to keep warm.

Add the spaghetti to the boiling water and cook until al dente. Drain, reserving ½ cup of the cooking water, and add it to the squid and broccoli mixture along with the spaghetti. Mix well over medium-low heat until hot.

Transfer the mixture to a platter. Sprinkle with the cheese, if desired, and add a good grinding of black pepper. Serve at once.

*Serving cheese with fish dishes has long been frowned upon by Italians who claim it competes with the delicate flavor of the fish. You be the judge.

Salt to taste

2 pounds squid rings

½ cup extra-virgin olive oil

2 cloves garlic, peeled

1½ teaspoons red pepper flakes, or more to taste

1 medium head broccoli, broken into small florets

1 pound spaghetti

1 cup grated Pecorino Romano cheese (optional)*

Freshly ground black pepper to taste

Pesce al Cartoccio

Fish in Paper

This is a popular way to cook fish in Italy. It is both healthful and very quick, and impressive enough for company. Wrapping the fish in parchment paper keeps it moist and creates tasty juices. Paper-thin slices of vegetables are cooked along with the fish, providing a complete meal with no cleanup. In the summer, wrap the fish in foil and put it on the grill. Any firm-fleshed white fish works well in this recipe. **Serves 4**

Preheat the oven to 450°F. Place a large sheet of parchment paper or aluminum foil on a rimmed baking sheet large enough to hold the fish in a single layer. Brush the paper or foil with 1 tablespoon of the olive oil.

Spread out the spinach on the paper or foil and place the fish pieces side by side on top. Place the fennel leaves on the fish and scatter the vegetables over them. Drizzle with the remaining 2 tablespoons olive oil and season with salt and pepper. Place a second sheet of paper or foil over the top and fold in the edges to seal.

Bake the fish for 10 to 12 minutes, depending on the thickness. Carefully unwrap the fish. Serve the fish with some of the vegetables and juices spooned over the top.

3 tablespoons extra-virgin olive oil

4 (6-ounce) fish fillets, such as cod, haddock, salmon, halibut, monkfish, sea bass, or flounder

4 cups fresh spinach

½ fennel bulb, sliced paper-thin, plus 4 fennel leaves

1 onion, sliced paper-thin

1 carrot, sliced paper-thin

Salt and freshly ground black pepper to taste

Capesante Grigliate agli Agrumi

Citrus-Marinated Grilled Scallops

Grated zest and
juice of 2 medium
lemons

¼ cup extra-virgin
olive oil

1 teaspoon minced
garlic

Salt and freshly
ground black
pepper to taste

2 pounds dry sea
scallops

Italian scallops are very sweet. The best ones I ever had were in landlocked Umbria! One day, while staying in Perugia, the capital, I drove to a nearby fish market that had the most beautiful display of succulent-looking scallops still in their colorful tortoiseshell-patterned shells. I asked one of the fishmongers what his secret was for cooking them. He looked at me with amusement while he quickly opened a scallop shell, scooped out the pearl-colored meat and popped it into his mouth! But don't worry, in this recipe they are grilled. Be sure to always buy dry scallops as opposed to wet scallops, which have been treated with water and sodium tripolyphosphate. **Serves 4 to 6**

In a shallow dish large enough to hold the scallops in a single layer, combine the lemon zest, juice, olive oil, and garlic. Season with salt and pepper. Add the scallops and toss to coat them well with the marinade. Cover the dish and refrigerate for 1 hour.

Heat the grill and lightly brush the grill grate with oil. Thread 5 or 6 scallops on individual skewers and place them on the hot grill. Grill, basting occasionally with the marinade and turning the skewers, just until the scallops are cooked through, about 3 minutes. Serve immediately.

Gamberetti al Rosmarino Grigliati e Marinati

Grilled and Marinated Rosemary-Scented Shrimp

Shrimp are grilled first, then marinated, in this clever and tasty dish.
Serves 4

Heat the grill and brush the grate with a little olive oil.

In a shallow nonmetal dish, whisk together the olive oil, vinegar, garlic, and rosemary. Season with salt and pepper. Set aside.

Thread 5 or 6 shrimp on individual skewers and grill the shrimp for about 2 minutes on each side. Remove the shrimp from the skewers and add them to the marinade, tossing to coat them well. Cover and refrigerate for several hours, turning them frequently in the marinade.

Allow the shrimp to come to room temperature, in the marinade, before serving them with some of the marinade as a sauce.

Note: Soak a couple of whole rosemary sprigs in water and throw them on the grill just before cooking the shrimp. This imparts a wonderful rosemary-smoked taste to the shrimp.

½ cup extra-virgin olive oil

3 tablespoons red wine vinegar

2 cloves garlic, finely minced

2 tablespoons fresh rosemary needles

Salt and freshly ground black pepper to taste

1 pound medium shrimp (26–30 count), peeled and deveined

Gamberi in Salsa di Birra Piccante

Shrimp Cooked in Beer

I can't say that I ever took a liking to beer, but it makes a great brothy sauce for shrimp. Peroni and Moretti are Italian brands that are available here in the States. Beer plays nicely off of the spicy peppercorns and the sweetness of the leeks.   **Serves 4**

Toast the peppercorns in a small skillet for a couple of minutes until fragrant. Transfer them to a spice mill, add ½ teaspoon of the coarse salt, and grind them to a powder. Transfer to a small dish and set aside.

Combine the beer, sugar, and ½ teaspoon salt in a baking dish; add the shrimp. Cover and marinate in the refrigerator for a couple of hours.

When ready to cook, pour the chicken broth into a saucepan and bring it to a boil. Add the farro and cook until tender and the liquid is absorbed. Stir in 1 tablespoon of the olive oil and the remaining ½ teaspoon salt; keep warm while the shrimp are cooking.

Heat the remaining 2 tablespoons oil in a sauté pan; add the leeks and cook over medium heat until they soften. Add the shrimp with the marinade and cook until the shrimp turn pink. Stir in the ground spice mixture and toss well.

Divide the farro among 4 soup bowls and ladle in some of the shrimp with the broth. Serve hot.

½ teaspoon whole black peppercorns

¼ teaspoon whole pink peppercorns

¾ teaspoon coarse salt

1½ cups light-colored beer

1 tablespoon brown sugar

2 pounds large shrimp (21–25 count), peeled and deveined

3 cups chicken broth, homemade (page 38) or store-bought

1¼ cups farro

3 tablespoons extra-virgin olive oil

½ cup diced leeks

Gamberetti alla Salsa di Rucola

Shrimp in Arugula Sauce

2 tablespoons distilled white vinegar

2 pounds large shrimp (21–25 count), in the shell

1½ cups packed arugula leaves

1 teaspoon coarse salt

1 cup extra-virgin olive oil

1 soft-boiled egg, yolk only

1 sweet red bell pepper, cored, seeded, and diced

Lemon wedges, for serving (optional)

Arugula, also called "rocket," is a member of the chicory family, and its spicy, sharp peppery flavor lends itself to many uses. Add it to the salad bowl for sure, but also try it as a sauce for shrimp. The vibrant green sauce is a nice contrast against the pinkish shrimp. Serve with good crusty bread for dipping in the sauce.   **Serves 8**

Bring a large pot of water to a boil over high heat. Add the vinegar and shrimp, cover, and bring back to the boil. Cook until the shrimp shells turn pink, about 2 minutes. Drain the shrimp and let cool. Peel and devein them.

Combine the arugula and salt in a food processor or blender and pulse to puree it. With the motor running, slowly add the olive oil through the feed tube. Add the egg yolk and pulse until the mixture is smooth.

Arrange 5 or 6 shrimp on individual salad plates. Drizzle some of the sauce over the top and sprinkle the shrimp with the diced red pepper. Garnish each plate with a lemon wedge, if desired.

Vongole con Vermicelli

Clams with Vermicelli

I got lost in Venice a few years ago in a confusing maze of narrow streets, but that turned out to be a good thing because I discovered a group of fishmongers displaying gorgeous-looking seafood on ice-covered wooden tables. The variety was spectacular, with everything from orange-red spiny lobsters to tiny glistening clams. That night I had dinner at La Barcaiola and ordered little clams with vermicelli. They were delicate and sweet. Littleneck clams are used in this recipe; use whatever is available in your area.   **Serves 4**

3 dozen littleneck clams in the shell

¼ cup water

2 tablespoons chopped fresh flat-leaf parsley

½ cup extra-virgin olive oil

3 cloves garlic, chopped

7 medium plum tomatoes, peeled, seeded, and diced

½ cup dry white wine

Salt and freshly ground black pepper to taste

1 pound vermicelli

Rinse the clams well in cold water and discard any with cracked shells. Soak the clams in a bowl of cold water for about 45 minutes, changing the water frequently.

Drain the clams, put them in a large sauté pan, and add the ¼ cup fresh water. Cover the pan and cook over medium-high heat until the clams open, about 5 minutes. Remove the clams from the pan, discarding any that have not opened, and strain the cooking liquid into a bowl. When cool, remove the clams from their shells and place them in a small bowl. Add the chopped parsley and toss to mix.

In the same pan, heat the olive oil over medium heat. Add the garlic and cook until it softens. Add the tomatoes and cook for 5 minutes. Add the wine and reserved clam liquid and cook for about 5 minutes, or until the sauce has reduced by a third. Add the clams and season with salt and pepper. Cover and keep warm over very low heat.

Bring a large pot of water to a boil over high heat. Add 1 tablespoon salt and the vermicelli and cook until it is al dente. Drain the vermicelli, reserving ¼ cup of the cooking water, and transfer it with the vermicelli to the clam mixture. Mix everything well over medium-low heat and serve.

Insalata di Mare

Seafood Salad

3 lemons, 1 cut into ¼-inch slices and 2 juiced

Coarse sea salt to taste

1 pound large dry sea scallops, cut in half crosswise

1½ pounds large shrimp (21–25 count), unpeeled

1 pound squid rings

⅔ cup extra-virgin olive oil

1 teaspoon coarse sea salt

¼ teaspoon celery salt

8 ounces lump crabmeat

Coarse colored Margarita salt (optional)

½ cup minced fresh mint

2 large blood oranges or navel oranges, 1 juiced and 1 cut into 8 wedges

This rich and succulent seafood medley is best when allowed to marinate for several hours or overnight. The presentation is nice, too.
Serves 8

Fill a medium saucepan with water; add the lemon slices and a pinch of salt and bring to a boil. Lower the heat to a simmer, add the scallops, and gently cook them for about 3 minutes, or just until they look opaque. Remove the scallops with a slotted spoon to a large bowl, keeping them in a pile. Set aside.

Add the shrimp to the saucepan and cook them for about 2 minutes, just until the shells turn pink; remove the shrimp with a slotted spoon. Cool, peel, and devein the shrimp. Place them in the bowl with the scallops.

Add the squid rings to the saucepan and simmer them for about 20 minutes, or until they are tender. Cooking them too fast over high heat will make them tough. Remove the squid rings with a slotted spoon and add them to the bowl.

Pour the olive oil into a 9 x 12-inch glass casserole dish. Stir in the lemon juice, celery salt, and 1 teaspoon salt. Mix well. Add the scallops, shrimp, squid, and crabmeat to the olive oil mixture. Stir to combine well. Cover the dish with plastic wrap and refrigerate it for at least 3 hours or overnight.

When ready to serve, have 8 martini glasses or small ice cream sundae dishes ready. Wet the rims of each glass and dip the rims in Margarita salt, if desired.

Stir the mint into the seafood mixture and spoon it into the individual glasses. Pour a little of the fresh orange juice over each dish. Make a small knife slit in the center of each orange wedge and anchor one over the rim of each glass. Serve.

Ancileddi cu Pumaruoru

Baked Fish, Sicilian Style

2 tablespoons
extra-virgin olive
oil, plus more for
greasing the pan

2 pounds (½-inch-
thick) tuna steaks

1 clove garlic, finely
minced

4 cups Fresh Tomato-
Basil Sauce
(page 141)

1 tablespoon
chopped fresh
flat-leaf parsley

Salt and freshly
ground black
pepper to taste

I have known Giovanni Iapichino for years; he is from Palermo but studied in the States. He is passionate about Sicilian cooking and gave me this quick recipe for fish cooked in tomato sauce. Swordfish and tuna are two of the most popular fish on the island, but any firm fish will do. **Serves 4**

Preheat the oven to 450°F.

Oil a baking dish large enough to hold the tuna steaks in a single layer and place them in the dish. Brush the fish lightly with the olive oil and sprinkle with the garlic. Spoon the tomato sauce over the fish and sprinkle with the chopped parsley; season with salt and pepper.

Cover the dish with aluminum foil and bake for 20 minutes, or until the internal temperature registers 145°F on an instant-read thermometer. Serve immediately.

Meat and Poultry

In my opinion, the best way to get to know Italy's cuisine is to spend some time in the *mercato publico* (local market). Saturday is a big market day all over Italy, but small towns also have a market day during the week. All the best that Italy has to offer in the way of fresh foods can be experienced on market day.

Going to market is serious business. Elderly women in black dresses, carrying string shopping bags, walk arm in arm from stall to stall commenting on the freshness of the fruits and vegetables. A stylishly dressed young couple argues with the meat vendor about the size of the scaloppini. The fishmonger has all he can do to keep up with the scores of people waiting to take home fresh-caught eels, shrimp, octopus, spiny lobster, squid, trout, and more. Groups of men stand around and talk about the latest soccer game with their *amici intimi* (buddies) and the *bambini* (children) are hugged and kissed by everyone.

The meats for sale look good enough to eat raw. The cuts are lean and with good color. Lamb, pork, beef, veal, horse, donkey,

Cooking school in Martina Franca

and goat are available in many cuts, and there are even signs that direct you to *carne per i gatti e cani* (meat for cats and dogs). There is a special section for rabbit, pigeon, chicken, duck, or turkey, and your choice will be freshly dressed while you wait.

In Italy meat is eaten in small portions, and in the past was considered a luxury only to be enjoyed on special occasions. There are many, well known regional meat specialties, including *bistecca alla fiorentina*, the famous grilled porterhouse steak of Florence served rare with a drizzle of extra-virgin olive oil and a squirt of lemon juice. *Cotoletta alla Milanese*, the classic veal cutlet dish of Milan, is coated in breadcrumbs and fried in clarified butter. In Rome, *abbacchio al forno* (tender spring lamb) is roasted to perfection. In Umbria, *porchetta* (whole roasted suckling pig) is the star, with its bronzed crackling skin and rosemary-scented meat that lures lines of shoppers to stop and buy a *panino di porchetta* (roast pork sandwich).

Artisan cured meats (salumi) from many regions are represented, including prosciutto di Parma ham cured only with air, salt, and time. Delicious mortadella di Bologna, a cooked pork sausage in a casing, is made from finely ground pork and studded with *lardelli* (small pieces of fat); it has a delicate taste and velvet texture, while *soppressata di cinghiale* (cured wild boar sausage) from Tuscany is bold and complex in flavor. There are many more. Some of these products, like prosciutto di Parma, prosciutto di San Daniele, and speck are available in the States, while FDA rules prohibit the entry of many other salumi.

For the most part, Italians like their meats and poultry cooked simply, either boiled, grilled, baked, or fried.

The Ham That Wears the Crown

The heavy steel doors to the refrigeration room are rolled open, and my face immediately prickles from the cold air. Suspended above me is an aerial display of hundreds of hams taking time to rest and cure. Each one is a unique, artisan product, the result of the work of salting masters who know just the right amount of salt to rub into them to sufficiently cure them without drying them out and destroying their delicate flavor. These are not your average run-of-the-mill hams; this is prosciutto di Parma, known the world over as the king of ham, and each one, when fully cured for a minimum of twelve months, will sport a fire-branded five-point ducal crown on its skin to prove its authenticity. Italy produces over 9 million of these hams per year, 1.1 million of which are exported worldwide—more than six hundred thousand to the States alone.

I have made the trip to Bedogni Egidio, the *prosciuttificio* (prosciutto factory) in Langhirano, in the province of Parma, to see the carefully orchestrated process of producing these hams. The Bedogni Egidio factory alone produces more than one hundred thousand hams per year. The tradition of producing these hams goes back centuries, to a time when ancient tribes of Cisalpine Gaul bred pigs and cured the meat in the area between the Via Emilia and the Enza River. Because of the geographic presence of the Apennine mountains, a near-perfect environment exists for curing the hams with nothing more than salt, time, and mountain air.

Pork products have always had a place of honor on the Emilian table and, like the production of Parmigiano-Reggiano cheese, the making of prosciutto di Parma is controlled by law, with its production overseen by the Consorzio del Prosciutto di Parma, the body responsible for establishing the rules governing the production of these hams. Once the hams are cured and final inspection takes place by trained specialists, the five-pointed crown is branded on the ham, certifying its authenticity.

Prosciutto di Parma is a DOP (Protected Designation of Origin) product and, as its name implies, can be made only in and around the province of Parma from special breeds of pigs eating a controlled diet of whey (the leftovers of the cheese-making process), grains like barley and corn, and fruits. Approximately 150 Parma ham producers belong to the Consorzio del Prosciutto di Parma. The pigs must come from northern or central Italy, be slaughtered between ten and twelve months old, and weigh between 350 and 440 pounds. A fat pig is ideal because the amount of fat is a key factor in preventing the meat from drying out as it cures. The hind leg of the pig is selected after slaughtering, and *la salagione* (the salting process) begins. This is where the experience and innate sense of the *maestro salatore* (salting master) comes into play. First, coarse salt is rubbed onto the leg and the meat is refrigerated for three weeks, after which time a second salting is applied. Salt and cold air draw out the moisture; that is where the name *prosciutto* comes from, since *prosciugare* means "to dry out." The mastery comes from knowing just what areas of the leg need salt, and how much. After a resting period of two months, the hams are washed of excess salt and hung to dry for several days. As the aging process continues, the hams are covered with lard and placed in cool, airy attics, where

they are hung on special wood frames called *scalere* to further develop their unique flavor. The amount of airflow is very important; to that end, a series of shuttered windows are opened and closed with attention paid to internal and external humidity.

After twelve months, the traditional tapping of the ham takes place by inspectors to determine the quality of the ham. Using the femur bone of a horse, which is odorless, the inspector punctures the ham in several places, and the smells emitted onto the bone are ones that he recognizes that can pronounce the ham ready for its crown, the stamp of approval. Once branded, the hams are ready for market, although some can be aged for up to thirty-six months.

Prosciutto di Parma shows up in many Italian dishes, but the best way to serve it is on its own as an antipasto, the salmon-pink meat sliced paper-thin, with a white line of creamy fat outlining its edges. Slices are draped or curled into "roses" on a serving plate and enjoyed alone or with an accompaniment of bread, melon, or figs. Perfect Parma ham has a mild flavor, with a smooth, silken texture that is neither too salty nor too bland.

Recent studies in Italy have produced some interesting facts relating to the health benefits of eating prosciutto di Parma. The most interesting findings come from the analysis of the fats, which showed that Parma ham has a high percentage of oleic acid, the main component of olive oil, which we know to be beneficial in preventing hardening of the arteries. The cholesterol content is comparable to that of beef, veal, chicken, or rabbit, and a 1-ounce serving has only 75 calories and 6 grams of fat .

From a nutritional point of view, prosciutto di Parma is easily digestible and better for the digestive process than any other meat. It is also rich in free amino acids, which is one reason it is recommended for athletes. And the fact that there are no additives, except for salt, makes it an excellent food for everyone. With all that in its favor, it's no wonder that prosciutto di Parma is the ham that wears the crown.

Stufato di Manzo

Beef Stew

A beef stew has rich flavor if care is taken to marinate the meat first. In this recipe, a rump roast soaks in aromatic vegetable and wine before it is cooked.   **Serves 6 to 8**

With a small knife, make l-inch-deep incisions all over the meat and insert the pancetta. Put the roast in a deep nonmetal dish and scatter the celery, carrots, and onion around the meat. Tie the herb sprigs together with kitchen string and add to the pot, along with the cinnamon stick and bay leaf. Pour the wine over the meat. Cover and let marinate in the refrigerator for at least 8 hours, or overnight, turning the meat occasionally.

In a large Dutch oven or heavy-duty pot, heat the olive oil over medium heat. Remove the meat, reserving the marinade, and dry the meat with paper towels. Brown it on all sides in the olive oil.

Add the reserved marinade to the pan and season with salt and pepper. Bring to a boil, then lower the heat, cover, and simmer for about 2 hours, or until the meat is very tender.

When the roast is nearly done, make the sauce. In a saucepan, melt the butter over medium heat. Add the pancetta and cook until it is crisp. Add the pearl onions and cook for about 5 minutes, turning to glaze them in the fat, until browned. Add the mushrooms and cook until soft. Set aside.

Transfer the roast to a cutting board. Strain the meat juices into a bowl, pressing on the solids with the back of a spoon to extract as much as possible. Discard the solids. Add the pancetta and mushroom sauce to the cooking juices and cover to keep warm.

Carve the meat into serving pieces, arrange them on a platter, and spoon some of the sauce over them.

BEEF

1 (3-pound) rump roast

2 (¼-inch-thick) slices pancetta, diced

1½ cups sliced celery

1½ cup sliced carrots

1½ cup thinly sliced onion

1 sprig fresh rosemary

1 sprig fresh thyme

1 sprig fresh sage

1 small cinnamon stick

1 bay leaf

4 cups dry red wine

3 tablespoons extra-virgin olive oil

Salt and freshly ground black pepper to taste

SAUCE

3 tablespoons unsalted butter

½ cup diced pancetta

12 small pearl onions, peeled

1½ cups sliced button mushrooms

Spiedo Misto

Mixed Grill

In Umbria at La Stalla, a rustic outdoor ristorante, I sat under a grape arbor at a long picnic table covered with red-and-white checked table-cloths. Everything on the menu was cooked in the classic Umbrian style, *alla griglia* (grilled on an open fire). I ordered spiedo misto, which was more than a wise choice because it prompted the other diners at the table, who were all locals, to engage me in a delightful conversation about the merits of Umbrian foods.   **Serves 8**

Cut the meats into l-inch pieces. Season the pork with salt and pepper and rub with the garlic. Season the beef or veal with salt and pepper and sprinkle with the minced sage. Season the chicken with salt and pepper and sprinkle with the minced rosemary. Set aside.

In a sauté pan, heat the olive oil over medium heat and cook the peppers until they are crisp-tender. Add the wine and cook until the liquid is reduced by about half.

Thread metal skewers in this order: pork, bell pepper, chicken, pancetta, sage leaf, beef or veal, bell pepper, and sausage. Do not crowd too many pieces on each skewer. Place the skewers in a nonmetal dish large enough to hold them in a single layer and drizzle the lemon juice and olive oil over them. Let them marinate for several hours in the refrigerator, basting and turning them often.

Heat the grill and lightly oil the grill rack. Remove the skewers from the marinade; place them on the grill, and baste with the marinade. Grill, turning and basting the skewers, until done to taste, 8 to 12 minutes.

---

1 pound boneless pork loin

1 pound boneless beef or veal loin

1 pound boneless, skinless chicken thighs

Coarse sea salt and coarsely ground black pepper to taste

3 cloves garlic, peeled and crushed

2 tablespoons minced fresh sage, plus a small bunch of fresh sage leaves

2 tablespoons minced fresh rosemary needles

¼ cup extra-virgin olive oil

3 medium bell peppers (an assortment of red, green, and yellow), cored, seeded, and cut into 2-inch squares

¼ cup dry white wine

4 thick slices pancetta, cut into 1-inch squares

12 ounces sweet or hot Italian sausage, cut into chunks

½ cup fresh lemon juice

extra-virgin olive oil to drizzle on top

Carbonada Valdostana

Beef Stew with Polenta

1 (2-pound) chuck roast, cut into 1-inch cubes

Salt and freshly ground black pepper

½ teaspoon grated nutmeg

1 cup unbleached all-purpose flour

4 tablespoons (½ stick) unsalted butter

1 large onion, finely minced

2 sprigs fresh thyme

2 sprigs fresh sage

2 sprigs fresh flat-leaf parsley

1 bay leaf

1 whole cinnamon stick

2 cups dry red wine

Polenta (recipe follows), for serving

Val d'Aosta is Italy's smallest and least-known region, located in the northwest corner of the Italian Alps. It is known for its rustic cooking, and one of its most famous dishes is a beef stew originally made from salt-preserved beef that was very dark in color, like coal; hence the name *carbonada*, meaning "carbon." This is a very flavorful stew marinated in red wine, herbs, and spices. The stew is traditionally served over polenta.   **Serves 4 to 6**

Place the meat in a large bowl and season with salt, pepper, and nutmeg. Cover and refrigerate overnight. When ready to cook, bring the meat to room temperature.

Put the flour in a large paper bag and add the meat cubes. Close the bag and shake to lightly coat the cubes. Shake off the excess flour and transfer the meat cubes to a plate.

Melt the butter in a stew pot over medium heat and brown the meat cubes, in batches, on all sides. Transfer the cubes to a dish as they brown.

Add the onion to the pan and cook gently until soft. Season with salt and pepper. Return the meat to the pan with the onion.

Tie the herb sprigs, bay leaf, and cinnamon stick together with kitchen string and add to the pot. Pour in the wine. Bring to a boil, then lower the heat to low. Cover and simmer for about 2 hours, or until the meat is fork tender. Remove and discard the herbs and cinnamon stick.

Pour the polenta onto a serving platter, add the beef cubes and sauce, and serve hot. Alternatively, you can spread out the cooked polenta on an oiled rimmed baking sheet and refrigerate it until firm, then cut into slices and lightly pan-fry them in olive oil. Serve with the beef.

Polenta

Combine the cornmeal with 2 cups of the water in a bowl; cover and let stand for several hours or overnight. This will cut down on the cooking time.

When ready to cook, transfer the cornmeal to a heavy-duty saucepan and add the remaining 2½ cups water and the salt and stir the mixture well. Bring to a boil, lower the heat, and cook, stirring often, until the mixture thickens and begins to bubble and leave the sides of the pan, about 30 minutes.

4½ cups cold water
1 cup cornmeal
1 teaspoon salt

Crocchette di Cuneo

Croquettes, Cuneo Style

1 pound ground veal

1 Golden Delicious or Pippin apple, peeled and grated

1 large egg

¼ teaspoon salt

½ cup unbleached all-purpose flour, for dusting

2 tablespoons extra-virgin olive oil

½ cup dry red wine

Apples are a common ingredient in savory dishes from Cuneo, in the Piedmont region. I have come to be very fond of these little veal croquettes flavored with grated apple. They are so easy to make and very addicting. Serve them for dinner or lunch or as an antipasto.   **Serves 4**

In a bowl, combine the veal, apple, egg, and salt. With wet hands, form the mixture into 2-inch ovals. Put the flour in a shallow dish and coat each croquettes in the flour; set aside.

Heat the olive oil in a large sauté pan over medium heat and brown the croquettes on all sides. Add the wine and reduce the heat to low. Cover the pan and cook for 20 minutes. Serve hot.

Salsicce di Maiale con Lenticchie e Porri

Pork Sausage with Lentils and Leeks

1 tablespoon extra-virgin olive oil

1½ pounds sweet Italian sausage links

¼ cup diced pancetta

1 large leek, white bulb only, cut into thin rings

2 ribs celery, diced

1 large carrot, peeled and diced

2 cloves garlic, peeled and minced

½ cup dry red wine

2 cups coarsely chopped plum tomatoes

Salt and freshly ground black pepper to taste

1½ cups lentils

5 cups beef broth, homemade (page 40) or store-bought, or vegetable broth

The region of Umbria is famous for many things, such as its olive oil, *porchetta* (roast suckling pig), and the creamy lentils of Castelluccio, which grow on the high plains near the Sibillini Mountains between the regions of Umbria and the Marche. The small round seeds are an ancient food, known in biblical times and found in many worldwide cultures. Lentils of Castelluccio have IGP (Protected Geographic Indication) status and are very different from other varieties. The seeds are flat and vary in color from green to brown and yellow. Lentils are planted in the spring, and the plants are harvested in late summer and left to dry in order to extract the seeds. The lentils of Castelluccio are not only creamy in texture but are thin-skinned, eliminating the need for soaking them. This versatile legume is often teamed with the delicious pork sausage that Umbria is noted for. Other uses include adding them to salads and soups. Lentils are a rich source of protein and vitamins.

Serves 4 to 6

Preheat the oven to 325°F.

Heat the olive oil in a heavy-duty oven-to-table pot over medium-high heat and brown the sausages and pancetta. Transfer the sausages and pancetta to a dish and set aside. Cook the leek, celery, and carrot in the pan drippings until they soften. Stir in the garlic and cook until it softens.

Raise the heat to high, add the wine, and allow it to come to a boil. Lower the heat to simmer and stir in the tomatoes. Season with salt and black pepper. Stir in the lentils. Return the sausages and pancetta to the pan and cover the mixture with the broth.

Cover the pan and bake for 35 to 40 minutes, or until most of the liquid has evaporated.

Abbacchio al Forno alla Romana

Roast Lamb, Roman Style

Roast lamb, considered a delicacy, takes the place of honor on the Italian table. The word *abbacchio* refers specifically to baby lamb weighing between 15 and 25 pounds and milk-fed. In Italy lamb is prepared in many ways—grilled on a spit, braised, and stewed—but Roman cooks take particular pride in their method of roasting it. **Serves 8**

1 (4-pound) leg of lamb, with shank bone attached

3 cloves garlic, slivered

3 tablespoons fresh rosemary

½ cup extra-virgin olive oil

1 tablespoon salt

1½ teaspoons coarsely ground black pepper

1 cup dry white wine

Wipe the meat dry with paper towels. With a small knife, make slits about 1-inch deep all over the meat and insert the slivers of garlic and rosemary.

In a small bowl, combine the olive oil, salt, and pepper and combine well. Spread the mixture all over the lamb, coating it well. Place the meat in a deep dish, cover it, and let it marinate in the refrigerator for 2 to 3 hours.

Preheat the oven to 350°F.

Place the lamb on a rack in a roasting pan and add the wine to the pan. Roast, basting the meat every 15 minutes with the pan juices, for 1 to 1½ hours, or until an instant-read thermometer inserted in the thickest part of the leg registers 135°F to 140°F for medium-rare or 160°F for medium. Transfer the roast to a cutting board and let it rest, loosely tented with aluminum foil, for 10 minutes before carving into slices. Serve with some of the pan juices.

Note: To make gravy, skim off the top layer of fat from the pan drippings and place the pan over two stovetop burners. Over medium heat, stir in 1 tablespoon flour and 1½ cups beef broth and whisk to make a smooth, slightly thickened sauce. Season with salt and pepper and serve on the side.

Involtini Messinese

Stuffed Veal Rolls, Messina Style

Call it *braciole*, *farsumagru*, or *involtini*, depending on where you are in Italy, and you are talking about meat, specifically thin meat slices that are rolled around a stuffing of breadcrumbs, cheese, herbs, and/or vegetables. These are usually cooked on the stovetop in butter or olive oil or braised in some sort of sauce or wine, though sometimes they are threaded onto wooden skewers and then grilled, baked, or pan-seared. In Messina, Sicily, they are stuffed with *molica condita*, a combination of breadcrumbs, parsley, garlic, and Pecorino Romano, caciocavallo, or provolone cheese. Tradition holds that the Spaniards introduced this dish to Sicily. Serve the involtini with Potato Salad with Oregano, Messina Style (page 309)   **Serves 4**

Preheat the oven to 325° F

In a bowl, combine ½ cup of the breadcrumbs, the parsley, Pecorino Romano cheese, garlic, salt, and pepper. Add enough water to just moisten the mixture enough so that when a small amount is compacted between your fingers, it holds together and does not fall apart. Spread this mixture evenly over the veal slices. Top each one with two slices of the caciocavallo cheese. Roll each slice up like a jellyroll and tie in several placed with kitchen string.

Spread the remaining 1 cup breadcrumbs in a large casserole dish. Brush the involtini with olive oil then roll them in the breadcrumbs on both sides.

Place the involtini side by side in the baking pan. Bake them for 12 to 15 minutes, or until an instant-read thermometer registers 150° F.

If using the stovetop, heat the butter in a large sauté pan over medium heat and brown the involtini on both sides until nicely browned, about 4 minutes. Remove the strings with scissors and serve hot.

Extra-virgin olive oil, for brushing the pan and the involtini

1½ cups dry breadcrumbs

¼ cup minced fresh flat-leaf parsley

½ cup grated Pecorino Romano cheese

1 large clove garlic, minced

½ teaspoon salt

¼ teaspoon freshly ground black pepper

About ¼ cup water

8 thin slices veal, each at least 3 inches wide and 4 inches long (about 1 pound total)

8 slices caciocavallo cheese, at room temperature

4 tablespoons (½ stick) unsalted butter or ¼ cup extra-virgin olive oil (optional)

When Saints Compete

They are ardently competitive and revered like rock stars. They have fans in the millions; their names are household words. Their images grace refrigerators and furniture. Some say that they have touched their lives in miraculous ways, while others daily implore them to do the impossible. They are saints—Ubaldo, Antonio, and Giorgio—and they are the honored holy ones in the medieval stone city of Gubbio. Every May 15 they mesmerize the local citizens and the world in a special way. In fact, no citizen of Gubbio would think of being anywhere else on that day but smack in the center of the Piazza Grande, young and old, packed like sardines, waiting in heightened anticipation to catch a glimpse of the saints as their likenesses are carried out of the austere-looking civic palace, the Palazzo dei Consoli, to begin a race. The statues of the saints are perched precariously atop twenty-foot-high intricately carved, missile-shaped wooden candles called *ceri*, weighing about one thousand pounds each. Each saint is carried by teams of runners through twisted, narrow eye-of-the needle streets up to Mount Ingino, and the arduous run finishes at the summit in the church of Sant'Ubaldo.

It is a privilege for me to be in the midst of this reverent frenzy, to see up close what la Corsa dei Ceri (the running of the candles) means to the people of Gubbio, who refer to this event as "the race of the crazies." The festivities are planned for all year long, and this is one of the oldest celebrations in Italy, even drawing fans from the States with Umbrian heritage. The event is documented in the Tavole Eugubine, the Eugubine Tablets, a set of prayers and rituals written in the Etruscan and Roman languages, dating from 250 to 150 BCE, and preserved in the Palazzo dei Consoli. Archaeologists have found stirring evidence of the longevity of this event from sacrificial offerings made high atop the mountains when it was a pagan celebration before it was Christianized in 1256.

May 15 is the eve of the anniversary of the death of Saint Ubaldo (1160), Gubbio's much-beloved bishop and patron saint. To prepare for the race, citizens from every walk of life take to the kitchens of the town's restaurants to cook a meatless feast for *la viglia* (the vigil). In the kitchen of the Taverna del Lupo, a well-known local restaurant, a group of men decked in aprons are singing as they prepare *baccalà arrosta* (roasted cod fish) and wrap hunks of cheese bread, and prepare to sell the fish and bread to the public for a few euros. At the same time, they prepare a feast for the privileged thousand or so guests, who along with town officials will eat together the next day in the Palazzo dei Consoli prior to the start of the race. The menu includes a cold seafood salad, seafood risotto, boiled salmon with caper sauce, roast pork with rosemary, chicken, frittata filled with seafood, mixed green salad, and a sponge cake filled with pastry cream in the shape of the candles. Umbrian wines flow in abundance while the crowd sings . . . all in anticipation of five o'clock in the afternoon, when the race of the saints begins. The irony of all this merrymaking is that the outcome of the race is already known, as it is each year. Saint'Ubaldo is the declared winner even before the race begins—of course this makes no sense to a foreigner, but it makes perfect sense to the people of Gubbio, who see this as an affirmation of their pride in being Eugubini. Everyone participates in the event, from declaring allegiance to a favorite saint and wearing that saint's colors to displaying the colors in flags that are draped from doorways, windows, and balconies. I get into the spirit, too, buying a red and yellow scarf in support of Sant'Ubaldo. Sant'Antonio fans wear black and Santo Giorgio, blue.

The roar of the crowd is at a fever pitch as the time grows closer for the race to begin, and red, yellow, black, and blue paper confetti rains down on everyone squeezed into Piazza Grande. Drums begin to beat, trumpeters in red and white medieval costumes pump out their sounds, people begin to chant, and the clang of the *campanile* (bell tower) erupts into an endless peal as the monstrous doors of the civic palace are opened to announce

each saint and its team of runners. I can feel the surge of energy in the crushing, deafening cry of the crowd as the first team races out carrying Sant'Ubaldo, who is soaring high atop his cero. He is whizzed through the crowd, resplendent in his pointed bishop's hat, clutching his staff with his gold cape flapping in the breeze. He reminds me of a soft-souled Santa Claus with his snowy white beard and sweet face, but in fact he represents the absolute authority of the church. Next comes Santo Giorgio, prancing on his mighty horse, his hands firmly on his silver shield and sword. He is all business, defender of the faith and symbol of military power. The crowd rocks with enthusiasm. Gentle Sant'Antonio, clothed in his humble brown garb, a symbol of the working class, closes ranks. Each saint is paraded four times around the square, and each is greeted with endless, frenetic chants. Before the race begins, all the saints stop at various high windows and balconies along the narrow streets from where the citizens of Gubbio pin money to their clothes, touch them with reverence, give them a pat on the back, and encourage them to do their best.

At the stroke of five o'clock, the race begins with Sant'Ubaldo leading the pack down the narrow, steep streets, followed by Santo Giorgio and Sant'Antonio. They are cheered along the route all the way to the church at the top of Mount Ingino, as if no one knows who will win, but of course they do know; it is the way the race must be run according to tradition. When darkness falls on the dark stone streets of Gubbio and the saints are once again returned to their resting places, the singing, dancing, and joy for this day continue long into the night, and plans are made for next year's race and the anticipation of who will win la corsa dei ceri will build once again in the souls and hearts of the Eugubini.

Friccò di Pollo all'Eugubina

Stewed Chicken, Gubbian Style

¼ cup extra-virgin olive oil

1 large white onion, coarsely chopped

1 (3½- to 4-pound) chicken, cut into 8 pieces and wiped dry with paper towels

¼ cup red or white wine vinegar

4 fresh sage leaves *or* 1 teaspoon dried sage

2 tablespoons fresh rosemary needles *or* 1 teaspoon dried rosemary

1 cup dry white wine

1½ cups pureed fresh plum tomatoes (3 to 4 medium), strained to remove seeds

Salt and freshly ground black pepper to taste

Friccò di pollo is a popular stewed chicken dish from Gubbio that is easy to recreate in your kitchen.   **Serves 4**

In a large sauté pan, heat the olive oil over medium-low heat. Add the onion and cook slowly for 5 minutes, or until soft. Raise the heat to medium-high, add the chicken pieces, and brown them on all sides. Add the vinegar and boil until it has evaporated. Lower the heat, add the sage and rosemary, and cook for 20 minutes.

Raise the heat, add the wine, and boil until it has evaporated. Add the tomato puree, season with salt and pepper, and reduce the heat to medium-low. Cook for 25 minutes, or until the sauce has thickened and the chicken is easily pierced with a fork and has reached an internal temperature of 165°F.

Transfer the chicken to a platter and spoon some of the sauce over the top. Serve immediately.

Mozzicone di Maiale con lo Smalto Balsamico

Fig and Balsamic-Glazed Pork Butt

This is not a traditional recipe but a composition of favorite ingredients drawn from various regions, like pork and balsamic vinegar from Emilia-Romagna, herbs from Tuscany, and figs to salute the many ways this beloved fruit is utilized. It is a fantasia but a delicious one.
Serves 6 to 8

1 (4-pound) boneless pork butt (shoulder roast)

1 tablespoon coarse sea salt

½ tablespoon coarsely ground black pepper

1 teaspoon Tuscan Herb Rub (page 284)

2 tablespoons extra-virgin olive oil

1 large onion, peeled and sliced into thin rounds

¼ cup warm fig jam

3 tablespoons Balsamic Glaze (page 30) or store bought

Bring the meat to room temperature about 1 hour before cooking. In a bowl, combine the salt, pepper, and herb rub. Rub evenly all over the meat. Tie it with kitchen string, and set aside.

In a Dutch oven or other heavy-duty stovetop-to-oven pan, heat the olive oil over medium heat until it begins to shimmer; cook the onion just until it wilts and begins to look glazed. Transfer the onion to a bowl. Raise the heat to medium-high and brown the meat on all sides. Turn off the heat and return onion to the pan.

Preheat the oven to 325°F.

Combine the jam and balsamic glaze in a small bowl and brush two-thirds of the mixture evenly all over the meat. Cover tightly and place the meat in the oven; cook for 1 hour. Remove the cover and spread the remaining jam mixture over the roast. Cover and return to the oven for about 25 minutes, or until an instant-read thermometer registers 160°F; the meat should be very tender. Remove from the oven and allow the meat to stand for 10 minutes before carving it into slices. Serve with some of the pan juices.

Costolette di Agnello di Luigi

Luigi's Lamb Chops

Whenever I am in Italy, I take the opportunity to learn about local foods from home cooks. Such was the case at the Di Majo Norante winery in Molise where winemaker Luigi Di Majo shared his favorite recipe for rack of lamb served with a delicious sauce made with wine from his estate.   **Serves 4**

If you plan to use rendered lamb fat, cut enough off the chops and melt it in a large pan to get 3 tablespoons and set it aside. In the same pan, raise the heat to high and brown the lamb chops on both sides. Set the meat aside.

In a Dutch oven or deep frying pan, combine the melted fat with the olive oil and add the chopped onions and pepper. Add the salt and mix well. Cook the mixture over medium heat for 5 minutes, then add ½ cup of the wine. Cook for 5 minutes, or until the vegetables have absorbed just about all the liquid. Add the lamb chops to the pan, pour in the remaining ½ cup wine, and cover the pan. Simmer for 1½ hours, or until the meat is fork-tender. Check the pan after about 20 minutes of cooking; if the mixture looks dry, add more wine, broth, or water.

Remove the cover and add the bay leaves and tomatoes. Simmer until the tomatoes soften, 10 to 12 minutes. Transfer the lamb chops to a platter and serve with some of the pan juices and vegetables.

1 rack of lamb, cut into chops (7 or 8)

3 tablespoons lamb fat, lard, or unsalted butter, melted

⅓ cup extra-virgin olive oil

2 red onions, coarsely chopped

1 small hot pepper, seeded and finely chopped

2 teaspoons fine sea salt

1 cup dry red wine, or more to taste

2 bay leaves

4 to 6 large plum tomatoes, peeled, seeded, and quartered, *or* 1 (16-ounce) can plum tomatoes, undrained

Pollo con Limone ed Erbe Aromatiche

Chicken with Lemon and Aromatic Herbs

¼ cup extra-virgin olive oil

1 large garlic clove, peeled and gently smashed

2 large fresh sprigs rosemary

2 fresh sage leaves

2 pounds boneless, skinless chicken thighs, wiped dry with paper towels

Coarse sea salt and freshly ground black pepper to taste

Grated zest and juice of 2 large oranges

In a rush and don't want to spend a lot of time preparing a meal? Chicken with lemon and herbs is *perfetto!*   Serves 4

In a large, deep skillet, heat the olive oil over medium heat. Add the garlic, rosemary, and sage. Cook until the garlic is soft and the herbs are wilted. Remove and discard the garlic and herbs.

Add the chicken pieces to the pan and brown them slowly on all sides. Season the pieces with salt and pepper and pour the orange zest and juice over them. Cover the pan, reduce the heat to medium-low, and simmer for 45 minutes, or until the chicken is tender.

Transfer to a serving platter and serve immediately with the pan juices.

The Road Not Taken

Bologna does not get the same kind of attention from tourists to Italy as, say, Rome, Florence, and Venice. And even though I love those three sister giants of culture and historical significance, I believe Bologna should get much more attention, for it is a grand city of learning, boasting the oldest continuing university in the world. For that reason it has the endearing name of La Dotta, "the learned." But it is also called La Grassa, meaning "the fat," in the sense that the cuisine is very rich.

My first trip to Bologna began at Tamburini, on Via Caprarie. This beautiful food emporium right in the heart of the city is an edible library of all the regional foods of Emilia-Romagna. There I met owner Giovanni Tamburini, a towering, jovial guy who is passionate about promoting awareness of the exquisite foods that this region has to offer and who was more than happy to give me a food tour and tasting that has had lasting memories.

All the big cured meat and artisan cheese players—mortadella, prosciutto di Parma, Parmigiano-Reggiano, culatello, and coppa—were brilliantly displayed. And while I love them all, I have great fondness for mortadella di Bologna. Giovanni explained that the word *mortadella* may have come from the word for *mortar*, a vessel that the ancient Romans used to grind meats and spices together. This signature cooked pork sausage of Bologna received IGP (Protected Geographic Indication) status in 1998, meaning that true mortadella di Bologna can be made only in certain areas and provinces beyond the region of Emilia-Romagna, including Piedmont, Lombardy, Veneto, Tuscany, Marche, and Lazio.

Mortadella is made with pork from the loin and shoulder area that is ground to a fine paste-like consistency, studded with *lardelli*, cubes of fat from the pig's neck area, and mixed with salt and spices like coriander, nutmeg, ginger, star anise, and black peppercorns. The mixture is piped by machine into natural casings and shaped into cylinders. Some of them can weigh as much as two hundred pounds! They are tied by hand with string and cooked by dry heat in large ovens, with cooking times dependent on their size. This is followed by a cooling period that helps the mortadella keep its shape.

Tamburini's mortadella was displayed in varying sizes; some almost as tall as me! It was time for a taste. Sliced tissue-thin, its fine pink texture reveals square patches of the lardelli and specks of black peppercorns. The taste is mild and the texture like velvet. Giovanni explained that mortadella is so beloved by the Bolognese that there are songs written about it, and he proceeded to entertain me with one as he strummed on his guitar.

As I listened to him and enjoyed this revered artisan product, I thought to myself that if I had not taken the road to Bologna, I would have missed one of its most beloved and classic dishes.

Lombata di Maiale alla Siciliana

Roast Pork Loin, Sicilian Style

The flavors of Italy linger long after I come home, and I am always eager to recreate them in my kitchen. This tender and very moist pork roast is coated in a paste made with familiar Sicilian ingredients like capers, oregano, peppercorns, and Sicilian sea salt from Trapani. Teamed with creamy potatoes and roast fennel, it makes a fine dinner. **Serves 6 to 8**

Preheat the oven to 425°F.

In a small grinder or food processor, combine the peppercorns, garlic, capers, oregano, and salt. Pulse until reduced to a powder. Transfer the mixture to a bowl and stir in ¼ cup olive oil.

With a small knife, make 6 deep slits in the top of the meat; fill each slit with ½ teaspoon of the olive oil mixture. With your hands spread the remaining olive oil mixture evenly over the top, bottom, and sides of the roast.

In a bowl, toss the onions, potatoes and fennel with 2 tablespoons olive oil and salt and pepper to taste. Set aside.

Place the meat on a rack in a roasting pan. Roast for 25 minutes. Add the onions, potatoes and fennel in the bottom of the pan. Pour in the wine along the sides of the pan. Lower the oven temperature to 375°F and continue roasting until an instant-read thermometer registers between 140°F to 145°F for medium.

Transfer the roast to a cutting board and allow it to stand, loosely tented with aluminum foil, for about 10 minutes. Carve and serve with the vegetables and some of the pan juices.

1½ tablespoons whole black peppercorns

1 large clove garlic, peeled

1 tablespoon capers in salt, well rinsed

1 teaspoon dried oregano

2 teaspoons coarse sea salt, plus more to taste

¼ cup plus 2 tablespoons extra-virgin olive oil

1 (3-pound) boneless pork loin, wiped dry with paper towels

1 large onion, cut into small chunks

3 medium potatoes, peeled and each cut into 4 wedges

1 medium fennel bulb, cut lengthwise into ½-inch-thick slices

Freshly ground black pepper to taste

1½ cups dry white wine

Erbe Toscane

Tuscan Herb Rub

2 cups fresh rose-
  mary needles
1 cup fresh sage
  leaves
4 large cloves garlic,
  peeled
2 teaspoons coarse
  salt

Keep a jar of Tuscan herbs on hand for rubbing into pork roasts and chicken and for mixing it into sautéing vegetables and soups. It makes a great little culinary gift, too. The most favored herbs are rosemary, sage, and garlic. This is a great way to utilize the herbs in your garden.
Makes about 3 cups

Make a pile of the rosemary, sage, garlic, and salt on a cutting board. Mince the ingredients together. Spread the mixture out onto paper towels and allow it to dry overnight. Transfer the mixture to a jar and keep it in the refrigerator.

Bologna Street Market

Salad

Salad has always been an integral part of the Italian meal, traditionally served after the main course as a digestive. This practice still exists in many places, but in larger cities, salad is often served with the main course.

The word *salad* comes from *sale*, "salt," and is also the root of our word for *salary*. In ancient times, salt was a necessary preservative for fish and meat and for making sauces. It was a form of currency paid as salary to the Roman legions, and the phrase "he is not worth his salt," meaning not worthy to be paid, comes directly from ancient Rome.

Ask for a salad in Italy and the standard choices will be an *insalata verde* (green salad with no vegetables) or an *insalata mista* (a mixed salad with vegetables like shaved carrots, radicchio, tomatoes, and fennel). Salads are typically dressed with extra-virgin olive oil and red wine vinegar or fresh lemon juice. In restaurants, cruets of oil and vinegar are brought to the table for you to dress your own. Some regions offer more than just green or mixed salad. In Milan, I enjoyed a splendid salad with a Gorgonzola cheese dressing. In Tuscany, *panzanella* (bread in a swamp) is a classic raw vegetable salad made with the addition of small stale bread cubes soaked in red wine vinegar. In Sicily, *rinforzata* (reinforced salad) contains cauliflower and other vegetables that are added each day to the original salad. Fennel and blood oranges make an unusual flavor combination in Sicilian salad. In Amalfi, the ubiquitous *insalata Caprese* (Capri style) can only mean juicy tomatoes, fresh mozzarella cheese, and basil leaves with a drizzle of extra-virgin olive oil. Creamy cheese from Puglia is the inspiration for burrata and roasted pear salad.

Italians prefer their salad greens on the bitter side. A mix of radicchio, with its gorgeous deep purple leaves and white

veining, sturdy escarole, romaine, and dandelion greens is popular. Romans adore bitter-tasting *puntarelle alla romana*, a chicory with lime green shoots that grows in the countryside from fall to early spring. The name comes from its pointy stems, and there is even a special tool called a *tagliapuntarelle* for cutting them. Puntarelle greens are tossed with an anchovy and olive oil dressing. And, as if you thought it couldn't get any more bitter, there is *agretti*, a wild springtime green with long, chive-like foliage and a strong taste; it

Piedmont

can also be braised in olive oil and served as a side with seafood or incorporated into a frittata.

A salad starts with the freshest ingredients and in the case of a green salad, crisp lettuce that has not been water sprayed to death, a practice in many grocery stores. To get limp lettuce crisp again, revive it by soaking the leaves in ice water for about 30 minutes; drain and then spin the leaves dry in a salad spinner to remove the excess water from the leaves, otherwise the dressing will not adhere very well.

Do not saturate the leaves with too much dressing; if puddles of dressing remain in the bottom of the bowl, you have used too much. The leaves should be lightly coated with the dressing. A ratio of one part extra-virgin olive oil to two parts vinegar works well, but that is a personal choice. Toss the leaves with the olive oil, then the vinegar, and last the salt. Some cooks dissolve the salt in the vinegar first before adding it to the salad.

Whether salads come before, with, or after the main course, they remain a healthy component of the Mediterranean diet.

Insalata di Agretti

Agretti Salad

1 bunch agretti

¼ cup extra-virgin olive oil

Grated zest and juice of 1 large lemon

Salt

¼ cup toasted sunflower seeds

½ cup shaved Asiago cheese

Agretti, also known as *salsola soda* or *barba del frate*, is a wild springtime green that grows near salty water. This annual has long, chive-like foliage and an assertive grassy taste. It is eaten raw in salad or braised in olive oil and served as a side with seafood or added to a frittata or pasta dish. Farmers' markets are your best bet for finding agretti, or you can order seeds from GrowItalian.com.   **Serves 4**

Soak the agretti in a bowlful of ice water for 10 minutes. Drain and spin dry. Transfer to a salad bowl.

In a small bowl, whisk the olive oil with the lemon zest and juice and salt to taste. Pour the dressing over the agretti, add the sunflower seeds and mix well. Sprinkle the cheese shavings over the top and serve.

Insalata Rinforzata alla Siciliana

Sicilian Reinforced Salad

From Caltanissetta, Sicily, home of my maternal grandmother, comes this reinforced cauliflower salad. Whatever was left from one day's salad was saved and added to the salad bowl the next day, intensifying the flavors and always keeping the salad interesting. **Serves 6**

Separate the cauliflower into small florets. Bring a large pot of water to a boil over high heat. Add 1 tablespoon salt and the florets and cook until al dente, about 5 minutes. They should retain some crunch. Drain and transfer to a bowl.

   Pour the olive oil over the cauliflower and toss to coat well. Add all the remaining ingredients and toss to mix well. Let the salad marinate for several hours at room temperature, stirring occasionally, before serving.

1 medium head cauliflower, outer leaves and core removed

Salt and freshly ground black pepper to taste

½ cup extra-virgin olive oil

2 teaspoons minced garlic

3 tablespoons red wine vinegar

½ cup pitted and diced black oil-cured olives

½ cup diced red onion

½ cup diced sweet red bell pepper

3 tablespoons capers in brine, drained

3 tablespoons chopped fresh flat-leaf parsley

Insalata di Rucola, Radicchio e Romana

Arugula, Radicchio, and Romaine Salad

Arugula is a spicy chicory that is very easy to grow and lasts well past the first frost. It is also available in most grocery stores. It is best partnered with other greens for an *insalata verde* (green salad), rather than served alone. It can also be made into a smooth sauce for pasta. **Serves 4**

Wash and spin dry all the lettuce leaves, or dry them well with a towel. Place them in a salad bowl. Add the olive oil and toss well to coat the leaves; add the vinegar and toss again. Season with salt and pepper and toss to combine well.

1 cup torn radicchio leaves (bite-size pieces)

1 cup torn arugula leaves (bite-size pieces)

1 cup torn romaine lettuce leaves (bite-size pieces)

1 heaping tablespoon extra-virgin olive oil

2 tablespoons red wine vinegar (or more to taste)

Salt and freshly ground black pepper to taste

The Jewel of Treviso

No one in my cooking group was enthusiastic about getting up early and leaving the hotel in Venice for an hour's bus ride to see, in their words, "lettuce growing." But this was no ordinary food foray; this would be an opportunity for them to see how the jewel of Treviso, *radicchio rosso di Treviso*, became the city's symbol and a defining food of the region of the Veneto.

We arrived at the Bellia Claudio farm in Cappella di Scorze, where the prized radicchio is grown, processed, and sold. We were met by Damiano and Giorgio, two enthusiastic, young growers, who know everything about radicchio, right down to its name being derived from the Italian *radice*, meaning "root" (which is also where we get the word *radish*). The radicchio produced here is of two types—an early variety called *precoce* and a late variety called *tardivo*—and they are both stunning to look at. Precoce is planted in early summer and harvested from late August to mid-November. It has tightly closed elongated leaves with an intense red-purple color and white veining. Its leaves are crisp and taste bittersweet, while tardivo, with its brilliant deep red wine–colored leaves and white veining, resembles an open flower and is often called "the flower of winter." The leaves are crisp and slightly bitter. Tardivo is planted in the summer and harvested after several hard frosts during the winter months. Only after repeated hard frosts is it dug up and kept in the dark in large tubs of cold water. Then the magic happens, as it begins to grow again, sending out its crisp yet tender white and crimson shoots. After three weeks, the field-grown plant has rotted away and is trimmed and discarded, leaving only the blanched heart.

There are many other types of radicchio, and the area of production involves several communes in the province of Treviso, two in the province of Padua and five in the province of Venice.

Growing radicchio in Treviso is a huge industry, and there is even a series of tours offered to the public called Strada del Radicchio (Radicchio Road) managed by the association Strada del Radicchio Rosso di Treviso e Variegato di Castelfranco, to promote tourism in the area.

Giorgio handed out blue booties to the group to slip over our shoes so as not to contaminate the plants growing in the fields. As we stood on the edge of a vast field of radicchio, Giorgio and Damiano couldn't emphasize enough how it is the spring water as well as the soil in this particular area that accounts for the quality of the plants. We learned that when precoce is harvested, it is washed

and the outer leaves stripped away. When tardivo is harvested, the leaves are tied together and left for a week. The plants are put in water and kept in a dark place where the lack of light prevents chlorophyll from developing, thus causing the plants to lose green pigmentation. The outer leaves are then stripped away to reveal the inner leaves boasting their brilliant deep red color. In the Veneto, Radicchio Rosso Tardivo di Treviso is always branded with the initials IGP, meaning that the radicchio was grown and harvested in a designated area and according to specific rules.

There is documented evidence that radicchio existed as far back as the fifteenth century in the Veneto and Trentino regions of Italy. But it was not an Italian who engineered the development of modern-day radicchio. It was a nineteenth-century Belgian agronomist, Francesco Van den Borre, who came to the Veneto to help establish a garden for a local nobleman and there developed a technique called *imbianchimento* (whitening) to force the plants to produce the dark red leaves with white veins.

I have been growing radicchio in my garden for years; the common type here is called Chioggia; it is round and about the size of a small cantaloupe. I have also had good luck with the variegated Castelfranco variety, with its pale yellow leaves dotted with red splashes.

Radicchio is an extremely healthy food, providing vitamins C, E, and K, along with folic acid and an abundance of antioxidants, more than is found in other fruits and vegetables. This versatile and noble chicory is not just for salads, which in the Veneto means simply tossing the leaves with a good extra-virgin olive oil, salt, and vinegar, but is also delicious as a sauce for pasta, cooked into risotto, or cut into wedges and grilled and served as a side dish. Giorgio's mother treated us to her homemade radicchio marmalade and marinated radicchio, both of which were delicious and taught us all clever new ways to use the jewel of Treviso.

A Juicy Story

My Sicilian nonna, Maria Assunta, came from Caltanisetta, the sulfur-mining area of central Sicily and was a great storyteller. One of my favorites was about oranges, specifically blood oranges. Nonna was about to be married in an arranged marriage to a man she hardly knew, who was already in L'America, as she put it. Her mother prepared a sack of blood oranges for her to take on her ocean passage to Ellis Island.

Alone and in steerage, Nonna had a hard time overcoming the seasickness of the long voyage. Unable to eat the soup or stew provided, she existed on those blood oranges. But years later when retelling this story, she let me know that once in America, she never wanted to see an orange again!

Every winter, I look forward to California-grown blood oranges available in supermarkets, and even though they are not the same as the ones from Sicily, they are quite delicious. If you are lucky, sometimes you can find the Italian tarocco variety in specialty stores. They come individually wrapped in beautiful papers.

Blood oranges and other citrus fruits were cultivated in Sicily during the Arab domination of the ninth and tenth centuries. The Italian word for orange is *arancia*, probably derived from the Arabic *naranj*. Gradually the cultivation of these oranges spread throughout the Mediterranean region; Sicily, with its perfect growing conditions, is a major producer of blood oranges and other citrus from lemons to citron.

Once you cut into a blood orange, you will understand how it got its name. The flesh is reddish-purple due to a pigment found in it called anthocyanin. It is a powerful antioxidant that many believe can prevent diseases such as cancer.

Insalata di Zucca Arrostita

Roasted Squash Salad

Roasted zucchini and yellow squash combine in this delicious salad. It is best to use small, firm ones that have few seeds and less water. This makes a delicious appetizer served over grilled slices of bread.
Serves 4

Preheat the oven to 350°F. Lightly oil a rimmed baking sheet.

Cut all the squash into ¼-inch-thick round slices. Spread them in a single layer on the baking sheet and bake them, turning once, until soft but not mushy, about 20 minutes.

In a bowl, combine all the dressing ingredients and whisk until well blended. Pour 2 tablespoons of the dressing into a shallow serving dish. Arrange the squash in the dish, slightly overlapping the slices and alternating the colors for a nice visual effect. Pour the remaining dressing over the squash. Cover the dish and marinate at room temperature for several hours, or overnight. Tilt the dish occasionally to move the dressing up and over the squash. Serve at room temperature.

- 2 small zucchini
- 2 small yellow summer squash
- ½ cup extra-virgin olive oil
- 2 cloves garlic, minced
- 3 tablespoons red wine vinegar
- 3 tablespoons minced fresh basil
- 2 tablespoons minced fresh mint
- Salt and coarsely ground black pepper

Insalata di Arancia Rossa e Finocchio

Blood Orange and Fennel Salad

3 tablespoons pine nuts

6 medium blood oranges or navel oranges

1 small fennel bulb, trimmed and thinly sliced crosswise, plus 2 tablespoons finely minced fennel leaves

⅓ cup extra-virgin olive oil

Salt and freshly ground black pepper to taste

Romaine lettuce leaves

One day I took a cooking group to visit the Marchesi di San Giuliano, an estate on the eastern side of Sicily near Villasmundo, where citrus has been growing for over 200 years. It is owned by the Ferragamo family and is famous for producing organically grown fruit like blood oranges, bitter oranges, grapefruit, lemons, and other citrus that go into its marmalades. Production runs from November to May.

Moro, Tarocco, and Sanguinello are the blood orange types grown here, and they are far different in look and taste from the domestic variety grown in California. Sicilian varieties are dense and heavy and have high concentrations of anthocyanins, which account for the deep red flesh. As the estate manager explained, the temperature fluctuation of hot days and cold nights is also responsible for the blood red color. The blood oranges of Sicily are unique and cannot be successfully cultivated in other areas because of climatic differences.

The combination of blood oranges and fennel has long been a favorite Sicilian salad. When I make this salad at home, I use California blood oranges, available during the winter months; lacking those, you can use navel oranges. **Serves 6**

In a small nonstick pan, toast the pine nuts over low heat until they begin to brown and smell fragrant. Watch carefully as they can burn quickly. Transfer them to a small bowl and set aside.

Peel the oranges and remove as much of the pith (white membrane) as possible. Slice the oranges into ¼-inch-thick rounds and place them in a shallow dish, slightly overlapping them. Scatter the fennel slices and leaves over the top. Drizzle the olive oil over the top and season with salt and pepper. Cover the dish tightly with plastic wrap and marinate at room temperature for several hours, tilting the dish every so often so that the oil and juices that have collected flow over and around the oranges.

To serve, arrange the salad on a bed of romaine lettuce leaves and pour the collected juices over it. Sprinkle the pine nuts over the top and serve.

Lake Como Garden

Insalata di Fagioli e Soppressata alla Toscana

Tuscan Bean Salad with Soppressata

1½ cups dried cannellini beans

4-ounce chunk soppressata, diced

¼ cup chopped red onion

1 clove garlic, minced

⅓ cup extra-virgin olive oil

2 teaspoons Dijon mustard

2 tablespoons chopped fresh flat-leaf parsley

Salt and freshly ground black pepper to taste

In June, fresh cannellini beans are harvested in Tuscany and used in pasta dishes, soups, sides, and salads. Fresh beans require just a little cooking time and the simplest seasoning, like extra-virgin olive oil and a good grinding of black pepper. Dried cannellini beans need to soak overnight before cooking; this helps plump up the beans and cuts down on the cooking time. (Canned beans that are well rinsed can also be used.) Soppressata, spicy dry-cured Tuscan salame, gives an added punch to this salad. **Serves 8**

Soak the beans overnight in water to cover. Drain them and put them in a pot; add fresh cold water to cover. Bring to a boil and cook until tender, 30 to 35 minutes. They are cooked when you can easily slip off the outer skin between your fingers. Drain the beans well and put them in a large bowl. Add the onion, garlic, and soppressata and combine well.

In a small bowl, whisk together the olive oil, mustard, and parsley. Pour the dressing over the bean mixture, tossing well. Season with salt and pepper and toss again. Serve.

Condimento di Gorgonzola

Gorgonzola Cheese Dressing

¼ cup Gorgonzola dolce

1 teaspoon Dijon mustard

6 tablespoons extra-virgin olive oil

¼ teaspoon salt

¼ teaspoon freshly ground black pepper

4 cups mixed lettuce greens

Gorgonzola cheese takes its name from the town of Gorgonzola, near Milan, where it is made; its production is said to date back to the fifteenth century. This cow's milk cheese, with its distinctive blue veining, comes from penicillin mold. Gorgonzola dolce has a mild taste, while the longer-aged Gorgonzola forte has a sharp taste. Gorgonzola is a great table cheese but is also used in cooking for sauces and fillings. It can dress up a salad, too.   **Make about 1 cup**

Put the cheese and mustard in a food processor or blender and pulse until smooth. With the motor running, slowly add the olive oil through the feed tube in a thin, steady stream and process until well blended. Add the salt and pepper and mix well.

Put the lettuce greens in a salad bowl and toss with ½ cup of the dressing. Transfer the remaining dressing to a bottle and refrigerate. It will keep for up to 2 weeks.

Panzanella
Swamp Salad

Panzanella means "bread in a swamp" and is a summer salad that is popular all over Italy. It originated in Tuscany as a clever way to use up stale bread and was considered a country dish that was eaten for breakfast or for a snack. Tomatoes and bread are enough to make this salad satisfying, but many cooks add other raw vegetables like cucumbers and bell peppers. I cannot stress enough that the quality of the bread, as well as in-season tomatoes and a good extra-virgin olive oil, are all critical to the flavor of this salad. Use a good sourdough, boule, or other tight-crumb bread. Soft bread does not work and will only disintegrate. Make this early in the day and hold it at room temperature so all the flavors can mingle and the bread becomes saturated with the juices of the tomatoes. **Serve 6 to 8**

In a bowl, toss the tomatoes with the sugar; set aside.

Dip the bread cubes quickly into a bowl of room-temperature water and squeeze out the water with your hands. Put the bread in a salad bowl. Add the tomatoes, onion, parsley, and basil and toss gently.

Whisk together all the dressing ingredients. Pour the dressing over the salad and toss again. Cover the salad and allow it to sit at room temperature for several hours. Just before serving, gently toss the salad again.

Note: Save the bread crusts to make into breadcrumbs.

2 cups ripe cherry tomatoes, halved, *or* 4 ripe heirloom tomatoes, chopped

1 teaspoon sugar

8 to 10 cups (1-inch) stale bread cubes, crust trimmed

½ cup thinly sliced red onion

¼ cup minced fresh flat-leaf parsley

Small bunch basil leaves, torn into pieces

Dressing

6 tablespoons extra-virgin olive oil

3 tablespoons red wine vinegar

2 cloves garlic, minced

Salt to taste

Insalata di Pere e Burrata

Pear and Burrata Cheese Salad

2 tablespoons
unsalted butter

2 large ripe Anjou
or Bartlett pears,
halved lengthwise,
cored, and
each half sliced
crosswise into
4 (¼-inch-thick)
slices

2 (4-ounce) balls
burrata cheese,
well drained and
each gently cut in
half

Warm honey or
Balsamic Glaze
(page 30), for
drizzling

New interpretations of traditional foods are a sign that the cook is always thinking of clever ways to present ingredients. Burrata cheese and pears have a natural affinity for one another, as evidenced in this combination salad that could almost double as dessert! **Serves 4**

Melt the butter in a nonstick sauté pan over medium heat and cook the pear slices until they just begin to brown on the edges; flip and cook the other side. Arrange 4 pear slices on each of 4 salad plates. Add a cheese half on top of the pears, then drizzle with warm honey or balsamic glaze. Serve.

Insalata di Melanzane e Burrata

Roasted Eggplant and Burrata Cheese Stack Salad

¼ cup extra-virgin olive oil, plus more for drizzling

Coarse sea salt

1 medium eggplant, trimmed and cut into 8 (¼-inch-thick) rounds

2 large beefsteak tomatoes, each cut into 4 thick slices

2 (4-ounce) balls burrata cheese, well drained and each gently cut in half

Fresh basil leaves, shredded

Roasted eggplant, garden tomatoes, and luscious burrata cheese stack up beautifully in this summer salad.   **Serves 4**

Preheat the oven to 350°F.

Pour the olive oil into a medium bowl and stir in ¼ teaspoon salt. Add the eggplant slices and toss them in the oil. Arrange them in a single layer on a nonstick rimmed baking sheet and bake them until they begin to brown. Cool.

Place 1 eggplant slice on each of 4 salad dishes. Top each with 1 tomato slice, then repeat with another eggplant slice and another tomato slice. Top with a burrata half and a sprinkling of basil. Drizzle the tops with extra-virgin olive oil and sprinkle with salt. Serve.

Insalata di Patate e Origano alla Messinese

Potato Salad with Oregano, Messina Style

No cloying mayonnaise masks the flavor of this potato salad, which is a perfect partner to meat, fish, or poultry. In Messina, it is often served with Stuffed Veal Rolls, Messina Style (page 269). Yukon Gold potatoes work best in this recipe, lending creaminess as well as color. **Serves 4**

Wash and dry the potatoes and poke them in several places with a small knife. Microwave or boil them until tender. Once they are cool enough to handle, peel and cut them into ¼-inch-thick rounds. Layer them in a rectangular serving dish. Sprinkle the olives and tomatoes over the slices.

In a small bowl, whisk the garlic and olive oil together and season with salt and pepper. Pour the dressing over the potatoes and scatter the oregano leaves over the top. Cover and marinate at room temperature for several hours before serving.

4 medium Yukon Gold potatoes

2 tablespoons chopped black olives

8 cherry tomatoes, cut into quarters

1 clove garlic, minced

6 tablespoons extra-virgin olive oil

Salt and freshly ground black pepper to taste

2 tablespoons fresh oregano leaves, torn into bits

Balsamic Vinegar

Ancient records show that balsamic vinegar (aceto balsamico) was being made as early as the seventh century by the Romans. *Balsamic* means "aromatic," according to Signorina Bona Tirelli, an expert on the production of balsamic vinegar and a native of Modena, where the famed vinegar is made. She stressed that even today it is a closely guarded secret as to how it is made among the Modenese, who for centuries have been passing down their particular formula to the next generation.

Balsamic vinegar is made from the Trebbiano grape, grown on the middle hills of Modena and the border areas of Bologna. The Modenese believe that only these areas have the right mixture of air temperature, humidity, and soil to produce the grapes for the vinegar. They must be picked at just the right moment and left to dry for a week on mesh screens. They are then squeezed by foot to extract the juice, because a machine crushing would be too brutal a process. As the grapes are crushed, the juices run through square openings in the casks to waiting tubes.

The *barili* (casks) used for holding, fermenting, maturing, and aging the vinegar must be made by hand. The casks are constructed from a combination of fruitwoods, including cherry, apple, and pear. The wood for the casks must be cut at certain hours of the day and certain times of the year, usually from October to March, when the trees are dormant. The casks must conform to a certain size and thickness to allow for enough evaporation to occur.

The grape juice is cooked in special copper pots for twelve to twenty-four hours, and this is the most critical step. Active vinegar bacteria is then added, along with wine vinegar. The mixture is put into the first cask and left to rest for one year. After a year, half of the contents of the cask are put into a second cask and left to rest for another year. What is left behind in the first cask is the "mother" for the production of balsamic vinegar. The vinegar in the second cask is put into a third cask for four years. Finally, after six years, the first bottle of *aceto balsamico giovane*, or young vinegar, can be tapped. At this point, the color is transparent, and the acidity count varies from 6 to 18 percent. Vinegars allowed to age for twelve to twenty-five years develop a deep mahogany color and a flavor that is extremely concentrated. The classification of this vinegar is set by law and is judged for its acidity, cleanness, and taste by experts like Tirelli.

Very few bottles of this prized flavor enhancer are produced in any given year. Since 1956, the Friends of Aceto Balsamico have presented an award for the best vinegar. Bona Tirelli let me sample her prized vinegar, which was kept in an etched glass bottle. She reverently poured a few precious drops onto a tiny silver spoon; the intense flavor was sweet and sour, with a thick velvety texture.

Tirelli explained that the Modenese use the vinegar in their everyday food preparation. It is never exposed to cooking heat, as this would destroy its unique flavor and burn off the alcohol content. The oldest vinegars are used very sparingly, often sprinkled over slivers of Parmigiano-Reggiano cheese served after a meal. Scant drops are sprinkled over boiled meats, and it is used as an accompaniment to steak. One teaspoon of a younger vinegar is enough to dress a green salad or perk up fresh fruits like strawberries or peaches.

Tirelli also stressed that in the past and even now, the most prized and expensive bottles of aceto balsamico tradizionale are given as wedding presents.

Sweets and Fruit

Duomo, Modena

Sweets are traditionally reserved for special occasions, although my observations in Italy tell me otherwise. *Pasticcerie* (pastry shops) seem to be around the corner in every town and city. The dizzying and tempting display windows play with your senses, teasing you with tiers of biscotti, dense jam tarts, and whole fruit tarts, glistening like jewels; plus towering snowball puffs of meringues, fluffy-looking powdered sugar donuts, and much more. Two of my favorite shops are Sandri's on Corso Vanucci in Perugia, famous for its signature torciglioni, a snake-shaped pastry filled with dried fruits, and Nannini's on Via Banchi di Sopra in Siena for its panforte, a dense spice cake filled with almonds and candied fruit.

From morning to late afternoon, Italians wander into these sweet paradises to select delectable treats to have with their espresso. Bringing a sweet gift to someone is part of the pastry shop scene as well. Whether you pick out a dozen cookies or just one, it will be beautifully wrapped in a flourish of ribbons and bows and sealed with an artistic sticker. Yes, the Italians know how to do everything with style.

As tempting as Italian desserts are, and as rapidly as old traditions are changing, sweets on a daily basis are rare. Holidays, feast days, name days, and other special occasions are when serious desserts are enjoyed. Some, such as tiramisù and cannoli, are known worldwide, but there are hundreds of lesser-known desserts like the fabulous pistachio cake from Bronte, Sicily or the apple cake from Mondovì.

But most of the time, it is still customary to have fresh fruit to end a meal, and Italy grows many varieties of fruit. Apples, grapes, and pears tumble down from the Aosta Valley in the north to the rest of Italy. Smooth, juicy apricots and tart golden lemons—some the size of grapefruits!—grow in terraced rows on the hillsides ringing Lake Garda; black currants come from the northern region of Friuli Venezia Giulia. Rich, red cherries as shiny as glass marbles thrive

Afternoon coffee in Rome

in Liguria. The most wonderful white peaches I have ever tasted come from Emilia. There are also scarlet-red strawberries and plump melons from Rome, purple plums and exotic pomegranates from Naples, prickly pears and delicate figs from Basilicata, and sugar-sweet blood oranges, tangerines, and citron from Sicily.

Italians, naturally, have a wonderful way of serving fresh fruit at the table. The fruit is presented in a bowl of cool water, and each diner chooses a fruit and eats it with a fork and knife—even a banana. Of course, fruit is also incorporated into many desserts, from fresh fruit tarts glistening under a transparent sugar glaze to *semifreddo*, chilled fruit and cream combinations. Stuffed and baked fruits, especially pears and peaches with *amaretti* (almond cookies), are popular, too, as well as fruits macerated in wine or liqueur.

La dolce vita is alive and well in Italy!

Tanti Biscotti

A Lot of Biscotti

5 tablespoons unsalted butter, cut into bits

1¼ cups sugar

6 large eggs

3¼ cups unbleached all-purpose flour

3¼ teaspoons baking powder

½ teaspoon salt

1 tablespoon vanilla extract

1 tablespoon brandy

¼ cup unsweetened cocoa

½ cup diced dried fruit, such as apricots, cherries, raisins, or figs

½ cup slivered almonds

½ cup chopped white chocolate

½ cup diced orange peel

GLAZE (OPTIONAL)

½ cup coarsely chopped white chocolate

1 teaspoon vegetable oil

Crunchy and dry, biscotti are never far from a cup of espresso or a glass of Vin Santo. Italians eat them for breakfast, too! *Biscotto* is the generic word for cookie, but more specifically, *biscotti* means "twice baked," for cookies that are shaped into a log, baked until firm, then cut and baked again to toast them. The best part is that with the basic dough recipe below, you can easily make a variety of flavored biscotti. Create almond biscotti, mixed dried fruit biscotti, white chocolate chunk biscotti, or chocolate and candied orange peel biscotti. But don't stop there—come up with your own special ingredients to add to the dough and have a biscotti baking good time. They make great gifts, too.   **Makes about 4 dozen**

Cream the butter and sugar in a stand mixer or in a bowl with a handheld mixer until the mixture is smooth and fluffy. Beat in the eggs, one at a time, on medium speed.

On a sheet of wax paper, sift the flour, baking powder, and salt together. Add the flour mixture to the butter mixture and blend well on medium speed.

Transfer half of the dough from the mixer to a bowl. On low speed, mix the vanilla into the remaining dough. Scoop the vanilla-flavored dough onto a sheet of wax paper. Set aside. Return the plain dough to the mixer and on low speed blend in the brandy and cocoa until the dough is a uniform chocolate color. Scoop the dough onto a second sheet of wax paper. Wrap each dough separately and refrigerate for 1 hour.

Preheat the oven to 350°F. Line 2 baking sheets with parchment paper.

Unwrap the vanilla-flavored dough and divide it in half. To one half mix in the dried fruits; to the other half add the almonds. Unwrap the chocolate-flavored dough and divide it in half. To one half add the white chocolate; to the other half add the orange peel.

With floured hands, form each section of dough into a log 12 to 14 inches long and 1½ inches wide. Flatten the logs slightly. Place two logs on each baking sheet, spaced 3 inches apart.

Bake the logs for 12 to 15 minutes, or until they are firm to the touch. Allow them to cool for 10 minutes before slicing them crosswise on the diagonal into ½-inch-thick slices. Place the biscotti back on the baking sheets, cut sides down, and toast them in the oven for about 5 minutes, or until they are light brown and dry. Remove and cool.

If desired, glaze the biscotti: Fill a small saucepan halfway with water and bring to a boil. Remove the pan from the heat. Combine the white chocolate and vegetable oil in a heatproof bowl and place it on top of the saucepan. Allow the chocolate to melt, then stir to blend the oil and chocolate. When smooth, dip the ends of the biscotti in the chocolate, allowing the excess to drip off. Place the biscotti on a cooling rack until the glaze is dry.

Dolce di Varese (Amor Polenta)

Varese Cornmeal Cake

How spectacular can a cornmeal cake be? As good as this one from the province of Varese in the region of Lombardia. There it is called dolce di Varese or amor polenta. The genesis of this cake was coarse-ground cornmeal mixed with other common cereal grains. I imagine it was crumbly, dry, and not very tasty. But with time, all that has changed. A trinity of cornmeal, all-purpose flour, and almond flour combine with butter and eggs to create a moist and well-textured cake, just right for any occasion. I like it as a snack cake with tea but sometimes dress it up with whipped cream and sliced apricots, blueberries, or raspberries, or even ice cream. This cake gets its traditional ridged log shape from a Moravian cake pan (available from Fantes.com), but it can also be made in an ordinary cake pan or even a loaf pan. **Makes one (10-inch) cake**

8 tablespoons (1 stick) unsalted butter, at room temperature

½ cup granulated sugar

2 large eggs

¾ cup yellow cornmeal

¾ cup unbleached all-purpose flour

¾ cup almond flour

1½ teaspoons baking powder

¼ teaspoon salt

Confectioners' sugar, for sprinkling

Preheat the oven to 350° F. Generously butter a Moravian pan, 10-inch cake pan, or 9 x 5-inch loaf pan and dust it with cornmeal. Shake out the excess cornmeal.

In a bowl, cream the butter and sugar until very smooth and pale yellow in color. Beat in the eggs, one at a time, and blend well.

In a separate bow, mix the cornmeal, all-purpose flour, almond flour, baking powder, and salt together. Beat the flour mixture into the egg mixture.

Fill the pan with the batter and bake for 20 to 35 minutes, or until the cake is nicely browned and firm to the touch; cool completely in the pan, then unmold.

Heavily dust the top of the cake with confectioners' sugar, slice, and serve.

Mantovana di Prato

Prato Almond Cake

1¼ cups unbleached all-purpose flour

1¼ teaspoons baking powder

¼ teaspoon salt

1 cup sliced almonds

¾ cup sugar

8 tablespoons (1 stick) unsalted butter, melted and cooled

2 large eggs

Grated zest and juice of 1 large lemon

Confectioners' sugar, for sprinkling

The city of Prato in Tuscany fascinates me not just because of the food and wine but because of a book I read a long time ago called *The Merchant of Prato*. In it, Francesco di Marco Datini, a wealthy merchant, chronicles his daily life in fourteenth-century Prato. I was especially drawn to the remarkably preserved letters he wrote to his wife Margherita while he was absent on long business trips. In them, he told her what he wanted to eat when he got home! I can only surmise from Margherita's letters that he loved the chickpeas, chestnuts, capers, beans, figs, and raisins that she often sent him. But Datini would not have known about this elegant cake known as Mantovana di Prato because the original recipe dates from the nineteenth century and is said to have been created by nuns from Mantua and given as a gift to Antonio Mattei, who opened the Biscottificio Mattei in 1858. There he sold the famous biscotti di Prato that are still being turned out today, as well as the Mantovana. **Serves 8**

Preheat the oven to 350°F. Butter an 8-inch round cake pan and line it with parchment paper.

In a bowl, combine the flour, baking powder, salt, and ⅔ cup of the almonds. Set aside.

In another bowl, whisk the sugar and butter until well blended. Whisk in the eggs, one at a time. Whisk in the lemon zest and juice.

Add the flour mixture to the butter mixture and mix well. Spread the batter in the pan, then sprinkle the remaining ⅓ cup almonds on top. Bake for 30 to 35 minutes, or until the cake is set and nicely browned.

Cool, then sprinkle with confectioners' sugar. Slice and serve.

Torta di Mele di Mondovì

Mondovì Apple Cake

The humble apple can most certainly be declared the most powerful of all earthly fruits when we consider its ancient biblical origins and the consequences eating one had for Adam and Eve.

Italy is the world's sixth largest producer of apples, and one in five apples sold in Italy comes from the Trentino-Alto Adige area. The region produces over four million apples annually, of all varieties. Two of the most popular types are Golden Delicious and Renette, which are related to our Pippin. They are often paired with veal and pork to make savory crochette or used to make such classic sweets as apple strudel. I stumbled upon Renette apples in the outdoor market in Mondovì in the province of Cuneo in Piemonte and was completely taken by their beauty and size. Their yellow-greenish skin is splattered with red checks, and their flesh is juicy and firm with a clean, almost lemony taste. Italians love to use Renette apples for making this torta di mele, an exquisite apple cake from Mondovì, which is perfect for fall and winter eating.   **Serves 8**

3 large Golden Delicious or Pippin apples, peeled, cored, and thinly sliced

1 cup plus 2 tablespoons sugar

¼ cup dry Marsala wine

5 tablespoons unsalted butter, softened

3 large eggs, separated

1⅓ cups unbleached all-purpose flour

1 teaspoon baking powder

¼ teaspoon salt

Put the apple slices in a bowl, sprinkle with 2 tablespoons sugar, and stir in the Marsala. Set aside for 30 minutes.

Preheat the oven to 350°F. Butter a 9-inch springform pan and line it with parchment paper.

In a bowl, cream the butter and remaining 1 cup sugar until light and fluffy. Beat in the egg yolks, one at a time, until well blended.

Drain the apple slices in a small sieve set over a bowl and add the resulting liquid to the egg yolk mixture; stir well.

Sift the flour, baking powder, and salt together and add to the egg yolk mixture. Stir until combined. Beat the egg whites in a clean bowl until soft peaks form; fold the whites into the batter.

Spread half of the batter in the prepared pan. Arrange the apple slices in several layers over the batter. Cover the apples with the remaining batter, smoothing it evenly over the top. Bake for 45 to 50 minutes, or until golden brown and a cake tester comes out clean when inserted in the center of the cake.

Cool for 10 minutes before unlatching the sides. Cut into slices and serve warm.

Crostata di Prugne al Balsamico

Dried Plum and Balsamic Vinegar Tart

This intensely flavored dried plum tart is always in demand in my house. The simple dough is pressed into a tart pan, with no rolling involved. What makes this tart a winner is the balsamic vinegar reduction. It is a cold-weather treat when fresh plums are all but a memory. **Serves 8**

Preheat the oven to 400°F.

Mix the flour, butter, sugar, and baking powder together in a bowl. Add the egg and vanilla to form a dough. If the dough is too dry, add a few drops of cold water. Flour your hands and press two-thirds of the dough into the bottom and sides of a 9-inch tart shell with a removable bottom. Crumble the rest of the dough into small bits and set aside. Bake the crust unfilled for about 8 minutes. Set aside to cool while you make the filling. Lower the oven temperature to 375°F.

Combine the dried plums and water in a saucepan and bring to a boil over medium heat. Lower the heat to a simmer and cook until they soften. Drain well and transfer them to a food processor; pulse until a thick, smooth paste is obtained. Transfer to a bowl.

Wipe out the saucepan and add the vinegar. Cook over medium heat until it thickens and is reduced to about ½ cup, about 10 minutes. Cool for 10 minutes.

Add the balsamic reduction to the plums, along with the brown sugar, salt, and zest. Combine well and transfer it to the cooled shell. Smooth the filling so it is even. Scatter the remaining dough bits evenly over the top and sprinkle the coarse sugar over the dough.

Bake the tart for about 30 minutes, or until the top crust is nicely browned.

Cool on a wire rack. Loosen the sides of the tart pan and carefully remove it. Place the tart on serving dish, cut into wedges, and serve.

PASTRY CRUST

1½ cups unbleached all-purpose flour

8 tablespoons (1 stick) cold unsalted butter, grated

½ cup granulated sugar

1 teaspoon baking powder

1 large egg, lightly beaten

1 teaspoon vanilla extract

FILLING

1 (18-ounce) box pitted dried plums

⅔ cup water

4 cups balsamic vinegar

¼ cup brown sugar

¼ teaspoon salt

Grated zest of 1 large orange

2 tablespoons coarse sugar

Sebadas

Sardinian Cheese-Filled Pastry

CHEESE FILLING

1 pound young
   Pecorino Romano
   cheese, cut into
   small chunks

2 tablespoons water

Grated zest of
   2 oranges

DOUGH

3 cups durum
   semolina flour

3 tablespoons lard or
   extra-virgin olive
   oil

¼ teaspoon salt

1 cup water, plus
   more if needed

Olive oil, for frying

½ cup warm honey,
   for drizzling

Sebadas, thought to be of Spanish origin, is a sweet and savory cheese-filled country pastry made all over Sardinia. Sebadas were traditionally made to celebrate the shepherd's homecoming from pasturing flocks during the long migration known as the *transumana*. Today they are a holiday treat for Easter and Christmas. Made with semolina, Pecorino Romano cheese, honey, and sugar, they have layers of flavor both sweet and salty.   **Makes 18**

Line a rimmed nonstick baking sheet with parchment paper.

In a medium saucepan, combine the cheese and water and cook over medium heat until the cheese melts. Remove the pan from the heat, stir in the zest, and combine well. Spread the cheese mixture onto the baking sheet in a ¼-inch even thickness. Cover and refrigerate for 1 hour.

Meanwhile, dump the flour onto a work surface and make a hole in the center. Add the lard or olive oil, salt, and enough water to make a soft dough. Cover and let rest for 30 minutes.

Roll the dough out into a large diameter and use a 3-inch round cutter to cut circles. Reroll the dough scraps to make more; you should have 36.

Cut 2-inch rounds of the chilled cheese and place one piece on top of each of 18 circles. Cover the cheese with the remaining circles and seal the edges well with your fingers. Use a pasta wheel to crimp the outside edges. Place the sebadas on towel-lined baking sheets as you form them. (The sebadas can be frozen at this point; wrap them individually and freeze on a baking sheet, then transfer to freezer bags. Defrost the sebadas before frying.)

Heat the oil in a large, deep pot to 375°F and fry the sebadas, a few at time, until they are golden brown. Drain them on absorbent paper. Place the sebadas on individual plates and drizzle with the honey while they are warm; serve immediately.

Torta Caprese

Capri's Chocolate-Almond Cake

I was introduced to torta Caprese when I made my first trip to the stunning island of Capri in the Bay of Naples. After touring Villa San Michele, I was famished and decided on octopus salad for lunch. It was beautifully and simply flavored with olive oil and was accompanied with local lemons cut into wedges and plump green olives. For dessert, a decadent flourless chocolate cake tempted me, and so I said *sì!* Dense, moist, fudgy, and full of almonds, this cake also wins many gluten-free fans.   **Serves 8**

Preheat the oven to 350°F.

Butter a 10-inch springform pan and line it with parchment paper, then butter the parchment.

Beat the butter with the sugar in a bowl until creamy.

Beat the eggs in a separate bowl until light and lemon colored, then mix them into the butter and sugar. Stir in the rum. Fold in the almonds, baking powder, and chocolate and scrape the batter into the pan. Bake for 45 to 50 minutes; it should still be moist but not wet in the center.

Cool on a wire rack, then remove the sides of the pan. Place the cake on a serving dish and dust heavily with confectioners' sugar. Cut into thin wedges to serve.

12 tablespoons (1½ sticks) plus 1 tablespoon unsalted butter, at room temperature

1 cup granulated sugar

6 large eggs

1 teaspoon rum

2 cups whole almonds, finely chopped

2½ tablespoons baking powder

8 ounces bittersweet chocolate, finely chopped

Confectioners' sugar, for dusting

Torta alle Mandorle e Limone alla Siciliana con Limoni Canditi

Sicilian Almond and Lemon Cake with Candied Lemons

3 large lemons

1½ cups granulated sugar

6 large eggs, separated

2¾ cups finely ground blanched almonds

2 teaspoons baking powder

½ teaspoon salt

Confectioners' sugar (optional)

Confectioners' Glaze (recipe below; optional)

Candied Lemon Slices (recipe below; optional)

Fresh mint sprigs (optional)

In March, the pink and white flowers of the almond trees are in full bloom, and a huge *sagra* (festival) is held in the city of Agrigento to celebrate the coming of spring. In the fall, the almonds are harvested and are used to make some of the most classic and unusual Sicilian desserts, like this intensely flavored almond and lemon cake.   **Serves 8**

Butter a 9-inch springform pan and line it with parchment paper, then butter the parchment.

Put the lemons in a pot, cover them with cold water, and bring it to a boil. Lower the heat and cook just under the boil for about 45 minutes. Drain the lemons and let cool. Trim the ends of the lemons, cut them in half, and remove the seeds. Coarsely chop the lemons, rind and all, and transfer to a food processor. Add ½ cup of the sugar and process until smooth and creamy.

Preheat the oven to 350°F.

Beat the egg yolks with the remaining 1 cup sugar in a medium bowl until the yolks are pale yellow and frothy looking; beat in the lemons and the ground almonds. Stir in the baking powder and salt.

In a separate bowl with clean beaters, whip the egg whites into soft peaks. Fold the beaten whites into the lemon mixture and pour the batter into the pan.

Bake the cake for about 45 minutes, or until a cake tester inserted in the middle comes out clean. Be careful not to let the cake brown too much; it should be golden brown.

Cool the cake slightly, then remove the sides and let the cake cool completely. Dust it with confectioners' sugar or cover it with confectioners' glaze, then decorate with candied lemon slices and mint sprigs, if desired.

continued on page 328

continued from page 326

Confectioners' Glaze

1 cup confectioners' sugar, sifted, plus more if needed

½ teaspoon orange extract

A few drops milk

Mix all the ingredients until a consistency like that of chocolate syrup forms, and spread it thinly over the cooled cake. Add several candied lemons and some sprigs of mint for garnish.

Candied Lemon Slices

1 cup granulated sugar, plus coarse sugar for coating the slices

1 cup water

2 medium lemons, thinly sliced and seeded

Combine the granulated sugar and water in a 12-inch skillet and heat until the sugar dissolves and the mixture looks clear. Add the lemon slices in single layers (use two pans if necessary) and simmer gently until the liquid is reduced and turns syrupy and the lemons look glazed.

Transfer the lemon slices with tongs to a lightly oiled rack to cool slightly; when cool enough to handle, coat each slice several times in coarse sugar. Let them dry completely on a wire rack before using them to garnish the top of the cake. (These can be made several days ahead and allowed to dry.)

Formaggio di Mascarpone

Mascarpone Cheese

Mascarpone is a high-butterfat, creamy-smooth white cheese made famous in the classic dessert tiramisù. The region of Lombardia lays claim to its origins, dating back to the sixteenth century. Mascarpone began life not with milk, but with the cream that was skimmed off the top of whole milk. The cream was heated and then some sort of acid was added to thicken it; the more acid used, the thicker the final consistency. In the past tartaric acid, the residue found on the inside walls of wine barrels and an ingredient found in cream of tartar, was used. Fresh lemon or lime juice is also perfect for thickening the cream. The cheese should have a smooth texture and a slightly sweet and tangy taste.

Mascarpone has many uses. It can become a smooth sauce for pasta or vegetables, made into a dip flavored with spices and fresh herbs, used as a filling for cheesecake or cannoli, or eaten fresh with berries or other fruits. Drizzle it with honey and nuts for a quick dessert, or add a dollop to pureed soups. **Makes 2 cups**

2 cups heavy cream
2 tablespoons freshly squeezed lemon juice
Pinch salt

Pour the cream into a 1-quart saucepan, attach an instant-read or candy thermometer to the side of the pan, and cook over low heat until the temperature reaches 180°F. Stir in the lemon juice and continue cooking until the cream thickens and coats the back of a spoon, 5 to 8 minutes. Stir in the salt. Turn off the heat and allow the cream to cool for about 45 minutes.

Line a fine-mesh strainer with cheesecloth or a clean towel and place it over a bowl. Pour the cream slowly into the cheesecloth. Cover the bowl and refrigerate the cheese for at least 5 hours before using. Use it within 4 days.

Say Formaggio

The day started out cloudy as I made my way to Azienda Cucchiara near Salemi, Sicily, to watch the process of making Pecorino and ricotta cheeses. At the *caseificio* (cheese house), I was greeted by the cheese maker, Baldo Cucchiara, and his sons, Salvatore and Liborio, who, along with eight other men, milk eight hundred sheep twice a day, every day, by hand! I was in awe of the work ethic of these men, who took such pride in making an artisan product. Baldo took me through the steps of how the milk is heated to a certain temperature, with rennet added to coagulate it to create the curds that will become Pecorino cheese. Pecorino is a salty table cheese that becomes a grating cheese as it ages and hardens. I was offered samples of Pecorino with black peppercorns, with hot red pepper flakes, and with pistachio nuts!

The leftover liquid whey from the cheese-making process is reheated with rennet and becomes ricotta cheese (*ricotta* means "recooked"). It tasted warm, creamy, and delicate—and so unlike the commercial product.

Just when I thought that there could be no more sampling, out came the most gorgeous cannoli that I have ever seen. The huge, blistered golden-brown shells were as thin as potato chips and were filled with sweetened sheep's milk ricotta, sugar, and bits of chocolate. I bit into this flaky queen of all Sicilian desserts and knew that this cannolo would be the benchmark by which I judged all future cannoli, even my own. After eating one, I wanted to know the secret for making those beautiful shells. I have made cannoli hundreds of times, using my grandmother's well-worn bamboo forms, but these were outstanding.

In the kitchen area, a woman was cleaning up. I approached her and mentioned how much I loved the cannoli. I am sure that my enthusiasm amused her. Did you use flour, sugar, butter or lard, and a little wine to make the shells? *Sì*, she answered with a quizzical grin. I knew better than to ask for a recipe since the standard response for most Italian ingredients is "quanto basta," or however much is needed. Italians cook by intuition, experience, and feel. My intuition told me that lard, not butter, was responsible for the flakiness of those shells and that white wine, Marsala wine, or vinegar was the liquid used with flour and sugar to make the dough. As much as I will forever remember those cannoli, I will never be able to duplicate them at home. I have come close, but for me, the best cannoli can only be experienced in Sicily.

Ricotta

Ricotta Cheese

2 quarts whole milk

1 cup heavy cream

¼ to ½ cup fresh
   lemon juice
   (2 to 3 lemons)

½ teaspoon salt

I learned how ricotta cheese is made years ago from Totò, an exuberant man who had been making Pecorino cheese for over thirty years. He knew his craft and his flock, sleeping outside in a straw hut when they were out to pasture. Totò made Pecorino cheese for the Tasca d'Almerita family wine estate, Regaleali, located in the middle of Sicily. I had come here with a television crew to film the cheese-making process that began early in the day. Twice a day from June to November, Totò makes cheese for the estate like clockwork, just as his father taught him from the age of fourteen.

Early in the morning when I enter the *caseificio* (cheese house), I find Totò already at work, starting the fire with trimmed olive and grapevine branches to heat the huge cauldrons of milk. He moves quickly through the cheese-making process like an orchestrated dance. When the milk is heated, he adds *caglia* (rennet) to coagulate it. Originally, the stomach lining of sheep or cow was used to thicken the milk and form the curds because of the lining's acidity. Today, commercially prepared rennet is used. In about twenty minutes, the curds form, and the first cheese—called *tuma* (unsalted)—is placed in baskets. It can be eaten immediately, and Totò hands me a spoon to taste the delicate texture of the cheese.

Next he salts the remaining curds, filling round baskets with what will become aged Pecorino. He adds black and green peppercorns to some of the curds and hot red pepper flakes to others. The cheese ages on wooden boards for up to three months, some even longer. The rind becomes deep brown and the texture dry and good for grating.

Totò heats the leftover liquid whey with more caglia to make creamy ricotta and ricotta salata. This is where the name *ricotta* comes from, meaning that the whey is "recooked."

Ricotta salata, salted ricotta, is a drier version of creamy ricotta and is an essential ingredient in the classic dish pasta alla Norma. Fresh sheep's milk ricotta, Totò says, is the only authentic cheese used to fill the classic Sicilian cannoli that we would enjoy after dinner.

Totò bids us goodbye, sending us off with our own aged Pecorino cheese with peppercorns. **Makes about 3 cups**

Line a fine-mesh colander with several layers of damp cheesecloth and place it over a large bowl. Set aside.

Pour the milk and cream into a large stainless steel soup pot. Attach an instant-read or candy thermometer to the side of the pan. Heat the mixture to 220° F. Add the lemon juice and stir only once.

As the curds form, gather them with a slotted spoon and transfer them to the colander. Allow the curds to drain at room temperature for at least 2 hours. Transfer the cheese to an airtight container and refrigerate. Use within a week.

Note: the leftover liquid (whey) can be saved and added to yeast dough.

Cannoli Decostruiti

Deconstructed Cannoli

1½ cups whole-milk ricotta cheese, homemade (page 332) or store-bought, well drained

3 tablespoons confectioners' sugar, plus more for dusting

2 teaspoons ground cinnamon

1½ cups heavy cream

¾ cup minced semisweet chocolate

¾ cup minced pistachio nuts

1 cup unbleached all-purpose flour

1 tablespoon granulated sugar

1 tablespoon unsalted butter

4 to 5 tablespoons Marsala wine

2 cups vegetable oil

Here is an unconventional way to make cannoli without having to wrap dough around a tubular form. Instead, roll and cut the dough into round disks and fry them, then sandwich the rich ricotta filling between the disks. It is difficult to find sheep's milk ricotta, but if you can, use it for this recipe. **Serves 8**

In a bowl, whip the ricotta cheese, confectioners' sugar, and cinnamon together until smooth. In another bowl, whip ½ cup of the cream into soft peaks, then fold it into the ricotta mixture. Stir in ½ cup of the chocolate and ½ cup of the nuts, cover, and refrigerate. Whip the remaining 1 cup cream into soft peaks and refrigerate.

To make the dough, combine the flour, granulated sugar, and butter in a bowl or food processor and mix with a fork or process until the mixture resembles coarse meal. Slowly add the wine and mix or process until a ball of dough forms. Add additional wine if the dough appears too dry; it should be soft but not sticky. Knead the dough on a floured surface until smooth, about 3 minutes. Wrap the dough and refrigerate it for 45 minutes.

Unwrap the chilled dough on a floured work surface and divide it in half. Work with one piece of dough at a time; keep the remaining dough covered. Roll the dough out into a very thin rectangle about 14 inches long and 4 inches wide, either by hand or using a pasta machine set to the highest setting. Cut the dough into 3-inch circles. Place them on a towel-lined baking sheet.

Heat the vegetable oil to 375°F in a heavy-duty pot. Fry the dough disks a few at a time until golden brown. Remove them with a slotted spoon and drain them on absorbent paper. Cool to room temperature.

To serve, lay one disk on an individual dessert plate and spread about 2 tablespoons of the ricotta filing over the disk. Top with a second disk and spread 2 more tablespoons of the ricotta mixture. Top with a third disk and add a dollop of whipped cream. Sprinkle with some of the remaining chocolate and nuts. Dust with confectioners' sugar over the top. Serve at once.

Fragole al Vino

Strawberries in Wine

3 cups fresh strawberries, hulled and cut in half

½ cup sugar

¾ cup dry red or white wine, such as Chianti or Pinot Grigio

Nemi, a dear little town situated on volcanic Lago di Nemi, in the region of Lazio, is noted for something special during the months of May and June: its famed wild strawberries. Many visitors come to take part in the *sagra della fragola* (strawberry festival), where they eat everything concocted from these extremely small strawberries that have an intense flavor found nowhere else. The strawberries from Nemi never go far because the good people of Nemi know a good thing when they eat it, so most of them remain a local treat. Strawberries and other fruits like peaches are often served in wine for a refreshing end to a meal. In Modena, where the famed aceto balsamico tradizionale is made (page 310), fruit is drizzled with just a few drops of the sweet and sour condiment. **Serves 6**

Toss the berries in a bowl with the sugar and wine. Cover and refrigerate for a couple of hours before serving.

Bigne

Cream Puffs

Bigne are cream puffs and go by other names as well, including zeppole and sfinge. They are popular at holiday time and definitley a must for the feast of Saint Joseph on March 19. Bigne require simple ingredients, flour, eggs, buter, water, salt, and flavoring. The goal is to create cream puff shells that have dry not wet interiors. The solution is to add egg whites, which have drying properties, along with the whole eggs.   **Makes 8 large or 16 small**

Preheat the oven to 450°F. Butter and lightly flour two rimmed baking sheets or line them with parchment paper.

Combine the water, butter, sugar, and salt in a 1-quart saucepan and bring to a rolling boil. Add the vanilla. Remove the pan from the heat and stir in the flour all at once; stir vigorously until it forms a ball of paste.

Return the pot to the stove and "dry" the paste over medium heat by stirring it in one direction to remove as much water as possible; this will allow the eggs to be absorbed better and produce a light puff. When the paste is really dry looking, remove it from the heat. Allow it to cool for a few minutes, then transfer the paste to a food processor fitted with a steel blade. Beat the paste for a few minutes until it is warm. Through the feed tube add 1 egg and process the mixture until it is well blended. Add the second egg and process again. Add 1 egg white and process, then the second egg white. Add the third egg only if the mixture does not hold up in a mass when scooped with a spoon. (Alternatively, you can do this by hand, using a wooden spoon to add the eggs and whites individually as explained above.) The paste should be shiny and smooth and thick and be able to fall from the spoon with a thick consistency.

Spoon the paste into a pastry bag with or without a plain tip. Fill the bag only three-quarters of the way or the paste will ooze out the top. Twist the top of the bag closed and pipe out 1½-inch rounds onto the baking sheets, spacing them 1 inch apart. For miniature puffs, pipe ¼-inch rounds, spacing them apart. Smooth the tops of each puff by dipping your finger in water and rounding the tops. (Alternatively, you can use two spoons instead of a pastry bag to make the puffs.)

Bake for 12 to 15 minutes, or until they are puffed and beginning to brown. Lower the heat to 300°F and continue baking for 20 to 30 minutes, or until the puffs are golden brown and dry. Do not remove them until they are browned and dry, otherwise they will collapse. Leave the puffs in the oven with the door ajar after turning off the oven. Make a small slit in each puff to allow steam to escape.

Cool the puffs on racks to allow for good air circulation. The baked puffs can be wrapped individually and frozen for up to one month, then defrosted and filled.

To make the pastry cream, heat the milk in a 2-quart saucepan to just under the boil.

Combine the sugar, flour, cornstarch, and salt in a bowl and stir into the hot milk. Stir in the eggs and whisk until the mixture thickens. Remove from the heat and stir in the almond extract and butter. Transfer the mixture to a bowl, cover, and chill.

When ready to serve, beat the cream in a separate bowl until soft peaks form and fold it into the pastry cream until well blended. Fit a pastry bag with a plain tip and fill the bag three-quarters of the way with the pastry cream. Puncture the side of each cream puff with the pastry tip and fill.

Place the cream puffs on a serving dish and sprinkle the tops with confectioners' sugar and serve immediately.

Rame di Napoli

Sicilian Chocolate Spice Cookies

1 cup plain tea biscuit cookies, such as Stella D'Oro, ground into coarse crumbs

1 to 1 ¼ cups milk

4 cups unbleached all-purpose flour

1 cup sugar

1 teaspoon baking powder

2 large eggs

7 tablespoons unsalted butter, melted

1 tablespoon honey

1 tablespoon orange marmalade

1 tablespoon vanilla extract

⅞ cup unsweetened cocoa powder

1 tablespoon ground cinnamon

1 teaspoon ground cloves

CHOCOLATE GLAZE

1 cup dark chocolate chunks

4 tablespoons (½ stick) unsalted butter

1½ cups coarsely crushed pistachio nuts

Rame di Napoli are spicy chocolate cookies prepared especially for the Day of the Dead, November 2, and are given to adults and children as a gift in memory of their deceased relatives. Even though the name suggests that these cookies are Neapolitan, they are in fact Sicilian because Sicily and Naples were once part of the Kingdom of the Two Sicilies, lasting from 1815 until 1860. The capitals were Naples and Palermo. *Rame* means "copper," and these cookies were meant to resemble the copper coins that were minted to replace the gold and silver ones when the kingdom of Sicily was annexed to the Kingdom of Naples.   **Makes about 28 large cookies**

Put the cookie crumbs in a medium bowl and just barely cover them with milk. Allow them to sit and soak until the crumbs have absorbed the milk, then stir well until the mixture reaches a creamy consistency.

In a separate large bowl, mix together the remaining ingredients. Add the milk-soaked crumbs to the mixture and combine well. Add more milk to the batter, a little at a time, and, using a wooden spoon, stir it until the mixture reaches the consistency of a thick paste, like that of pastry cream. The amount of milk added will depend on the type of cookies used, but should not be more than 1½ to 2 cups. Look for a somewhat loose and creamy consistency that still holds its shape on a spoon and is not runny or liquid. Let the batter rest at room temperature for 1 hour.

Preheat the oven to 325°F. Line several baking sheets with parchment paper.

Use a ¼-cup measure or scoop to form the batter into rounds, spacing them 1 inch apart on the baking sheets.

Bake for 15 to 20 minutes, or until the tops of the cookies appear dry. Remove them from the oven and cool completely on a cooling rack. Begin making the glaze only when the cookies have cooled completely.

To make the glaze, melt the chocolate and butter together in a double boiler over low heat, stirring constantly. Once the chocolate has completely melted and the consistency is a thin liquid, remove it from the heat and pour it into a bowl. Dip the top of each cookie into the glaze, coating the surface evenly, and place them on cooling racks to dry. Sprinkle the tops of each cookie with some of the pistachio nuts while the glaze is still warm, then cool completely.

Torta di Mascarpone con Mirtilli

Mascarpone Cake with Berries

1½ cups plus
  1 tablespoon cake
  flour

1 teaspoon baking
  powder

½ teaspoon salt

2 tablespoons grated
  orange zest

5 tablespoons
  unsalted butter,
  melted and cooled

¾ cup plus
  2 tablespoons
  granulated sugar

2 large eggs

½ teaspoon almond
  extract

1 cup mascarpone
  cheese,
  homemade
  (page 329) or
  store-bought

2 cups fresh
  blackberries,
  blueberries, or
  raspberries

2 teaspoons
  cornstarch

Confectioners sugar,
  for dusting

This delicate, not-too-sweet cake is studded with fresh berries. Mascarpone cheese makes it moist and a good keeper. Cut yourself a wedge to go with tea or coffee for an afternoon snack. **Serves 8**

Preheat the oven to 350°F. Butter an 8½-inch cake pan and line it with parchment paper.

In a bowl, combine 1½ cups of the flour, baking powder, salt, and orange zest.

In a separate bowl, use a handheld mixer or a whisk to beat together the butter, ¾ cup sugar, eggs, almond extract, and cheese until smooth. Mix the dry ingredients into the egg mixture.

Dust 1 cup of the berries with the remaining 1 tablespoon flour and fold them into the batter. Transfer to the pan and bake until firm and golden brown, about 35 minutes. Cool on a wire rack.

Combine the remaining 1 cup berries, 2 tablespoons sugar, and cornstarch in a small saucepan and stir to combine. Cook over medium heat until the berries begin to exude their juice. Lower the heat and continue cooking until the mixture thickens slightly. Cool and set aside.

To serve, dust the cake with confectioners' sugar and cut into wedges. Serve with some of the warm berry sauce.

Tiramisù al Cioccolato e Ciliegia

Cherry-Chocolate Tiramisù

Here is a twist on the classic tiramisù: Ladyfingers are dipped in cherry liqueur, then layered with cooked Bing cherries, mascarpone cheese, and cream. Make these in individual goblets or wine glasses for a really nifty presentation. Be sure to use hard Italian ladyfingers for this; if you attempt to make this with soft cake-like ones, they will simply disintegrate. **Serves 4**

Combine the cherry halves, ½ cup of the sugar, and salt in a medium saucepan and cook over medium-high heat until the mixture begins to thicken; lower the heat and cook for 5 to 8 minutes. Transfer the cherry sauce to a bowl and refrigerate.

Beat the mascarpone cheese with the remaining ¼ cup sugar until smooth. In a separate bowl, beat the heavy cream until stiff; fold the cream into the mascarpone and refrigerate.

Pour the cherry liqueur into a shallow bowl and dip each ladyfinger quickly into the liqueur; do not let them get mushy by overdipping them. Scoop a small amount of the mascarpone mixture into each goblet; layer a ladyfinger or two in the goblet, then spoon on some of the cherry sauce. Continue making layers of mascarpone, ladyfingers, and cherry sauce, ending with mascarpone. Place two cherries in the center of each goblet and sprinkle some shaved chocolate over the top. Refrigerate for at least several hours or overnight before serving.

1 pound Bing cherries, cut in half and pitted, plus 8 whole cherries for garnish

¾ cup sugar

½ teaspoon salt

½ cup mascarpone cheese, homemade (page 329) or store-bought, at room temperature

1½ cups heavy cream

24 dry ladyfingers

2 tablespoons cherry liqueur

4 ounces bittersweet chocolate, shaved

Torta Mimosa

Mimosa Cake

I wonder how many of us know the significance of March 8 for women in Italy and around the world. It commemorates the annual Festa delle Donne (International Women's Day), and I must confess that before I made my first trip to Italy many years ago, I had never heard about it.

To put the day in context: In ancient Rome, the calendar year ended with February, the word meaning "month of ending" or "cleaning" in order to make way for the coming year, which began on March 1, considered the first day of spring.

Historically, March 8 was commemorated as a day sacred to Ariadne, the daughter of King Minos of Crete, who was abandoned while she was sleeping on the island of Naxos by Theseus, who had promised to make her his wife if she helped him kill her father's minotaur. His false promise led her to become the symbol for womanhood.

There are differing opinions as to when the Festa delle Donne actually took hold in some parts of Italy, with some saying that it began as a grassroots political and social movement in 1922 when women began to express their political, economic, and social demands. But it may well have had its roots outside of Italy in New York City, where on March 8, 1857, garment workers went on strike, leading to the formation of the first women's union. In 1945 the Union of Italian Women proclaimed that March 8 should be set aside to celebrate all women, and a year later it became a nationally recognized day for women.

The mimosa tree, which blooms in March with its bright yellow flowers and refreshing scent, became the symbol of La Festa delle Donne, and its perfumed branches are given by family and friends to the women in their lives as a gesture of appreciation and love. This practice is said to have originated in Rome after World War II, but no one knows for sure who started it.

continued on page 346

CAKE

4 extra large eggs

6 extra large egg yolks

1 cup plus 2 tablespoons granulated sugar

1 teaspoon vanilla extract

1⅓ cups cake flour

¼ cup potato flour or cornstarch

1 teaspoon baking powder

½ teaspoon salt

FILLING

2 cups whole milk

1-inch piece vanilla bean, split down the middle and seeds scraped out with a small knife, *or* 1 teaspoon vanilla extract

2 large eggs

2 large egg yolks

½ cup plus 2 tablespoons granulated sugar

⅓ cup unbleached all-purpose flour

Grated zest of 1 large lemon

2 cups heavy cream

SUGAR SYRUP

½ cup water

¼ cup granulated sugar

¼ cup Cointreau or limoncello

Confectioners' sugar, for dusting

continued from page 345

One thing is for sure, La Festa delle Donne is a day for women worldwide to demonstrate solidarity with each other and to showcase the important roles that women play for equality and justice. To celebrate, a spectacular-looking mimosa cake is made.   **Serves 8 to 10**

Preheat the oven to 350°F. Butter 3 (8-inch) cake pans. Line the pans with parchment paper and butter the paper.

In a stand mixer, beat the eggs and egg yolks with the sugar on high speed until the mixture turns light yellow, is smooth, and quadruples in volume. Stir in the vanilla. The mixture should be very thick.

In a bowl, sift the cake flour, potato flour, baking powder, and salt together. On medium speed blend the flour mixture into the egg mixture.

Divide and pour the batter into the cake pans. Bake for about 25 minutes, or until the cakes are firm to the touch and light golden brown. Cool the cakes to room temperature. Remove them from the pans and peel away the parchment paper. Let cool completely.

To make the filling, pour the milk into a 1-quart saucepan and stir in the vanilla bean seeds or extract; cook over medium heat until the milk just begins to bubble at the edges. Remove from the heat.

In a separate bowl, beat the eggs, egg yolks, and ½ cup of the sugar with a handheld mixer until light yellow. Beat in the flour, a little at a time, until smooth. Beat in ⅓ cup of the hot milk and blend well. Add the mixture to the remaining milk in the pan and cook until the mixture thickens and coats the back of a spoon. Remove from the heat and stir in the lemon zest. Pour the pastry cream into a bowl and cover with a buttered sheet of wax paper. Refrigerate for several hours.

Whip the cream with the remaining 2 tablespoons sugar and fold it into the pastry cream. Refrigerate until ready to fill the cake.

To make the sugar syrup, pour the water into a small saucepan, stir in the sugar, and bring it to a boil. Lower the heat, and when the mixture looks clear, remove it from the heat and stir in the liqueur. Cool and set aside.

To assemble, cut each cake in half horizontally to get 2 layers. Set aside 3 layers. Trim the outside dark crumb of the remaining 3 layers if necessary and cut the layers into ½-inch cubes. Place them on a baking sheet in a single layer and cover until ready to serve the cake.

Line an 8½ x 4¼-inch-deep glass bowl with plastic wrap, allowing it to overhang the pan by 4 inches. Place one cake layer in the base of the bowl and gently press it down so that it is touching the base of the bowl. Brush the cake with one-third of the sugar syrup and spread with one-third of the pastry cream. Repeat with another layer of cake, sugar syrup, and pastry cream. Place the third cake layer on top. Fold the overlapping plastic wrap over the cake and gently press on it to settle and even the cake. Refrigerate it for at least 1 hour.

When ready to serve, unwrap the top of the cake and place a cake plate over the top of the bowl. Turn the bowl upside-down to release the cake and gently pull back the plastic wrap and discard it.

Spread the cake with the remaining pastry cream, covering it completely. Press the reserved cake cubes onto the top and sides of the cake. The cake can be refrigerated at this point, loosely covered with aluminum foil. When ready to serve, sprinkle the cake with confectioners' sugar and cut into wedges with a serrated knife.

'Mpanatigghi
Modica's Chocolate Cookies

PASTRY DOUGH

3½ cups unbleached all-purpose flour

½ cup granulated sugar

½ teaspoon salt

½ cup vegetable shortening or lard

1 large egg, lightly beaten with a fork

½ cup Marsala wine

2 tablespoons water, plus more if needed

FILLING

1½ cups sliced almonds

1 (3½-ounce) bar bittersweet (85% cacao) dark chocolate

1 cup granulated sugar

1 teaspoon ground cinnamon

⅛ teaspoon salt

1 tablespoon grated lemon zest

4 ounces very finely ground lean veal

2 large egg whites

Confectioners' sugar

Modica, in southeastern Sicily, is a UNESCO world heritage site, known for its magnificent baroque buildings, including the imposing cathedral (Duomo) dedicated to Saint George, the revered patron saint of the city. Every year in April, a huge festival occurs in his honor, when the saint is carried out of the cathedral on his mighty white steed and paraded through the streets of upper and lower Modica.

Of course, food is a big part of the celebration, because besides the fame of Saint George, the city is known for its outstanding quality chocolate, introduced by the Spaniards, who brought it from Mexico, courtesy of the Aztecs, who used it in drinks and in cooking. The chocolate was very bitter and used to enrich sauces for meats, grated for vegetable dishes like eggplant, and eaten on its own. It was just a matter of time before the most famous chocolate and pastry shop in Modica, Antica Dolceria Bonajuto, dating back to the 1880s, would mix chocolate with finely ground meat as a way of preserving it and use it as a filling for cookies called 'mpanatigghi, meaning to wrap or cover. (The name is derived from the Spanish word *empanada*.) At first, I thought the combination was strange, but one bite and I was a believer.

Still following the original formula, Modica chocolate is made from cacao beans, without soy lecithin, and has a grainy texture due to lower temperatures, which create the coarse sugar crystals. There are many flavors, from vanilla to hot chile pepper. According to renowned Sicilian author Leonardo Sciascia, the quality of Modica chocolate is unmatched anywhere in the world: "Modican chocolate is unparalleled in flavor and tasting it is like reaching the ultimate, the absolute. Chocolate produced elsewhere is an adulteration, a corruption of the original."

Modica chocolate is available online and at specialty chocolate shops; if you can't find it, 85 percent bitter dark chocolate is a good substitute for these unusual cookies. **Makes 5½ dozen**

continued on page 350

continued from page 348

Combine the flour, sugar, salt, and shortening in a food processor and pulse three or four times. Add the egg through the feed tube with the Marsala and process until a ball of dough begins to form. Add the water and continue processing; if the mixture seems dry, add additional water until the dough is moist but not sticky and holds together when squeezed between your fingers. Wrap the dough and refrigerate it for 1 hour.

Put the almonds in the food processor and grind them until fine but not powdery. Transfer to a bowl.

Break up the chocolate and add it to the food processor; process until the chocolate is in small pieces. Transfer it to the bowl with the almonds. Add the sugar, cinnamon, salt, and lemon zest to the almond mixture and stir to combine. Set aside.

Cook the meat in a medium nonstick sauté pan over medium heat until it turns gray. Transfer the meat to the food processor and pulse until it is very fine. Return the meat to the pan. Add the almond mixture to the meat and cook over low heat just until the chocolate begins to melt and the mixture is well coated with the chocolate. Transfer the mixture to a bowl and set aside to cool for 5 minutes.

In a separate bowl, beat the egg whites until soft peaks form; fold the egg whites into the cooled almond and meat mixture until well blended and the mixture looks shiny. Set aside.

Preheat the oven to 350°F. Line 2 rimmed baking sheets with parchment paper.

Divide the chilled dough into 4 pieces and work with one piece at a time, keeping the rest covered.

Roll the dough out to a thickness of about ⅛ inch. Use a 3½-inch round cookie cutter to cut out circles. Place a generous tablespoon of the filling in the center of each round. Moisten the edges with a little water. Fold in half to make a turnover and pinch the edges closed. Place the cookies on the baking sheets. Use scissors to make a slit in the center of each one. Bake for 20 minutes or until lightly browned. Cool completely, then dust the tops with confectioners' sugar. Repeat with the remaining dough and filling.

Where Cheese Is King

If I could be offered only one cheese in a lifetime, it would have to be Parmigiano-Reggiano, which is a far cry from what Americans call "parmesan." The creation of this cheese is the pride of the region of Emilia-Romagna; it is the king of the table. Making this exquisite cow's milk cheese by hand goes back over eight centuries, and the process has not changed much in all that time. To witness the actual "birth" of this region's most famous product is a rare experience. Each time that I have been privileged to do so, I am in awe of the elements of nature and man working in harmony to create such a unique artisan product.

So it was with great excitement early one morning that I found myself an invited guest to one of the six hundred *caseifici* (cheese houses) in the region to learn about the process. My destination, Baganzolino, was a half hour's drive from my hotel in Soragna.

Parmigiano-Reggiano is made every day from raw cow's milk from both an evening and a morning milking. Strict rules surround its production. Only the provinces of Reggio Emilia, Parma, Modena, Bologna (west of the Reno River), and Mantua (east of the Po River) are authorized to make the cheese. Cows must be fed only chemical-free grasses that come from these designated areas. The quality of the raw ingredients, along with ideal soil and climatic conditions, are the conduits for making Parmigiano-Reggiano. But there is also another element that cannot be overlooked: the ability of human hands to turn these raw materials into this superior cheese.

Once the milk is obtained, it is heated in huge copper cauldrons that look like gigantic inverted church bells. Whey from the previous morning's milking is added, along with calf's rennet. This coagulates the milk in twelve to eighteen minutes and forms the cheese curds. A huge wire whisk is used to break up the curds into pea-size pieces. These tiny pieces are allowed to set, and as

they do they form a solid mass that is brought up from the base of the cauldron with a large wooden paddle. The curds are cut in half to make two cheeses known as *gemelli* (twins). They are placed in round wooden molds. A stamped plate with pin dots spelling *Parmigiano-Reggiano*, and indicating which cheese house made it and the month and year of production, is placed between the cheese and the mold. This will leave an impression of the words on the rind as it ages, and it gives the maker and the buyer a historical record of the cheese's origin and authenticity. After three days of being in the molds, the cheese is added to a salt brine, where it is turned often and aged for twenty-four days. Next comes the aging process, which takes place in the maturing room, where the large wheels are stacked on wooden shelves. Wheels age for an average of two years, during which time cheese testers use special hammers to tap the entire surface of the cheese to make sure that it makes a uniform sound. As the cheese maker puts it, the cheese must make its own fine music, and if it does not, it is rejected. Testers also look for uniform color, pleasant smell, and no gaping holes in the interior. As the cheese ages, amino acids begin to form, which crystalize into tiny white dots visible when the cheese is cut open. These grainy bits give Parmigiano-Reggiano its unique texture. Once the governing body, the Consorzio del Formaggio Parmigiano-Reggiano gives its approval that the cheese has passed all the criteria, the wheels are stamped with the oval seal that signifies that it is worthy to take its place in the world marketplace.

Watching the grand opening of a wheel being cut is almost a spiritual experience. Anticipation builds, and silence falls as my eyes are riveted on the cheese tester, who uses a special almond knife to score the eighty-five-pound wheels across their diameter and down both sides. The wheel is turned over, and the line is completed on the other side. Then a half-inch-deep cut is made along the cutting line all around the wheel with a hooked rind cutter. Next a pointed spatula knife is inserted into the center of the top line. Almond-shaped knives are positioned diagonally into opposite corners of the wheel as the cheese tester grasps them and pushes one forward and the other backward to pry the wheel open. (After watching this tedious process, I have infinitely more respect for buying a wedge of Parmigiano-Reggiano already cut into wedges in my local supermarket!) When the interior texture is revealed, it is rough, with peaks and valleys like the surface of jagged stone mountains, and its sunny yellow color and aroma fill one's senses.

Tasting its delicate flavor right in the cheese house was an unforgettable experience, and for those accustomed to purchasing those canisters of artificial "parmesan" from the supermarket shelves, this comes as true enlightenment.

Parmigiano-Reggiano is a near perfect food, low in fat and sodium, high in calcium, and full of vitamins and other minerals. No wonder it was chosen as the cheese to send into space with Russian cosmonauts. Luckily we need not go that far, since it is available in supermarkets and specialty food stores nationwide.

Asiago DOP: Mountain Cheese

Caseificio Pennar in the town of Asiago was my destination to see how Asiago DOP cheese was made. This venerable cheese can be made in only four provinces of the Veneto region: Vicenza, Trento, Padua, and Treviso. To be given the coveted DOP certification of authenticity, Asiago must be made from the highest-quality milk produced from cows grazing on high-altitude mountain farms.

When I arrived, I suited up in hair net, white lab coat, and blue booties. The cheese maker was taking no chances. Asiago, a cow's milk cheese, is named after the town where it is produced and has over a thousand-year history. Originally it was made from sheep's milk, but since the sixteenth century, it has been made with cow's milk.

Stepping into the *caseificio* (cheese factory), I see a team of men in gleaming white lab coats and high rubber boots working in silent unison, stirring the milk in huge copper cauldrons to which *caglio* (calf rennet) is added to coagulate the milk.

Asiago pressato, made from whole milk, is a pressed cheese that is aged for twenty days. It is pale yellow, with random-size holes and a mild buttery flavor, making it not only a good table cheese but a good melting cheese for pasta sauces and fillings. Asiago d'allevo is made with partially skimmed milk and aged from four months to two years. Asiago mezzano is aged for a minimum of four to six months, giving it a semisoft texture and mild flavor. Asiago vecchio, aged for ten to fifteen months, is drier in texture and can be grated. Asiago stravecchio, aged over fifteen months, is more pronounced in flavor and has a firmer texture.

Identifying marks on wheels of Asiago DOP cheese indicate its authenticity, including the imprinted word *Asiago* on the rind of each cylinder, as well as the number of the dairy where it was produced and a certification code and the DOP mark.

The Passport

Stepping off the plane at Punta Raisi Airport outside Palermo, Sicily, I reached inside my purse to make sure that it was still there in the zippered pocket where I had put it. My aunt Phoebe had given me my grandfather's passport for safekeeping a few years before she passed away. The thin, brown paper document was issued to Rosario Saporito in 1900 during the reign of Vittorio Emanuele III, king of Italy. Rosario was 63 inches tall and 24 years old when he left Sicily for New York. His passport was good for three years, and his reason for leaving was to find work. He was described as having black hair, a straight physique, and brown complexion.

That passport was going to take me to my grandfather's hometown of Santa Caterina Villarmosa in the province of Caltanissetta and would lead to an adventure. When I arrived, the town seemed stark, gray, and dull. It had been bombed heavily during the war, and many old buildings were destroyed. In the town piazza was a rather somber monument dedicated to the family. Men in sweaters and caps sat nearby at an outside bar playing cards and staring at me. I found the town office and went in, clutching the passport. I did not speak Sicilian dialect, so I tried in my best Italian to explain why I had come. "Aspett" ("Wait") came the reply from the receptionist. A few minutes later, out came a young man with dark skin, black hair, and rimmed glasses. He introduced himself as Antonio Fiaccato. I started to speak in Italian when he cut me short and said in English, "Come with me."

I was so relieved! We walked to the Chiesa Madre, the mother church, and on the way I gave him the story as I knew it of my grandfather. I was half expecting him to quickly give me all the information that I needed to find out more about his life in this town, where his house stood, and if I had any long-lost relatives still here. But there were no computers to instantly galvanize the information, only stacks of dusty books with handwritten entries of births and deaths. Antonio took the passport and, using Rosario's birth date of April 28, 1876, was able to quickly locate the dusty book containing his young life story in this town. He was born and lived here until he was twenty-four years old, and he was a *contadino*, a farmer. "Your great-grandparents," Antonio told me, "are buried in the catacombs under this church, and they were related to the first bishop of the town." As Antonio rattled off information, I scribbled in my notebook, listening carefully so as not to miss anything. Where was his house? Sadly, it was no more Antonio said, because during the war, much was destroyed. I thanked him profusely for spending time with me and started to leave to explore the town, when he invited me to have dinner with him and his grandmother and mother.

Antonio's grandmother was a petite woman living in two rooms, a tiny kitchen with a bed and a simple loft area for storage. When we arrived, the smell of tomato sauce cooking permeated the tiny kitchen. She had cooked so much food—spaghetti, lamb, meatballs, fennel, and artichokes—in such short notice, that I felt guilty thinking about how much this must have cost. But as Antonio explained, "You are family because your grandfather came from here." Before I knew it, the parish priest arrived to bless the food, and several of Antonio's friends joined us with sweets from the local pastry shop. The meal lasted for hours as two worlds came together in that tiny house.

When I left, I promised to keep in touch with Antonio, who wanted desperately to write plays and go to New York, a long shot to be sure, I thought.

Many years have passed, and I still recall that adventure and the dinner with total strangers who welcomed me as one of their own—and all because of a passport. Antonio never made it to New York, but he did become the mayor of Santa Caterina Villarmosa.

Acknowledgments

Writing is a process and often a lonely one. Putting words to paper and conveying a message is one thing but seeing those words materialize into a beautiful book makes the process worth it. I could not have written this book without the guidance of Deidre Randall, CEO of Peter E Randall Publisher. Thank you for embracing this project and making it a reality. Thank you to book designer Tim Holtz for the classy layout and to photographer John Hession for the eat off the pages photos smartly styled by Catrine Kelty, a dynamo in the kitchen and to Morgan Karanasios, photo assistant and cover stylist, whose sharp eye makes a set look bellissima! Mille grazie to copyeditor Karen Wise for her superb job and for her always welcome Italian emails. Thank you to Kate Crichton, the efficient behind the scenes publishing assistant, Leslie Brenner, proofreader and Melissa Hyde, indexer. Thank you to Kelly Lancaster for getting me ready for the camera. Thank you to my husband Guy, who always believes in my goals and gives me unconditional encouragement. Thank you to chef extraordinaire Jasper White, for the beautiful Foreword. Thank you cannot be said enough to Paul Lally, executive producer of Ciao Italia, who never says no. Thank you to Debra Woodward. Thank you to Jelena Todorovic Meisel and Zonin 1821 wines for help with the photography and to Sandy Block, Master of Wine, for introducing us. To Lisa Ekus and David Carriere for getting the word out about the book. To Michael Jones for his legal expertise and to Chris Obert, Jane Dystel, Joe Comforti, Jim Darroch, Marketing Director of Local Brands, and Michael Flamini for your valued advice and help. And thanks to Kate Belavitch and James Home for the use of their lovely kitchen for the front cover.

Index

Positano, Amulfi coast

Chef, author, and TV personality Mary Ann Esposito is the creator and host of the nationally televised PBS series *Ciao Italia with Mary Ann Esposito*™ (www.ciaoitalia.com). The author of twelve cookbooks, most recently, *Ciao Italia Family Classics*, Mary Ann has worked beside world-renowned chefs Julia Child, Jacques Pepin, Martin Yan, Jasper White, and countless others.

Through *Ciao Italia* and appearances on other television programs—including *The Today Show*, *Regis and Kelly*, QVC, the Food Network, Discovery Channel, Fox, Martha Stewart Radio, RAI International, *The Victory Garden* and many others—she has shared traditional Italian cooking with audiences around the world.

Many organizations have recognized Mary Ann for her efforts to preserve the traditions surrounding Italian food and culture. In 2013 she received the Order of the Star of Italy Cavaliere from the President of the Italian Republic, as well as the Premio Artusi award for her work promoting Italian food. Johnson and Wales University presented her with the Distinguished Author Award. St. Anselm College conferred an honorary doctorate, and the Italian Trade Commission named her a 2010 Hall of Fame honoree. The Order Sons of Italy in America (OSIA) honored Mary Ann with the 2009 Lifetime Achievement in the Culinary & Cultural Arts of Italy, as did the National Italian American Foundation.

As part of the focus of *Ciao Italia*, Mary Ann established the Mary Ann Esposito Foundation (www.ciaoitalia.com/foundation), whose goal is to continue fostering the traditions of Italian regional cooking in the United States by providing scholarships for the next generation of chefs. When not filming *Ciao Italia*, Mary Ann can be found in Italian kitchens giving hands-on cooking classes all over the "boot."